Making Space For God

Repositioning Your Life for Kingdom Living

JOANNE ELLISON

CONTENTS

INTRODUCTION
INTERIOR DESIGN: AVAILABLE SPACE

Early in the movie Contact the main character asks her father if he believes there is life on other planets. The girl's dad looks up at the night sky and tells her, "It'd be an awful waste of space if there isn't. "

Our hearts, minds and souls are God's home. When we invite Jesus in, though, He often finds very little room in which to live. His freedom to live in and through us is directly proportional to the space we turn over to Him. Like rooms filled with excess furniture, bric-a-brac and junk, our hearts can be so cluttered that the only room we have left for Jesus is the scant space at the edges – standing room only. Jesus stands at the margins, looks into our hearts and sees a potential living area that we have filled with our anxiety, fear, and self-centeredness: an awful waste of space.

The inspiration for this book came from a series of teachings I based on requests from people who are struggling with issues relevant to all of us. As I read and thought about their requests, I realized that many of the trials people face – and the choices we make in the midst of our struggles – are dramatically affected by whether or not we have made space for God in our lives. Not just Sunday-morning space or Bible-study space or prayer-time space, but openness at the very center of our lives – 24X7- space: the present, the right-now-where-we-are, the now here as Brennan Manning calls it.

Although we so often clutter and even squander the space God originally created in us, He still wants to live there. He is gently persistent, infinitely patient, unfathomably faithful. When we are ready and willing – if we allow Him – He promises to use whatever we make available. And God wastes neither time nor space: He will begin renovations as soon as He gets the go-ahead. There has never been an Interior Designer like this one. When we say Yes to His invitation and make our now-here space available, He will start the process of restoring the living room in us for His throne, His temple. And He works weekends and holidays. Talk about dependable.

The problem is that between heaven and earth there are blocks – stops and detours and dead ends: our hearts are caught up with the issues and stresses and cares of the world, and we allow those space-wasters to crowd Him out.

The best example I know in Scripture of making space for Jesus was Mary. Jesus was the guest of honor at her house that she shared with her sister Martha. Martha was busily preparing food for her guest and Mary chose to sit at His feet. Martha was irritated because she was doing all of the work but Jesus commended Mary for choosing the One needed thing--- sitting and worshipping at His feet. Mary chose to quiet her soul and sit at the Master's feet. And in the process the voices around her were drowned out—the demands of the world grew dim and in that moment as she chose Jesus above all else she was transformed. From the place of being filled with His Presence she was better able to be Martha. In order to be a better Martha, completing her daily tasks, she knew that she needed to be a better Mary. That is my hope for you as you read through this book; that in the process of reading this book, the world's demands will grow dim, and you will make space for the King. As you work through the book, my prayer is that you will be still and take the time to work through each chapter ridding your inner space of the obstacles that block worship. In the end you will be a better Martha, transformed by the Presence of God.

This book comes from my heart, the place of my own ongoing spiritual expedition to find peace and rest in Christ alone, and to prepare myself – my living room – for an invasion by heaven, here and now. Each chapter represents a rung on the ladder, another step or two of the journey, another way to make space for God by removing the things in our hearts that crowd out His kingdom rule.

Please join me on this interior design project. Let's make space for the Grand Designer and then be prepared to marvel at what He does with the room we give Him.

1 THE ONE NEEDED THING

Psalm 46 is a hymn celebrating Zion, the place and nation through which God will bless the world. The psalm describes a people who are secure even in tumultuous times because God is present:

> Be still and know that I am God; I will be exalted among the nations, I will be exalted in the earth. The Lord Almighty is with us; the God of Jacob is our fortress. [1]

In this psalm, God's voice resounds as He speaks to us through the psalmist: Be still and know.

Be Still

God's command to 'be still' comes from the Hebrew verb *rapha*, which means to be weak, to let go, to release; also *enough* or *stop*. It might better be translated as 'cause yourselves to let go or let yourselves become weak'. [2] The King of the Universe is telling His people to stop, to be still and see that His presence is the calm in the midst of the storm; that His voice causes the earth to melt as He declares that He – the sovereign Lord Almighty – is their fortress.

God is reminding His people that they can know and be assured of His presence in the stillness. God is saying, *Stop running and worrying and listening to the world's chatter.*

4

Cause yourselves to let go, and let me inhabit the stillness. In another psalm, David says:

> The Lord is my Shepherd; I shall not be in want. He makes me to lie down in green pastures, he leads me beside quiet waters, he restores my soul. [3]

God is speaking the same words today: *enough, stop. Calm down and let my Holy Spirit teach, lead, comfort and empower you.* God wants us to lie down in green pastures and be led to quiet waters. He wants us to stop long enough to allow ourselves to do the one needed thing: to worship the One who created us, and to allow Him to quiet our souls and fill our hearts.

Why is it so difficult to see that all God wants is for us to be still so that we can hear His voice and receive His peace?

What Is It ... And How Can We?

What does it really mean to worship God? How can we learn to quiet ourselves, to accept and enter the place of rest that He promises us? Both questions are answered in Luke's gospel:

> As Jesus and his disciples were on their way, he came to a village where a woman named Martha opened her home to him. She had a sister Mary, who sat at the Lord's feet listening to what he said. But Martha was distracted by all the preparations that had to be made. She came to him and asked. "Lord, don't you care that my sister has left me to do the work by myself? Tell her to help me! "Martha, Martha, the Lord answered, "you are worried and upset about many things, but only one thing is needed. Mary has chosen what is better, and it will not be taken from

her. [4]

Martha, Mary and The One Needed Thing

Imagine the scene. Martha has invited an honored guest into her home. She had heard about many of the incredible things Jesus had done and was more than a bit nervous. Martha wanted everything to be perfect for Jesus – and there was so much to do! She is distracted – running around, setting the table, making sure the meal is cooked – and suddenly she can't find her sister Mary.

Then Martha finds Mary sitting at the feet of Jesus! What? With all that needs to be done,
Mary is just sitting there? So Martha complains to Jesus. *It's so unfair, Jesus. I'm working so hard and no one is helping me – by the way, I'm doing this for you, Savior! Won't you do something about this? Get my sister to help me, will you?*

Have you ever done what Martha did? Does this sound as familiar to you as it does to me?

Well, Jesus cut to the chase and gently set Martha straight: *…you are worried and upset about many things, but only one thing is needed.*
Mary chose to stop and sit at the feet of Jesus and worship Him. She chose the one needed thing. And we need to do the same. Every time we find ourselves in overdrive, running in place, sweating the small stuff, forgetting what's most important, we need to come back again to the one needed thing.

Martha called out to Mary to help, but for Mary the doing paled in comparison to Jesus' voice. And for all of us, Jesus' voice must become greater than the voice of the crowds, the housework, the world's clamor.

Martha was busy preparing her home for the honored guest Jesus. Mary was sitting at His feet. In His Presence the clatter of the world grew dim. As Mary chose to be still, to sit at His feet something extraordinary happened. I believe that the clutter of her life began to lose its grip. The things that had taken up her 'internal space' were removed so that she only had space for Jesus. And in that moment.... I believe she was transformed. In that moment I believe she knew who she was—a king's kid, a friend of God transformed forever to live as Martha in the world but from a place of being a Mary. She knew that in order to be a better Martha, she needed to be a better Mary.

A Place of Abundance

Jesus said that He came so that we could have an abundant life and Mary knew that abundance could only be found in His Presence. Abundance comes from being filled with the presence of God, and worship is the way that we get filled. Abundance means *an extremely plentiful or over sufficient quantity or supply; an overflowing fullness.* When Jesus told us we would have an over sufficient supply, that we would be filled to overflowing, He was referring to Himself. He was telling us that He is our supplier of plenty, He will quench our thirst. In a life filled with an over supply, we can easily flow when in our Martha mode. Let's look at another scene with Jesus as He visits with another woman at a well. He tells her that He has an endless supply of water:

> Everyone who drinks this water (in the well) will be thirsty again, but whoever drinks the water I give him will never thirst. Indeed, the water I give him will

become in him a spring of water welling up to eternal life. [5]

At the pool of Siloam during the Feast of Tabernacles, Jesus declared that if anyone was thirsty they needed to drink the streams of living water that He offers. [6] Imagine that scene at the Feast: at the moment the water is being poured out on the altar as an act of ceremony, Jesus announces that He is that water. He says: *Be still. Enough. It's time to stop and worship.* Mary knew that she had to be still and worship if she was ever going to be a good Martha.

The Choice Between Worthy and Worthless

Worship comes from the word meaning worth or value. When we worship we recognize and give our voice to the worth of the One who created us. All our activity is focused on Him. It is all about Him – all the honor is His – and as we worship Him, we become more like Him.

In the Old Testament, God was concerned that the people only gave lip service to honoring Him:

> These people come near to me with their mouth and honor me with their lips, but their hearts are far from me. Their worship is made up only of rules taught by men. [7]

When I first read these words I realized that even worship can become meaningless – worthless – if it does not come from a genuine heart of truly honoring God. In certain periods of their history, the Israelites worshipped idols, worthless manmade images. They forgot the One true God and worshipped dead figures:

> From the rest he makes a god, his idol; he bows

down to it and worships. He prays to it and says, "Save me; you are my god. " They know nothing, they understand nothing; their eyes are plastered over so they cannot see, and their minds closed so they cannot understand. [8]

Do you fall into the trap of idol worship? I know I do. I find myself worshipping time, money, people-pleasing, perfectionism – you name it. And you know what? We become like the dead things we worship. Think about those wooden idols with their mouths and ears plastered shut. That's you and I whenever we worship anything or anyone besides God. Our spiritual eyes and ears get plastered over and we become like those things we worship.

Scary, isn't it?

But if we stop in the midst of the world's clamor and madness and idol worship – if we take the time to worship God as He has created us to – we will become more like Him:

> Now the Lord is that Spirit, and where the Spirit of the Lord is, there is freedom. And we, who with unveiled faces all reflect the Lord's glory, are being transformed into his likeness with ever increasing glory, which comes from the Lord, who is Spirit. [9]

Everything Except What's Needed: Doing Damage in the Middle of Nowhere

In *How to Worship Jesus Christ,* Joseph Carrol describes a scene in which a friend of his traveling in Japan stops to have his oil checked. A great army descends on the man's car, offering all kinds of service – washing the windshield, cleaning even his tires – but when he leaves he realizes that the one thing he needed (oil) he did not get. [10] Do you ever feel that way – that you do everything except the one needed thing?

I do. I run around on an empty tank using up all my energy and resources, wondering why I'm feeling drained – and suddenly I realize that my worship tank is empty. I have not been still. I have not been filled with God's Presence. I have not *let go and let God*. I have not been praising and worshipping Him. I've been worthlessing.

A few years ago I was in the middle of nowhere when my car got a flat tire. I decided to drive until I could get to a well-lit place. When I finally found a service station, the attendant told me that I should have stopped when I first noticed the flat tire. He explained that since I had continued to drive on the flat, I had ruined the rim. I had caused a lot more damage than I needed to.

When we forget to stop and worship God – when we fail to do the one needed thing – it is kind of like continuing to drive on a flat tire. It's like Martha running around her house like a chicken with its head cut off while the King of Kings was in the living room, waiting.

If we keep driving on the flat, if we allow the world and its ways to push us on, rather than stopping for a deep drink of Living Water, we cause more damage to our souls.

Bearing Fruit Requires Water
Worshipping our God is not just important – it's essential. When we worship, He breathes into us. When

10

we worship, He feeds us and gives us Living Water. When we worship, we live.

If we want to be fruit trees – that is, if we want to bear fruit – we must have water. Bearing fruit does not require more effort, more doing, on our part; it requires water:

> Blessed is the man who does not walk in the counsel of the wicked or stand in the way of sinners or sit in the seat of mockers. But his delight is in the law of the Lord and on his law he meditates day and night. He is like a tree planted by streams of water, which yields its fruit in season and whose leaf does not wither. Whatever he does prospers. [11]

The one needed thing is worship of the one true and everlasting God.

Rest For Our Souls

Dallas Willard describes the soul as the deepest level of life and power in the human being.
He says that when our soul is filled with God we are constantly refreshed and exuberant in all we do. Weariness is a sign of a soul not properly rooted in worship. [12]

We find rest for our souls when we are yoked with Jesus:

> Come to me, all you who are weary and burdened, and I will give you rest. Take my yoke upon you and learn from me, for I am gentle and humble in heart, and you will find rest for your souls. [13]

The Shadow of Your Smile

One night I was upstairs in my house, working in my office, when I heard my husband call to me from downstairs. I could faintly hear the sound of music coming from down there too, but I couldn't tell what it was. I told him I would come downstairs soon.

A few minutes later the music was louder, and again I heard him call to me to come downstairs. Again, I told him I would be there soon.

Finally the music was so loud I could hardly hear myself think, so I went downstairs. My husband was standing there in the middle of the music, waiting to dance with me. On the stereo was the first song we had danced to at our wedding: *The Shadow of Your Smile.*

He took me in his arms, and we danced and danced and danced.

Invitation to the Dance

Sometimes God calls out to us and invites us to dance. He wants to hold us, to lead, to enjoy our company – but we're too busy, too caught up in our own stuff. We don't have time. Still, God does not give up. He doesn't walk away from the dance floor. He keeps calling. He is willing to invite us again and again and again. He wants nothing more than for us to come to Him and spend time with Him.

Worship is the main way we connect with our Creator. It is a place and a time and a frame of mind and heart. Worship is the place where we stop and reach out our arms and say, *Yes, Lord, yes – let's dance. Please lead. Yes!*

Worship is the time when we open our hands and let go of our stuff and let our hearts rest and yoke ourselves to

Him.

The Key to Worship

A. W. Tozer says we are made to worship God:

> Here above all the creatures that I have made and created I have given you the largest harp. I put more strings on your instrument and I have given you a wider range than I have given to any other creature. You can worship me in a manner that no other creature can. "[14]

We were created to worship God. When we worship anything or anyone else we lose our identity; we lose our purpose; life is meaningless. Our soul is left empty.

Worship is not for us; it is not a time set aside for us to get through our prayer list. Worship is a time to honor God, to be still and know that He is the One and Only, to become more and more aware of His presence, recognizing that we can approach Him on the basis of the mercy seat:

> Therefore, brothers, since we have confidence to enter the Most Holy Place by the blood of Jesus, by a new and living way opened for us through the curtain, that is his body, and since we have a great priest over the house of God, let us draw near to God with a sincere heart in full assurance of faith, having our hearts sprinkled to cleanse us from a guilty conscience and having our bodies washed with pure water. [15]

Through His death on the cross, Jesus Christ made a way for us to worship and draw near to His Father. He became our High Priest. In the Old Testament, the High

Priest offered sacrifices over and over again. On the cross, Jesus was the offered sacrifice, the lamb who was slain, and He once and for all made a way for us to enter into the very presence of God.

He made a way, and He is the way.

That is how we worship. That's the key: we are able to enter because Jesus made a way for us. Worship is for and about *Him*, not us.

David's Passion

King David recognized that the one thing he lived for was to worship God:

> One thing I ask of the Lord, this is what I seek; that I may dwell in the house of the Lord all the days of my life, to gaze upon the beauty of the Lord and to seek him in his temple. [16]

All David wanted to do — his driving ambition — was to worship God.

Can you imagine beginning every day with worship? Maybe you already do that. Think of it as tuning an instrument (you!) first thing in the morning so that you can play your worship song all day long — so that you can be your song — whenever you think of Him, whenever you hear Him say, *Want to dance?*

A day or two before Christmas last year, I was in the drugstore and I heard a voice over the loud speaker: "Are you stressed? Are you burned out? Consider ways to rest — ways to alleviate anxiety during this season." The voice went on to suggest several stress- and anxiety-relieving strategies: read a good book, take yoga, seek counseling. But the voice did not mention the one needed thing. Didn't mention dancing with God (or even your spouse, for that matter).

The world offers all sorts of answers and strategies and solutions for filling our empty tanks, but the One who is Living Water is the only source that satisfies.

What Worship Reveals

As he was trying to understand a God who apparently demanded worship, C. S. Lewis discovered something that radically changed his outlook. He realized that God communicates His Presence through worship. Lewis came to recognize that it was when he worshipped – while he was authentically engaged in the process of worship – that God revealed Himself: His thoughts, His ways, His truth. [17]

Who wouldn't want to know the thoughts of God? We all want to hear from Him, don't we? And it is through worship that He reveals Himself. Mary knew that as she sat at the feet of Jesus and worshipped Him, she would be transformed by His Presence.

Worship Is Being

Worship is not necessarily reading the Bible, although that is needed. It isn't necessarily praying, although that is important. Worship is ... being. Worship is being with God ... and being content to be there. Worship is sitting at His feet in the living room, like Mary. It is the one needed thing.

Enemy Opposition

The enemy will do all he can to keep us from worshipping God. He will encourage us to stay too busy, keep us distracted, or cause us to worship something (or someone) other than God. Satan tried to get Jesus to worship him. He promised Jesus the kingdoms of the world if He would worship him. 18 Satan knows that we will serve the one we worship. Think about that for a minute. Do you get that you may be worshipping something (or someone) other than God? The enemy will try to divert you to spend your time elsewhere; he will tempt you with doubt, unbelief; he will even suggest that your time is better spent doing something more worthwhile. But you see, he knows: he knows you will become like Jesus if you worship the Son of God – that you will be changed – and that is exactly what our enemy does not want!

Satan knows that worship precedes service, and if you worship God, you will serve Him.

New Year
New Year's Day was two days away and I was beginning what has become a yearly ritual for me. I would spend time with the Lord seeking His will for the New Year. I'd ask Him questions, journal, and listen; and I would expect Him to lead me into the New Year focused and ready to do His will.

This year the word God gave me was surrender. I asked Him, *Haven't I already done that? Don't I do that every day?* Surrender. What is it about that word that I don't really understand?

Surrender and Worship

Abraham could not comprehend with his intellect why God told him to sacrifice his son.

Isaac was the son of the covenant, the one from whom the nation of Israel would be birthed, so killing Isaac made no sense whatsoever to Abraham. But he took his son to the mountain as God had instructed him, and he prepared to kill Isaac on the altar as an act of worship. [19]

The first act of surrender is worship.

One thing Abraham had to surrender on the way to Mount Moriah was his intellect. At that moment, for what God wanted him to understand, Abraham's intellect was a hindrance, not a help. No way could he have understood what God was asking him to do by thinking it through.

But one thing he did understand, one thing he did know how to do: worship. He prepared himself and his son to go to Mount Moriah to worship. He knew how to do that. And this time worship would require all. Abraham could not hold back anything, even his son.

He surrendered in worship, and God provided another sacrifice.

Okay, so this year my focus will be surrender. But I have to admit to you that it sounds scary to me, particularly since I already think I have been there and done that. But God spoke and now I have no choice.   Like Abraham, I have to go to my own mountain At   this moment, I don't know where or what my Mount Moriah is, but I have to be prepared to go and surrender.

Surrender – letting go and giving in – begins with worship; and worship engages our entire being   So   I intend to worship my God at every opportunity, and expect that the Holy Spirit of God will show me what it is I must surrender.

Fully Surrendered?

If the first act of surrender is worship, can you say that you are fully surrendered? That's the question of the day, the challenge we all face. Where and what is your Mount Moriah? What must be put on the altar as your act of worship? Your job? Your marriage?

What do you need to surrender to make more space for God?

Speaking of Surrender and Worship: Daniel

The King of Babylon besieged Jerusalem, and Scripture tells us that the King of Judah was taken captive. Nebuchadnezzar, King of Babylon, ordered his officials to bring in some of the Israelite males who were bright and handsome and qualified to serve in the palace. The boys were given a daily amount of food and wine from the king's table and were to be trained for three years and after that enter the king's service. Daniel and some of his friends were among these young men.

One day the Babylonian administrators talked Nebuchadnezzar into issuing a decree which stated that anyone who prayed to any foreign god (and not to Nebuchadnezzar) would be thrown into a very unique jail cell: a pit containing hungry lions. Well, Daniel and his friends had no intention of worshipping anyone but the One true God. They were surrendered to Him. And they continued to worship God three times a day.

Of course, when the Babylonian administrators found Daniel praying, they tossed him into the lions' den. They expected Daniel to be the lions' dinner that night.

Do you know the rest of the story? Actually, the king liked Daniel and was distraught at this turn of events. Nebuchadnezzar was sorry he had signed that decree into law. He said to Daniel: "May your god whom you serve continually rescue you!"[20] The king was so worried about Daniel that he couldn't sleep that night. And early the next morning he called out to Daniel:

> "Daniel, servant of the living God, has your God, whom you serve continually, been able to rescue you from the lions?"
>
> Daniel answered, "Long live the king! My God sent his angel to shut the lions' mouths so that they would not hurt me, for I have been found innocent in his sight. And I have not wronged you, Your Majesty."
>
> The king was overjoyed and ordered that Daniel be lifted from the den. Not a scratch was found on him, for he had trusted in his God. [21]

Daniel would not back down from worshipping His God. He let go and let God, he surrendered and worshipped with his whole being. And God delivered Him.

A Peek Into Heaven

Scripture tells us that worship is the activity that all lovers of God are engaged in. Can you imagine? All day worshipping the One who sits on the throne? Let's peek into heaven for a moment and see what worship looks like. Let's imagine we are standing around the throne of God, joining the angels as they praise God:

> After this I looked, and there before me was a door standing open in heaven. And the same voice I had first heard speaking to me like a trumpet said, "Come up here, and I will show you what must take place after this. " At once I was in the Spirit, and there before me was a throne in heaven with someone sitting on it. And the one who sat there had the appearance of jasper and carnelian. A rainbow, resembling an emerald encircled the throne. Surrounding the throne were twenty-four elders. They were dressed in white and had crowns of gold on their heads. [22]

Go closer. Can you hear the sound of the living creatures, the elders and the angels worshipping?

> Holy, holy, holy is the Lord God Almighty, who was, and is, and is to come. Whenever the living creatures give glory, honor, and thanks to him who sits on the throne, and who lives for ever and ever, the twenty-four elders fall down before him who sits on the throne and worship him who lives for ever and ever.[23]

Do you believe that putting God first in your life will deliver you from even the fiercest trials?

You may have a lion prowling around seeking to devour

you, but God will deliver you. He is faithful.

Mary sat at the feet of Jesus and worshipped Him. Abraham worshipped God in complete surrender and obedience on Mount Moriah, knowing that God was asking him to do the unthinkable. Daniel would not stop worshipping His God, no matter what.

They all knew that life flows like living water from worshipping our Creator. Life begins and ends, ebbs and flows around His royal throne.

Be still and know that He is God. And know that He loves you. And know that He will never forsake you. And know that He inhabits your praises.

And know that He will reveal Himself to you when you accept His invitation to the dance.

Notes

1. Psalm 46:10
2. John J. Parsons, Surrender: God's Irrepressible Care of the World; see www. hebrew4christians. net/Meditations/Be_Still/be_still. html
3. Psalm 23:1-2
4. Luke 10:38-42
5. John 4:13-14
6. John 7:37
7. Isaiah 29:13
8. Isaiah 44:17-18
9. 2 Corinthians 3:17-18
10. Joseph Carrol, How to Worship Jesus Christ, 20
11. Psalm 1:1-3
12. Dallas Willard, Renovation of the Heart, 209
13. Matthew 11:28-29
14. A. W. Tozer, Worship, 12, 23-24
15. Hebrews 10:19-22
16. Psalm 27:4
17. C.S. Lewis, Reflections on the Psalms, 90-91
18. Matthew 4:8-9
19. Genesis 22:1-13
20. Daniel 6:16
21. Daniel 6:19-23
22. Revelation 4:1-4
23. Revelation 4:8-10

2 HOSTING HIS PRESENCE

Mary knew that when she sat at the feet of Jesus she was not able to help prepare the feast for his arrival. Her sister was up to her elbows in bearing the load of preparation but Mary chose something else. She chose to partake in the real feast. The banqueting table that was set before her was the Presence of Christ. She heard a new sound; her spiritual ears and eyes were opened. She feasted on His Words and knew that the water He offered would quench her spiritual thirst.

In *The Prodigal God* Timothy Keller tells us that the end of human history (and the beginning of God's reign on Earth) will be marked by an incredible feast, a great celebration. Keller says:

> In Isaiah's predictions of the new heavens and new earth, he declares that, like all homecomings, this final one will be marked by the ultimate party-feast (Isaiah 25). Jesus, too, constantly depicts the salvation he brings as a feast. "Many will come from the east and the west," he said to his followers, "and will take their places at the feast with Abraham, Isaac and Jacob in the Kingdom of heaven" (Matthew 8:11). [1]

The Feast Starts Now

But we do not have to wait until Jesus' return to this little planet to experience the feast God has prepared for us. Jesus never intended for us to mark time and wait. He wants to live in us now; He wants to sit down and eat with us now and here.

Here I am! I stand at the door and knock. If anyone

hears my voice and opens the door, I will come in and eat with him, and he with me. [2]

Remember, Jesus told His followers (and tells us) that the Kingdom of God (the feast, the deepening relationship with the King) is both near[2] and within us. [3]

Later in the same section of his book, Timothy Keller says:

> Jesus' salvation is a feast, and therefore when we believe in and rest in his work for us, through the Holy Spirit he becomes real to our hearts. His love is like honey, or like wine. Rather than only believing that he is loving, we can come to sense the reality, the beauty, and the power of his love. His love can become more real to you than the love of anyone else. It can delight, galvanize, and console you. That will lift you up and free you from fear like nothing else. [4]

Christ In Us Transforms What's Around Us

Did you know that when a living-breathing-walking-talking-Christ-loving Christian enters a room the atmosphere in the room should change? Did you know that your presence as a Christian filled with the glory of God, which lives in you, should transform the environment? If that sounds radical to you, it should. It is radical. And it is absolutely true.

If the King of Glory lives in you, then His Presence, and an open invitation to the feast, goes wherever you go.

The more you yield to Jesus' life in you, the more interior space you make available to the King of Glory, the greater the impact you will have wherever He plants you – family, job, church, missions, relationships. Know why? Because if you allow less space for yourself and more for Him, it will mean more power, more love, more anointing in your life, and more of God's influence in everything you do and say. We all want that, don't we?

Or Do We?

Allowing more of God, accepting and extending the invitation to His feast, means making space for Him by tossing out the stuff of ours that gets in the way, giving up control, turning the management of our life over to the King and recognizing that in our weakness He is strong. To us skeptical hu- mans it seems better to be in charge doesn't it? It is much less scary to be strong and independent and free-thinking instead of weak and dependent and focused on an invisible God. Weakness is scary, right?

But the ways of God and His Kingdom are radically different from our ways and the ways of the world in which we find ourselves. The Kingdom of God and the Kingdom of Us could not be more dissimilar.

Giving Up Control Is Easy

Just kidding. Giving up control is hard. Anyone who has tried it knows just how difficult it can be. But what if you, a living temple of the living God, could offer invitations to the feast on the King's behalf ? What if you, filled with His Holy Spirit, could change the atmosphere in a room? Would that be worth giving up control of your life to the King?

If your family life changes because of the amazing influence of God in you; if your job and your relationship with your co-workers is transformed by Who you allow to live in you; if all your relationships take on new and deepened meaning because you carry the King's glory, isn't giving up control to Him worth it?

Do you have a better life – a better plan, a greater adventure – than that in mind?

Did you know you are a glory carrier? It's true. That's you.

Don't you think it is a more-than-fair exchange, His life for yours?

> Whoever finds his life will lose it, and whoever loses his life for my sake will find it.[5]

I would rather take on Jesus' life and invite Him to live in me than live without Him. He is the only One who can empower us to make a difference in the world. The King of the Universe's life for mine? Yes, yes, yes.

Called To Shine

You are called to shine in a dark world, and that requires making space for the lamp and the light of Christ in your life:

> You are the light of the world. A city on a hill cannot be hidden. Neither do people light a lamp and put it under a bowl. Instead they put it on a stand and it gives light to everyone in the house.[6]

Where do you need to shine? With whom do you need to share the light? To whom do you need to extend an engraved invitation to the feast?

Party Pooper or Light Bearer

I attended a party once and walked over to a group of girls who I discovered were gossiping about someone. Had I known they were gossiping, I would not have approached them. As I made my way to the group and understood what they were doing, I wondered if it would be better to be silent or to defend the poor soul who was on the gossip chopping block. I chose to be quiet and pray for discernment, and to my surprise the conversation quickly changed. I did not have to appear self-righteous and tell them to stop; I didn't have to defend the girl who was not present to defend herself. All I had to do was pray and listen to the group's conversation for a moment, and the Holy Spirit stopped the gossiping.

More of God and less of me. That's what I asked for. And the King stopped the backbiting and shifted the conversation.

How Much of Him Do We Want?

As we read about people in the Bible we often see the phrase *And God was with him*. Throughout Biblical stories – across the Old and New Testaments – we meet people (very much like us) who have God with them. Right? In the first chapter of Matthew Mary is told that she will have a baby who is to be called Immanuel. Immanuel means *God with us*, and Jesus was and is the living promise of God's Eternal Presence. But we can disregard God's promise to us of His Presence-Through-Jesus; we can turn down His invitation to the feast. The free will our Creator has given us makes our rejection of Him possible. We have a choice: we can choose not to accept the invitation; we can turn and walk away; we can fill our living space with anything and anyone we want.

How much of Him do we really want in our lives? Really.

Our response to this crucial question, the choices we make regarding interior space available to Him, will directly affect how much of God's Presence we experience.

The Song of Solomon, also known as Song of Songs, describes an exchange between two lovers and metaphorically between Christ and His bride, the church. It describes the magnificent feast at the banquet hall, and that is what Jesus offers us: a seat at the table with Him, a feast of His Presence. God proffers a celebratory feast beyond our imagination, and our response to the question about how much of Him we want will determine how much of the feast we will share in.

How much of Him do we want? Would we rather be in control and starve, or would we rather surrender and be filled?

> I delight to sit in his shade, and his fruit is sweet to my taste. He has taken me to the banquet hall, and his banner over me is love. [7]

Breathtaking Mystery: We In Him, He In Us

Paul said that in God we live and move and have our being. [8] And – what a wonderful mystery! – He wants to dwell and abide and remain in every corner of our lives. He doesn't just want to visit us every now and then; He wants to inhabit us and make our hearts His dwelling place. And we must consciously, intentionally make room for Him.

Think of the rooms in your house. Are some of the ones

in which you spend a lot of time cluttered with furniture or junk or just the accumulation of things you've collected over your lifetime? Stuffed with your stuff? Is there room enough for you to sit down and enjoy the room or for others to sit down with you?

Now think about your spiritual house. What does God find when He comes in? Does He find the living room cluttered with your stuff? Is He able to move freely? Is there space enough for all He wants to do in you?

Preparing the room is the key, if you want to make space for Him; if you want Him to fill you; if you want Him to overflow your heart with His glory.

The House That Solomon Built
Solomon's father David had it in his heart to build a temple, but God told David that Solomon would build it instead. Well, after David got over his initial disappointment, he rolled up his sleeves and set out to help his son build. David invested in the temple before he died and Solomon completed it. The glory of God filled the space:

> When the priests withdrew from the Holy Place, the cloud filled the temple of the Lord. And the priests could not perform their service because of the cloud, for the glory of the Lord filled the temple. [9]

Get it? You are the temple; God resides in you! That was His plan from the start. And when His glory fills His temple (you), all the doing and all the striving and all the activity ceases. He takes over. His life for your life. The feast is ready now. The table is set. You are invited.

What Is In You?

Nehemiah was a man of God who was called away from Babylon to help build the wall in Jerusalem that was broken down. He completed his assignment and returned to Babylon, but while Nehemiah was away from Babylon Tobiah, an avowed enemy of God's people, had filled God's temple with his own household goods:

> Some time later I asked permission and came back to Jerusalem. Here I learned about the evil thing Eliashib had done in providing Tobiah a room in the courts of the house of God. I was greatly displeased and threw all of Tobiah's household goods out of the room. I gave orders to purify the rooms, and then I put back in them the equipment of the house of God with the grain offerings and the incense. [10]

Nehemiah cleaned out God's house and filled it with God's things.

What is in your temple? What is in you? Are there things in you that need to be removed so that the God who wants to dwell in the center of your soul can live and move and have His being in you? What needs to be purified so that you can make more space for God?

It is simple but not easy: the first thing we must do to partake of the feast of God's Presence is to remove what is not of Him and fill the resulting available space with more of Him.

Prepare For The King

In the Old Testament the rubble and stones were removed from the highway that the King would travel. The way was prepared for the King to travel on it. We too must be willing to have the Holy Spirit declutter our rooms. We must prepare for the King. We must desperately want more of Him and less of ourselves.

Why do we need to increase God's Presence in our lives? Because His Presence brings us victory and rest, and it fulfills our destiny. It fulfills the plans He has for us.

Promises Then and Now: Victory and Rest

Moses was a man who made space for God. In fact, Moses would not go on assignment unless God went with him:

> Moses said to the Lord, "You have been telling me, 'Lead these people,' but you have not let me know whom you will send with me. You have said, 'I know you by name and you have found favor with me. ' If you are pleased with me, teach me your ways so I may know you and continue to find favor with you. Remember that this nation is your people. "The Lord replied, 'My Presence will go with you, and I will give you rest. ' Then Moses said to him, "If your Presence does not go with us, do not send us up from here. "[11]

Moses knew he needed God, and he was not about to go on assignment leading the Israelites out of Egypt unless God was going with him. God made some extraordinary promises to Moses: He told him that He would go ahead of him and drive out the enemy nations that were opposed to God; and even though Moses and the Israelites did have to face some brutal battles, God assured Moses of victory and rest.

God has given us the same assurance. He sent His Son to go ahead of us; He sent His Holy Spirit to lead and comfort us; and He has promised us that His Presence will defeat our enemies. The Israelites faced some very serious enemies, including:

- The Hittites, who were the third most influential people in the ancient Near East, rivaling the Egyptians and the Mesopotamians
- The Hivites, who were not warriors but were steeped in the arts of diplomacy and compromise
- The Cannanites, who were pantheistic and engaged in degrading cultic activity
- The Jebusites, who lived in the hill country

And we face the same enemies. The Hittites chase us too; they represent the fear that tries to divert our attention and undermine our confidence in God. The Hivites drive us to compromise when God tells us to stand and be unswerving in our purpose. The Canaanites try to oppress us with their counterfeit lures. And the Jebusites seek to create strongholds in our lives and take us to the high places of idolatry.

Moses was on assignment and he knew he would be toast if he tried to complete his assignment without God. When he asked God to go with him, God's response was that His Presence, His glory and His goodness would go before Moses.

On Assignment
How about you? Do you know that you are on assignment every day? And do you understand that, like Moses, you must ask God to go with you? He is not being coy; He wants relationship with you, and relationship is a two-way street. God does not just want you to ask Him to visit from time to time; He wants you to ask and keep

asking Him to stay with you, to dwell in you, to inhabit your life. To live in the temple that is you.

If God is omnipresent why did Moses ask Him to go with him? Why must we do the same?

God Fills the Space We Give Him

If we give God a corner, He lives in a corner. If we surrender our space, He invades and takes over. The truth is I do not give up my space readily to anybody. You know the expression *I need my space?* Well, I may not have coined that one, but sometimes I feel like I did. I do not easily give up control.

But that is exactly what it takes to make room for more of God.

How about you? What do you struggle with releasing to Him? Children, finances, habits, secrets, relationships, your very life? You will not find rest or victory in those people, places or things until you release them to Him. Believe me, I've tried to do it my way. But the more I hold on, the less I have victory and rest.

Moses got it, and he got it by *letting go and letting God.* He got it by giving God all the space He requested, by being obedient, by allowing God to abide in him. Or at least I think he did. What I know for sure about Moses is that he knew he was not capable of leading his people out of slavery in Egypt unless God was with him.

Picture yourself in a car. Do you picture God in the driver's seat or the passenger's seat? Or the back seat?

Take as much time as you need with this simple exercise. It may help you determine where you are in your journey with the making-space-for-God thing.

Preparing for The Feast: Three Spiritual Disciplines

There are many spiritual disciplines and practices that can help us prepare for the feast, clear space for the Presence of God, declutter ourselves and make room available for more of Him.

These disciplines can't save you; they can't even make you a holy person. But they can heighten your desire, awareness, and love of God by stripping down the barriers that you put up within yourself and some that others put up for you. What makes something a 'spiritual discipline' is that it takes a specific part of your way of life and turns it toward God. A spiritual discipline is, when practiced faithfully and regularly, a habit or regular pattern in your life that repeatedly brings you back to God and opens you up to what God is saying to you. [12]

Four spiritual disciplines or practices that have helped me make space for God are repentance, meditation, prayer and fasting. Chapter 19 (*Moving Mountains*) is all about prayer; so let's look into repentance, meditating on God's Word, and fasting now.

Repentance

Jesus told us to repent because His kingdom is at hand. He's telling us to get a hold of our minds and get rid of the stuff that crowds Him out. He is saying, "Change your minds and your direction. Turn away from the dead-end path you're on and come to me. Fill yourself with more of me and your actions will reflect it."

Repentance was our Lord's first instruction to us. He was saying, "Wake up, everyone! I am here to bring my Kingdom. Make space for me. " Repentance closes the door to the enemy and makes interior space, temple space, available to God: more of Him, less of me. Where the enemy cluttered the room with deception and confusion and stinkin' thinkin', repentance makes room for God.

I wish I could say it is a once-and-for-all thing we have to do, but it's not: repentance is a daily commitment, even moment to moment, depending on what kind of day you're having. It needs to happen as often as necessary. When we know we are headed in the wrong direction, away from His abundant life, toward death – when we realize we are on a dead-end path – we must simply, humbly, change our mind and change our direction. We must choose to turn away from the things of the world and turn back to our King.

Meditating on God's Word

You may have read some variation or other of this story on the internet:

> One evening an old Cherokee told his grandson about a battle that goes on inside people. He said, "My son, the battle is between two wolves inside us all. One wolf is Evil; it is anger, envy, jealousy, sorrow, regret, greed, arrogance, self-pity, guilt, resentment, inferiority, lies, false pride, superiority, and ego. The other wolf is Good; it is joy, peace, love, hope, serenity, humility, kindness, benevolence, empathy, generosity, truth, compassion and faith. "

The grandson thought about it for a minute and then

asked, "Which wolf wins?"

The old Cherokee replied, "The one you feed. "[13]

Jesus told us He is the bread of life and we are to feed on Him. He described how He (the Living Word) cleanses us:

> You are already clean because of the word I have spoken to you; remain in me and I will remain in you.[14]

Making space for God's Word in our lives requires a sacrifice of time. We must read and meditate on the Word for transformation, not just for information. Paul writes that God's Word renews our minds and reveals God's will. [15]

Making space for God through meditation on His Word cleanses us; it removes the clutter from our lives, sanctifies us, and renews our minds. Again: His life in exchange for ours: more of Him, less of us.

Fasting

Feasting on God increases His Presence and denies self. Through fasting we deny our natural appetites and sate our spiritual appetites. We all want more of God's power, anointing and infilling, but there is a cost, and as always it involves denial of self. I sound like a broken record, don't I? I know I'm repeating myself, but sometimes I think redundancy is necessary. The world tells us to celebrate ourselves, to make ourselves the center of the universe, to put ourselves and what we want above all. But that's not what our Creator says.

Deny self, deny self, deny self. Not a very inventive beat, and we probably can't dance to it ... but there is no shortcut; there will be no real victory or rest until we give up on our own plans and embrace God's plans for us; until we accept His invitation to the glorious feast; until we say Yes and go into the party and take a seat at the table. The feast has been paid for and prepared.

Deny self: maybe we cannot dance to it, but we can dance in it.

There are so many misconceptions about fasting that I want to be as clear as possible about what it is and how this spiritual discipline can help us make space for God. The purposes of fasting include:

- Opening ourselves to God's presence: our physical appetites scream for attention and we spend time thinking about, preparing and eating food. As we fast we gain the time we would spend on preparing and eating and give this time to the Lord. We can focus more on Him.
- Bringing our whole being (soma) into alignment with God by aligning our spirit, soul, and body under the power of the Holy Spirit; bringing our body, mind and spirit into submission.
- Tuning in to God: giving our spiritual ears and eyes a tune- up.

We do not fast to change God's mind; we fast to change our mind and to align with the mind of Christ.

We fast to put God in charge and to get our flesh, our plans, our opinions, our me-centered wants out of the way so the Holy Spirit can have His way in our lives.

We fast to prepare ourselves to be holy vessels, set apart for God's purposes. Fasting helps us to bring down strongholds in our lives, remove blocks; and it helps us to become more sensitive to the still small voice of God.

God's plan for fasting is not about us; it is about Him: more of Him, less of us.

Increasing The Feast

It is critically important to make space for more of God's Presence because we need to push back the forces that threaten to squeeze Him out. Around every corner there are fast food purveyors who will tell you that you have to eat on the run – there's no time to rest, no time to take a seat and partake in some elaborate 'feast'. Do not buy it. If run you must, then run toward the One Who is inviting you to the feast.

We need to give God space to live His life (and serve His feast) through us. He will do a much better job than we will. We need to decrease so that He can increase. When we do, we will find victory and rest.

When you accept His open invitation to the feast, when you increase the feast by seeking Him with everything you've got, you will begin to discover everything He's got. You will begin to see the road turn; your destiny will begin to unfold. His plan for you, the feast He has prepared specifically for you, will be served, one incredible, delectable course at a time.

His feast, His timing.

If you are willing to lose your life you will find it.

He is faithful.

Notes

1. Timothy Keller, The Prodigal God, 105
2. Revelation 3:20
3. Mark 1:15
4. Timothy Keller, The Prodigal God, 108
5. Matthew 10:39
6. Matthew 5:14
7. Song of Songs 2:3-4
8. Acts 17:28
9. 1 Kings 8:10
10. Nehemiah 13:6-9
11. Exodus 33:12-15
12. SpiritHome. com, Spiritual Practices and Disciplines: see http://www. spirithome. com/spirdisc. html
13. Jim Gustafson, The One You Feed, Ezine Articles; see http://ezinearticles. com/?The-One-You-Feed&id=342145
14. John 15:3-4
15. Romans 12:2

3 IN THE EYE OF THE STORM

Mary probably had a lot of storms in her life. We don't know for sure, but we do know that no one is exempt from storms—those things in our lives that wreak havoc. Perhaps as she sat at the feet of Jesus she had just experienced one. But you can be sure of one thing, when she sat at the feet of Jesus her storm was stilled. Perhaps the storm was within her own soul. You know the kind where you feel battered, wounded, depressed? My guess is the longer she remained at His feet the more the waves of peace washed over her weary soul. Perhaps she was a people pleaser longing to be set free and just be herself. As she sat at His feet even the hurricane wrath of her irritated sister drove all the people pleaser out of her. She simply wasn't going to get up and help in the kitchen. She preferred to sit in the peace waves.

Have you ever had a front-row seat for a hurricane? Ever been in the middle of a big one? I have. I was born and raised on America's southeast coast, in Charleston, South Carolina, and hurricanes are a fact of life where I come from. There have been many during my lifetime, and I expect more before I'm done.

Amazing Gracie
Maybe you are old enough to remember Hurricane Gracie. September 1959. Gracie was my first big storm, also the strongest during the Atlantic hurricane season that year, and the most intense to strike the United States since Hurricane Hazel in 1954. This was back in the days

when hurricanes were always given feminine names. By the way, what was that all about?

My grandmother was staying with us when Gracie hit Charleston because my parents were out of town on one of my father's medical trips. My sisters and I were quite young, and our grandmother kept us inside, even before the storm made landfall and people all over the city were out taking a look at the pre-hurricane panorama. As we looked out the tape-reinforced windows of our house, my sisters and I were very excited. It was thrilling. Looking back on it, I realize that for us the gripping anticipation outweighed any other emotional response. After all, this was something new for us, we were safe as far as we knew – I don't think we were even remotely aware of the elements of unpredictability and danger that lie in the dark hearts of hurricanes.

But for my grandmother the fear of a monstrous storm and the responsibility of caring for us must have been daunting. Greek grandmothers are not known for their calm, restrained demeanors. I'm pretty sure centuries-old DNA is involved. And my wonderful grandmother was no exception.

We kids weathered Gracie just fine. No cuts or bruises or close calls. It was a sensual treat: though we couldn't actually taste the hurricane, we could smell it and see it and hear it and, with our hands pressed against the trembling windows in our living room, we could almost touch it. It was wonderful! We thought it was fun. I have to admit I never checked back with my grandmother to see how wonderful she thought Gracie was, but I am willing to bet that 'fun' would not have been a word she would have chosen to describe her extreme-weather experience that day. Trees and parts of trees were strewn everywhere, and there were numerous opportunities to build forts with the debris for weeks after the storm had blown through Charleston and finally exhausted itself.

As far as I was concerned, the world had been extraordinarily rearranged – at least for a little while – and it seemed as though Gracie and the transformation she caused in our city was some kind of gift. For a child, it was a wonderland.

I cannot count the number of hurricanes that have beaten on the coast of South Carolina over the years since Gracie, but I do know that as I grew older my anticipation of imminent hurricanes – and my response to them – more closely resembled my grandmother's than the delighted reaction I had as a little girl. The sense of wonder and awe turned into fear, even dread, as I listened to the weather reports. Responsibility quite naturally came along with age, and the burden of broadened accountability often caused my sense of anticipation and excitement to give way to the stark reality of the terrible and irreversible things hurricanes can do.

I liked hurricane season better when I was a child. I liked it better when I could leave the fear and worrying and responsibility to my parents and grandparents. Maybe children don't worry so much about hurricanes because they are able (quite naturally) to find a safe place in the middle of the storm.

Hugo
The most devastating hurricane in my lifetime (so far) was

named Hugo. Sort of a serene name. You wouldn't think something named Hugo would do what that Hugo did. Who does name hurricanes? Anyway, that wind-and-water monster with the gentlemanly-sounding name hit Charleston like an enemy bombardment in September 1989, thirty years (almost to the day) after Gracie. And Hugo made Gracie look like an uppity summer shower.

On the Wednesday before Hugo made landfall over the weekend, it looked as though the storm couldn't make up its mind where to go; the experts told us there was a possibility we could get a hit, but there was uncertainty as to the hurricane's direction and target. As a responsible adult with kids of my own – no longer able to hide worry-free behind the safety of my parents (or grandmother) – I did what any right-thinking grandmother – Greek or not – would do: my sister and I did not wait around and reason it out – we packed up our cars, took our five children, and left Charleston, heading further inland. My husband stayed to fish. Go figure. My decision to leave was a bit premature, but as it turned out, it was a good call.

Hurricane Hugo, a Category 4 hurricane, slammed into the coast of South Carolina at Charleston on September 22, 1989. Winds reached 137 miles per hour. More than 26,000 homes were destroyed or severely damaged.

By the time I returned to Charleston it looked like a war zone. That has become a cliché around here as a description for the aftermath of a big storm, but it seems appropriate, at least in terms of the destruction a hurricane like Hugo leaves in its wake. I had a difficult time recognizing my neighborhood. It was eerie, dreamlike: fallen trees splitting houses in half, sailboats and yachts lining the streets, all manner of debris – from inside and outside houses and other buildings – strewn everywhere I looked. I felt like a stranger in an even stranger land. It was a sensation I had never experienced before, and one I'll never forget.

I did not stay in Charleston for Hurricane Hugo, but my in-laws did. My father-in-law was determined to ride out the storm in his house, and it is part of his account of the night Hugo hit that I want to share with you.

The Eye and the Eye Wall

The storm was raging, trees were falling everywhere. Some of them made a direct hit on my father-in-law's house; others missed literally by inches. He told me the storm sounded like a highspeed hundred-ton freight train roaring through town. And then suddenly the hurtling train stopped screaming and the trees stopped splitting and crashing to the ground. In an instant it was so quiet, so still, that my father-in-law wondered if it was over. But he knew that was unlikely. Storms don't just stop like that; they wind down, they blow themselves out over time and distance; they do their damage and then leave town like a freight train rolling off down the tracks. Was the monster taking a break – pacing itself – or was this a time and place in which the storm simply ceased to exist?

My father-in-law peeked outside and saw what he later described to me as the Eye of the Storm. We have all probably heard of it, even though we may not have known what it is. As a hurricane gains strength, its eye begins to form at the center, in the midst of the raging wind and water. Usually this happens once the winds reach about 80 miles per hour. The eye is a small area where the weather is calm, the sky is clear and the winds are gentle breezes. When viewed from above the eye is often circular, 20 to 40 miles in diameter.

Surrounding the eye is the Eye Wall, a ring of dense thunderstorm clouds that comprise the most violent part of the hurricane – the strongest, most damaging winds and most intense rainfall.

In the midst of Hurricane Hugo, my father-in-law observed the Eye of the Storm at eye-level. In the center of it all, between the two halves of Hugo's immense Eye Wall, he experienced a clear, calm stillness.

The Eye of the Storm: God's Presence

We have a place we can go when the storms of life threaten to overtake us. It is a place that is always available to us, no matter what the world says or suggests or presents. No matter the depth or breadth or intensity of the Eye Wall. This place is the Eye of the Storm, the center of God's Presence, where He promises to protect us from whatever it is that is raging around us.

The Eye of the Storm is the place where we can breathe easy and be calm, where His peace fills our souls in spite of the intensity and danger of the Eye Wall.

In his book, *A Place of Immunity*, Francis Frangipane describes the presence of God: "For those who dwell with God, His Presence is not merely our refuge, it is a permanent address. "[1] Frangipane's book is all about making space for God and understanding that in the midst of our frenetic lives we desperately need to make space for the only One who can guide us through the storms, through the Eye Walls. What we must trust and remember, especially in the midst of storms that are bigger than we are, is that our God is big enough to handle anything. His Presence is the Eye of the Storm (quite supernaturally), and we can rest in Him, storm or no storm. He is our safety, wherever we are.

Something we need to understand and recognize beyond the shadow of a doubt: the storms will come. Storms are one of life's guarantees. It is not a question of if; it is only a question of when.

So … what do we do when the inevitable storm hits?

A Storm Far From Home

Years ago my husband was in the army as a physician, and I found myself in Germany with three small kids, no friends or family, and a language barrier. We stayed in a small village near Ramstein Air Force Base, having chosen to live off base so that we could experience day-to-day living in a foreign country. The only problem was that I was lonely and I could not easily make friends. We stayed in that particular village for only six months, but it was a very difficult time for me. I'll never forget it. And I'll never forget the desperate longing to move back "home." Except this was my home now.

Those first months in Germany were a storm in my life. Loneliness and homesickness and the lack of a common language and the strange surroundings were the overwhelming elements of the Eye Wall, the intense winds and thunder and rain that raged around me in that little village in Germany. I felt as though there was no end in sight, no Eye of the Storm. It is fair to say I was miserable.

His Presence in the Midst of It

Then one day I cried out to the Lord and shared with Him my heart, my misery, my loneliness. I didn't hold anything back. I was desperate. And He answered. He took me to the eye of the storm; He surrounded me with His Presence; He became my best friend, and to this day I regard that storm-time and God's response to my heart's cry as a turning point, a defining moment in my life. I realized that wherever He is, I want to be. And the wonderful irony of God's presence: wherever I am, He is too.

He showed me – He proved to me – that He *is* the Prince of Peace, now-here and forever.

The word God spoke to me in the midst of my storm was in Matthew's gospel:

> Come to me all you who are weary and burdened, and I will give you rest. Take my yoke upon you and learn from me, for I am gentle and humble in heart and you will find rest for your souls. For my yoke is easy and my burden is light. [2]

The image Jesus uses is of oxen in a harness (yoke) and of their master pulling the load. Jesus spoke to me that day. He surrounded me and calmed me, and He told me – which is to say He promised me – that His yoke was easy. He said He would pull the load.

And He did. My husband and I met people who became friends-for-life, friends who have visited us here in the states. We learned enough German to get through our days with relative ease. We spent three years in Germany, and we loved our time there. We will never forget it. We grew in our relationship with each other and with God.

Superwoman Versus The Boulders

This week I am on vacation with my husband in the mountains of North Carolina. We love the outdoors, especially mountain climbing, and yesterday we went on a most unusual hike. We climbed on great BIG boulders, straight up and over a stream and a waterfall. At first I stood at the bottom of the mountain and could hear the falls above me; no, I don't mean the sound of people falling. It sounded huge, like Niagara Falls. My husband said, "Won't it be great to get to the top and see it?" and I'm thinking, *Won't it be great to get to the top and be alive?"*

But you know what? I forged ahead and led us up the mountain. No kidding. I was daring and un- daunted, very much like a great Indian scout leading the way across the raging river. I was amazing, I was incredible, I was – halfway into the hike when the boulders seemed to grow much larger, the waterfalls beneath us widened and the way became more slippery. I no longer felt like Pocahontas or Superwoman or whoever I had thought I was a moment ago. Suddenly I was less amazing, less incredible. It is fair to say I was scared.

The brave mountain climber was afraid and wanted to retreat. Climbing up the falls on the boulders was a little like solving a Rubiks Cube. Ever tried one of those? Well, I'm not much good at them either. As the leader, I had to decide which rocks to climb, which were the safest and the best to facilitate our ascent. When the boulders got bigger and fear creeped in, I gave up and asked my husband to lead.

With him guiding us, every risk I had feared melted away. He carefully and strategically led the way, and I felt safe. He took my hand and helped me up. He was fearless and a peace came over me. I followed with a grateful heart.

That is the way it can be with our Father in heaven. The only catch is that we have to say Yes to His invitation, His yoke; we have to take His hand and follow. We need to ask God to lead, and then allow Him to.

The problem is that we often (and quite naturally) forge out on our own, confident that our way is the best, secure in the belief that we can do it with our own strength and intelligence. And suddenly the inevitable and unpredictable storm comes, the wind picks up, seemingly from out of nowhere, the waves come crashing; the way becomes slippery and our self-confidence weakens as the boulders in our path grow much larger than they were only a moment ago. It is then we realize we need help. Big, powerful, experienced help. Help that is bigger than the boulders.

We need someone who can take us to the eye of the storm. We need someone who can lead us to safety.

Our Father whispers to us in the quiet, secure places of life, but when the storms come He must shout sometimes to be heard over the waves crashing around us. His word to us is repeated and clear:

> But now, this is what the LORD says – he who created you…

he who formed you…:
"Fear not, for I have redeemed you;
I have summoned you by name; you are mine.

"When you pass through the waters, I will be with
you; and when you pass through the rivers, they will
not sweep over you. When you walk through the
fire, you will not be burned;
the flames will not set you ablaze."[3]

A Lesson from Eagles

The Lord never tells us that He will keep us from the fire
or flood. But He tells us again and again that He will lead
us through. He promises to be with us in the middle of it
all – no matter what it is, no matter what shape the storm
takes.

In his book about leadership, Rick Joyner says:

Eagles are the noblest of birds. Few can soar to the
heights that eagles reach. It has been said that all of
nature fears storms except the eagle. That is because
eagles know if they approach opposing winds at the
proper angle they can be carried to even greater
heights with less effort. Remember, every opposing
wind is an opportunity to go higher, but you must
approach it at the right angle or with the right
attitude.[4]

This is our hope and our call. We are to be like eagles.
As the storms threaten to overtake us – to crush us, to fill
us with fear, to send us running away from where the
storms found us – as the winds blow fiercely around us,
we have to remember that there is a place of hope and
security. It is a place that is always available, always

offered; a place where there is always room for one more: the arms of our Father.

I love the deep mystery and irony of God in this. He loves us and He is Love; He leads us to the Eye of the Storm and He is the eye; He will give us peace as He leads us through the storm, and He is the peace.

The story about Jesus walking on the water really fits here. What a great storm story it is, always worth re-reading and re-imagining. Jesus told the disciples to take the boat and go on ahead of Him to the other side while He dismissed the crowd. After He released the people who had come to hear Him teach, He went up on the mountain to pray. He needed to be renewed, refueled. (Guess Who took Jesus by the hand as He made His way up the mountainside.)

When evening came, the disciples' boat was at a distance from land and the waves began to swell. The boat was tossed, and in the fourth watch of the night, Jesus went out to them walking on the lake. The disciples were terrified and at first thought He was a ghost. But Jesus saw their fear and told them to have courage. Peter, our impetuous friend, jumped out of the boat and began to walk on the water toward his Lord. But when Peter saw the wind-whipped waves he was afraid; he took his eyes off Jesus, and he began to sink.[5]

Like it or not, aren't we so like Peter? The storm is raging around us – our marriages are falling apart, our kids are rebellious, on drugs, unwilling to talk to us, our finances are a mess – and then we see God. At least we hope it is Him. Could be a ghost, could be wishful thinking. But we grab the life preserver, clinging to Him, because when we are faced with the towering Eye Wall, God is our only hope.

But the waves get bigger, and the storm rages on – fear and doubt creep (or rush) in – and we begin to sink. We cannot find His Presence, we can't find the Eye of the Storm. We forget what the eagles have taught us; we forget that if we approach the storm 'at the right angle (and) with the right attitude', the wind can lift us up instead of beating us down.

Wherever You Are, He Is

I love Psalm 139 because it reminds us that there is no place we can flee from God:

> O Lord, you have searched me and you know me; you know when I sit and when I rise; you perceive my thoughts from afar. You discern my going out and my lying down; you are familiar with all my ways…. Where can I go from your Spirit? Where can I flee from your presence? If I go to the heavens you are there; if I make my bed in the depths you are there. If I rise on the wings of the dawn, if I settle on the far side of the sea, even there your hand will guide me. [6]

Wherever you are, He is there. He is with you in any storm you encounter, no matter where or when. You cannot hide from Him, and He will never hide from you.

When I allowed my husband to lead me over the boulders, I entered a place of rest. Jesus was then and is now that place for each of us. I held my husband's hand, and I was yoked with Christ.

The Bible offers many examples of ordinary men and women who clung to Him in the midst of the storms in their lives. Again and again we are shown how people like you and I found God and entered the eye of the storm that threatened to overtake them.

Trust Is the Key

We can see that when ordinary everyday people trust God through their responses to the storms of life, they become extraordinary. We may not like it much, but we do know that storms are inevitable. And it is our response to them that determines whether we:

- become bitter or better
- simply weather the storm or become storm warriors
- give up and let the storm beat us up
- surrender to God and allow Him to lead us up the mountainside, over the boulders
- become like eagles and allow the storm to take us to the eye of His Presence

Job

Who had as many storms in his life as Job? Can you imagine? This faith-filled man lost his children, his home, and his livestock; then he suffered horribly painful lesions and boils all over his body; and then even his friends and wife turned on him. Amidst all of this – not just one hurricane but one after another, storm upon storm – Job responded by trusting God. He did not understand any of it, couldn't fathom why a loving Father would allow such an overwhelming Eye Wall onslaught. Job had a million questions and not one answer. And in spite of it all, contrary to the world's counsel, Job's response was: "Though he slay me, yet will I hope in him"[7] … and

"...he knows the way I take; when he has tested me, I will come forth as gold. "[8]

With the storms raging around him, with his wife telling him that death would be better than what he was facing, Job bet on God. Job trusted that God was as good as His word. And it paid off.

David

How about the boy who killed the giant with one stone? Anointed to be King of Israel, David's life hit the storm named Saul. (At that time in Israel, the weather service was willing to give storms masculine names.) King Saul, the first-and-current king of Israel, was jealous of David and relentlessly pursued him. Saul was obsessed with killing young David. In the midst of it all – running from the King and his army, hiding in caves, fearing for his life – David trusted God. He knew his time to be King would come, and he knew it beyond the shadow of a doubt because the true King of Israel, the eternal King had told him so. God was David's place of refuge in the middle of Hurricane Saul.

When David was hiding from King Saul in a cave at Engedi, he had a great opportunity to surprise Saul and be rid of him for good, but he chose not to. It was not time. He knew it wasn't time because the One he trusted, the One Who was leading him, told him so. David bet on God's timing and authority. And it paid off.

Mary

Mary the mother of Jesus hit an Eye Wall when the angel of the Lord told her she would become pregnant. This small-town teenaged girl was visited by an angel and informed that she would be the mother of the Savior of the world. Do you think this was part of Mary's plan? Do you think that upon hearing this news she thought it was a good plan? Do you think Mary thought she was 'right for the job'? She was engaged to Joseph and her out-of-wedlock pregnancy would be a profound disgrace. The Jewish religious laws at that time dictated that any girl pregnant out of wedlock should be taken to the edge of town and stoned to death.

How could Mary explain this to Joseph? How could she make him believe her story? She almost couldn't believe the story herself. "Uh ... the Holy Spirit impregnated me – I've never had a physical relationship with anyone, I swear – I don't exactly understand it either ... but it's true. Really. The King of the Universe has asked me to give birth to His son. I swear. "

Fat chance Joseph or anyone, including Mary's parents, friends and family, would believe that story. Would you? If Hugo was a Category 4 hurricane, I think it is fair to say that, at least to Mary, the hurricane named You'll-be-impregnated-by-the-Holy-Spirit-and-bear-God's-son was a Category 1000.

If God had not spoken to Joseph in a dream, it would have been a huge, tragic mess. No way could Mary have convinced her fiancé that she was a 'handmaid of the Lord'[9], chosen by God Himself. It would have been a Category 1000 mess with disgrace and exile, if not Mary's death, as the (quite natural) result.

But Mary chose to trust God. He had chosen her, and she said, "Yes." Where could she go to flee from His

Presence? Nowhere. Which is now here in one word. God is not only in the now here; He is also in the back-there and the up-ahead. He is anywhere and everywhere we are.

Mary bet on God's sovereignty and powers of persuasion, and it paid off.

Paul and Silas

One time in Philippi, Paul and Silas ended up in prison. (Actually prison was like Paul's home away from home.) The story of this particular stay in prison is found in the sixteenth chapter of the Book of Acts; and it is one of the Bible's most amazing, outlandish, crazy, fantastic stories about the Eye of the Storm. Here is part:

> The crowd joined in the attack against Paul and Silas, and the magistrates ordered them to be stripped and beaten. After they had been severely flogged, they were thrown into prison, and the jailer was commanded to guard them carefully. Upon receiving such orders, he put them in the inner cell and fastened their feet in the stocks.

> About midnight Paul and Silas were praying and singing hymns to God, and the other prisoners were listening to them. Suddenly there was such a violent earthquake that the foundations of the prison were shaken. At once all the prison doors flew open, and everybody's chains came loose. The jailer woke up, and when he saw the prison doors open, he drew his sword and was about to kill himself because he thought the prisoners had escaped. But Paul shouted, "Don't harm yourself! We are all here!"

> The jailer called for lights, rushed in and fell trembling before Paul and Silas. He then brought them out and asked, "Sirs, what must I do to be saved?"[10]

How many people do you know who would sing in prison? At best they would fear being beaten up, right? But Paul and Silas didn't fear the beating because they had already been beaten to bloody pulps before being thrown into prison.

How many people would stick around in prison once they had been released from their chains and their prison door 'flew open'? A case can be made that when a miracle like that happens, you're supposed to take advantage of it, right?

Paul and Silas did not do what any sane person would expect them to do because they knew that they were meant to be exactly where they found themselves. They were in the middle of this particular hurricane (and earthquake) because God intended for them to personally lead their fellow prisoners and their jailer to the Eye of the Storm.

In the midst of the storm, Paul and Silas trusted God. The chains of fear and despair were broken as they praised Him, and their physical chains were removed when they stood their ground and saved the jailer. Paul and Silas bet on God's promise to set the captives free, and it paid off.

When we find ourselves in chains of bondage or despair or paralyzing fear or loneliness, if we trust and praise

God, He will break the chains. The Presence of God replaces the chains of whatever prison we may find ourselves in. The storm may still rage, but looking for Him and praising Him and thanking Him in the midst of it will take us directly into the eye of the storm.

Elijah

Elijah was a nut case. He had an extraordinary encounter with God on Mount Carmel, and then he promptly forgot it. He confronted the 450 false prophets of Baal on the mountaintop and challenged them to call on their god to send fire on the sacrifice. Of course that never happened; after a ridiculous display of incantations to their supposed god, the gang of false prophets gave up. Then Elijah called on the One true God and fire fell and the offering was consumed.[11]

But poor Elijah hit an Eye Wall. Something happened after his mountaintop experience that made him run for his life out of fear. He stopped trusting the God who had just demonstrated that He was Lord of all the storms.

Elijah ran and when he could run no more he hid in a cave. Naturally God found him there. Remember the one place we can we flee from His Presence? Nowhere. God is anywhere we are, including nowhere.

God told Elijah to get a grip, to remember what God had just done, and to get back in the eye of the storm where safety was guaranteed.

As God met Elijah, He will meet you – anywhere, anytime, in the midst of any storm you face. Even when you are a nut case. Even when you are doubtful or fearful; even when it seems like the waves will consume you. Even when you find yourself in a cave.

He asks only that we trust Him to lead us through the storms and over the boulders. The place of immunity is the place of shelter in God. Once we find this place nothing we encounter in life can defeat us. Not any storm. Not even death. The Eye of the Storm, God's Presence, is the place where:

- Fear is replaced by His love
- Torment is replaced by His peace
- Satan's lies are replaced by God's Truth
- Discouragement and despair are replaced with hope and faith

Have you grown weary? Are you besieged by the storm waves of life, by the hurricanes you are facing? Find the place of rest in God. Make space for His Presence. His light will cast out any darkness that threatens to overtake you.

He waits patiently to take you into the eye of the storm. Be bold and cry out, say Yes, take His hand and follow.

Notes

1. Francis Frangipane, A Place of Immunity, 64
2. Matthew 11:28
3. Isaiah 43:1-2
4. Rick Joyner, Leadership: The Power of a Creative Life, 39-40
5. Matthew 14:22-33
6. Psalm 139
7. Job 13:15
8. Job 23:10
9. Luke 1:38, KJV: And Mary said, Behold the handmaid of the Lord; be it unto me according to thy word....
10. Acts 16:22-30
11. 1 Kings 18:17-40

4 I AM SPEAKS... THEN AND NOW

Mary figured it out. How did she do it? How did she know that the only voice that she needed to hear was the voice of her Savior? Even more than that how did she do it? How did she block out the clatter in the kitchen, the guests arriving and her sister fussing that she wasn't helping? Mary figured it out. And we need to figure it out too. We need I mean desperately need to hear the voice of God. The world is shouting all too loudly but Our Great Shepherd has promised us (His sheep) that we will hear His voice if we will only be still.

Speaking of listening... Life can be so funny. I was going to church to preach at our Wednesday night service and I had been praying about what the Lord had on His mind for the night. I had my prepared talk but sensed I had left something out. I live right around the corner from the church but I decided not to walk and took my car that night.

Tuned In, Tuned Out
As I was driving I heard the word Neuschwanstein. What? Was that my vain imagining? Was that God? If it was God, why was He talking in German? Did He forget how rusty my German is?

So I raced back home to get my German dictionary (in case it was God speaking) and then turned around and rushed back out to church, thanking God that the church is just around the corner from my house. I made it to the church parking lot in record time, and as soon as I had parked my car a police cruiser was there beside me with the flashing light. Hmm, I thought, I wonder why he's stopped beside me. Is he pulling someone over?

When the policeman got out of his patrol car and came over to my car – where I was busily leafing through my German dictionary to find Neuschwanstein – I looked up and realized that he wanted to talk to me. I rolled down my window and asked him if I could help him, more than a little irritated that he had interrupted my last-minute research project. He said, "Young lady, did you not see the stop sign back there?"

I liked him better already. Not everyone notices how young I look. "No, sir," I said, "I didn't. "

I cannot count the number of times I've not only seen that stop sign, but also actually stopped at it. I have lived here for years, and I have driven to my church only about six or seven million times.

"Well, you ran a stop sign and almost ran into an eighteen-wheeler. You could have seen the pupils in his eyes you were so close – an inch or so. "

"What? No, really? Me, sir?" You see, I wasn't operating in the now-here; I was living in *what- the-heck-does-Neuschwanstein-mean* time.

"What were you thinking?" he asked me.

I apologized and told him I was not thinking at all. "Actually I was praying," I said.

"Well, Ma'am," he replied without missing a beat, "do you pray with your eyes closed or open?"

I share this story with you because this was one of those times when God was talking to me. I am never completely sure when it is His suggestion or instruction or thought, but I always try to keep my spiritual antennae tuned in, in case He is communicating.

My grandfather had one of the earliest radios. You may have seen one like it – large, solid, rounded at the top, squared off at the base, beautiful wood. Anyway, as a child I used to fiddle around with that radio, trying to tune in different stations. One night I picked up an overseas station, and I could clearly make out people talking in a foreign language, though I cannot recall now what language they were speaking (or even if I knew then what the language was). I was stunned at the clarity and otherworldliness of this faraway connection. I can see myself now running to get my parents and tell them what I had discovered, as if maybe no one in the world had ever discovered it before.

But what stands out to me now is how I spent hours back-then trying to tune in – trying to find a faraway station without too much static or interference – and how thrilling it was when I did.

Often Mysterious

I am often on the wrong station when the King of the Universe speaks to me, or I'm tuned in to my own station, filled with my own thoughts, worries, to-do's. But this time, this Wednesday night on the way to church, He got through. And as so often has been the case in my experience, the word He said did not make immediate sense to me; it was mysterious. Truth be told, what I heard seemed a little crazy.

But as I said, I always check it out because I am always asking Him to speak. And I had to believe that it was not I who had come up with Neuschwanstein on my own in some random thought process. Right? Anyway, the word is the name of an ancient palace in Germany – the New Swan Stone palace – and, believe it or not, it had great meaning for me in that particular instance. It added value to the talk I was giving – it was the something I had sensed I'd left out.

God may speak to us in strange, mysterious ways, but that doesn't mean that what is spoken – a word or phrase, an instruction – isn't from God. I think for me He does this so I will pay attention. One thing I am certain of is that whatever He says will never contradict what He has already said in His written Word.

Think of the way Jesus spoke to His disciples. He spoke in parables, stories, metaphors. He spoke in ways that His followers often did not understand. But it got them asking questions, listening more closely, delving more deeply into what their Lord was saying.

If we allow Him, God never stops teaching us, expanding us, deepening us.

Maybe He uses mystery to entice us, to focus our wandering attention – to get us to tune in.

Patient Repetition for the Hearing-Impaired

Another time a friend asked me to pray for her and her daughter. Her daughter was 16 at the time, pregnant, and had decided to put her child up for adoption. They had reviewed several files on potential adoptive parents and were trying to make a decision. There was one couple in particular that they felt the Lord had told them was the right one.

I prayed for my friend and her daughter for three days, and each day after I prayed I stopped to listen. I try to do this regularly because I talk so much – even when God is speaking – and I often don't hear Him because of my own chatter. The first day I heard a name, but I dismissed it. I don't know why – why did I doubt what I heard? – because I'm human and was not willing to listen and trust even when I had set the time aside to do just that? The second day I heard the same name; and by the third day, the name repeated again finally got my undivided attention.

Was this God speaking? If so, I needed to share it with my friend. So although I thought it was risky, I told her. I told my friend that every time I prayed for them I heard a name; and I gave her the name. Immediately she dissolved in tears and fell into my arms like a limp rag. When she was able to compose herself she told me that the name I had given her was the name of the woman whom they had chosen to adopt the baby.

Coincidence? I know many would say so. But I call these things *Godincidences*. I am convinced that God spoke to me then, and that He speaks to His children all the time. He has spoken to us since the day He created us, and He has never stopped.

I am thankful that He is so patient and willing to repeat Himself for those (like me) who are hearing-impaired.

The Shepherd's Voice

I am convinced that Jesus was telling the truth when He spoke of Himself as a shepherd and His followers as sheep:

> ... the sheep listen to his voice. He calls his own sheep by name and leads them out. When he has brought out all his own, he goes on ahead of them, and his sheep follow him because they know his voice.[1]

Jesus convinces me that He is our Shepherd, He *does* call us, and we *do* hear His voice.

What's Better: Risk-Taking Faith or Play-It-Safe Denial?

Listen, I know it's risky to say we hear from God. I get that. Hey, I'm not crazy! (Or maybe I am, but we'll get to that later, when we talk about Elijah.) But these days I think: isn't it better, finally, to step out in faith and make a fool of ourselves than to ignore His voice and miss one mysterious and incredible opportunity after another?

I know this sounds kooky to some people. Over the years intellect and reason and the world's counsel have crowded out the possibilities that God is so personal. But ask the disciples. Ask the early church if God spoke to them. Ask modern-day risk-taking Christ followers if there have ever been times when God has spoken to them and they've acted on what He has said. While you're at it, ask if there have ever been events in their lives that they had to call miraculous because neither they nor any resident experts could come up with a better – even more *logical* – explanation.

If we conducted our own surveys on whether God speaks to His children – if we asked the disciples, the early church, and true believers today – I think we would all be surprised at their responses.

Why Wouldn't He?

If God spoke back-then, why wouldn't He speak now-here? Why wouldn't He? Why would He go silent? Did He get tired of our not listening to Him? Did we hearing-impaired so exasperate Him that He gave up on communication? Does that make any sense at all, even on a pragmatic, logical level?

God and His beloved son Jesus and their Holy Spirit live in the present, the now-here. They always have, always will. We humans are the ones who invented Time and split our story into the three not-so-neat divisions of Past, Present and Future.

Does it make any sense at all that the Father, the Son and the Holy Spirit would speak in and through and to us in the back-then (present) and not in the right-now (present)?

The first time God spoke to Moses, He said, "I am the God of your father, the God of Abraham, the God of Isaac and the God of Jacob. "[2] Then later during that same first meeting:
    Moses said to God, "Suppose I go to the Israelites

and say to them, 'The God of your fathers has sent
me to you,' and they ask me, 'What is his name?'
Then what shall I tell them?"
God said to Moses, "I am who I am. This is what
you are to say to the Israelites: 'I AM has sent me to
you. ' "³

So one of the very first times that God speaks directly to
His creation (the first time He speaks to Moses), He says
He is *Ehyeh asher ehyeh, I Am*. God tells us He is The
Present personified,

He lives in the Eternal Right Now.   And guess what?
Though *Ehyeh asher ehyeh* is generally interpreted to mean *I
am that I am*, it more literally translates as *I-shall-be that I-
shall-be*. Isn't that amazing, mysterious and wonder-full?
God is *I Am* and *I Shall Be* at the same time! He is
Forever Now; He is Now Forever.

I Am spoke to us and still speaks to us … then and now.

The Holy Spirit: God's Voice

Nearing the end of His life on earth, Jesus told His
followers that He had to leave the earth so that His Holy
Spirit could come and lead them (us) into all truth. Jesus
had to leave so that the Holy Spirit could come and stay.
Since Jesus left Earth to be with His Father in heaven, the
Holy Spirit has been His voice here and now. We have
just so often been tuned into the wrong station – Earth's
frequency instead of Eternity's.

I recently read this description of faith:
How dark the seeing. How fragmentary. Mostly it
consists of learning to freefall. Learning to trust the

constant somersaulting. Learning to live with spiritual vertigo. [4]

Patricia Garatti, a friend of mine in ministry, told me that living by faith and learning to listen to God's voice and to trust Him really is like freefalling, even though you know you have a supernatural parachute.

That's the way it is for me when I think I am hearing from God. I am not always sure it is He, but I do trust Him enough to know that if I fall He will open His parachute for me.

Is In Part Enough?

Paul put it this way: *Now we see but a poor reflection, as in a mirror. Then we shall see face to face. Now I know in part....* [5] Until we go to be with the Lord, we only hear and see in part; we are capable of seeing and comprehending only a piece of His wonderfully deep, complex and mysterious plan. Our station while we're here on Earth is often filled with the static of the world, our own thoughts and the things we see with our natural eyes. Right now we trust that He is here and that He is speaking to His sheep (us), but we hear only *in part*, and we see only a piece of the mosaic.

I don't know about you, but *in part* is enough to make me look for Him and listen for His voice daily. The promise of a piece of Him makes me want to tune into His station. And as I realize that what He gives me is only a part of the whole, I want to 'stay tuned for more'.

The Jewish people have a saying that one must stay close enough to the Rabbi to feel the dust from his shoes. It makes perfectly good sense to me that we Christ followers must stay close to *The* Rabbi, Jesus, so that when He speaks we can hear His voice. So that when He reveals Himself – even if only *in part* – when He shows us Truth, we can see with our spiritual eyes.

A Must Question

"Does God still speak today?" For an authentic now-here risk-taking God seeker, this is a must-ask-and-answer question. Isn't it? Is it even possible to believe in and trust and follow a God who does not speak into our lives as we are living them?

How we answer these questions will determine the course we take on our spiritual journeys. And the answers may well determine if we venture any further on those journeys at all.

Proof To Take Along

Again, if it really is He who is speaking, He will never contradict the Scriptures He has given us. He is consistent – in fact, He cannot help but be. He is always faithful. He not only tells the truth and leads us to truth – He is Truth.

Scripture tells us that *Jesus Christ is the same yesterday and today and forever.*[6] God is the same today as He was in the past. He has never changed. Though He speaks to each of us at different
times and in different ways, He has never stopped speaking to us:

> In the past, God spoke to our forefathers through the prophets at many times and various ways but in these last days he has spoken to us by His Son whom

71

He appointed heir of all things and through whom he made the universe. [7]

The words of Christ held more "weight" than the prophets' words. God spoke through the prophets but when Jesus came to live among us, God spoke through His Son. Jesus (*Yeshua* in Hebrew/Aramaic) was appointed heir of all things, and as the exact representation of God He spoke to us. While He was with us, He was God The Father's voice on the earth.
In the beginning was the Word, and the Word was with God and the Word was God.[8]

Jesus Christ is the Living Word; He came and spoke life and continues to speak life through His Holy Spirit today.
All of this I have spoken while still with you. But the Counselor whom the Father will send in my name will teach you all things and will remind you of everything I have said to you. [9]

So we know – because God tells us so through His Word – that the prophets spoke, Jesus spoke and now His Holy Spirit, living in and among us, speaks to God's people.

The Real Question
The question is not Does God speak today? The real question is: *How* does He speak?

One way to begin answering the question is to look at what Jesus tells His disciples when He's teaching them about His role as The Shepherd. One of the things I vividly remember from my time living in Germany was that I could drive for miles and miles and see only herds of sheep and open countryside. Maybe Jesus was looking out over just such a herd and countryside when He explained that He was the Good Shepherd.

> I tell you the truth, the man who does not enter the sheep pen by the gate, but climbs in by some other way, is a thief and a robber. The man who enters by the gate is the shepherd of his sheep. The watchman opens the gate for him, and the sheep listen to his voice. He calls his own sheep by name and he leads them out. When he has brought out all of his own, he goes on ahead of them, and his sheep follow because they know his voice. [10]

Maybe Jesus could see a court surrounded by walls, open to the sky, which was a common way the sheep were kept. The walls kept the sheep from wandering and protected them from predators.

Several different flocks may have been in the same pen, but a flock would respond only to their own shepherd when he called.

The Good Shepherd

Jesus explains that He is the Good Shepherd who lays His life down for His sheep. Can you imagine the questions that the disciples had for Him that day? Sheep pens were a familiar sight, and the disciples knew that God was known as the Shepherd of Israel,[11] but what was Je- sus saying – is He the Good Shepherd, is it His voice (and no other) that they needed to heed?

That is exactly what their Shepherd was saying to them (and to us); we are still His sheep; and He promised that His sheep will hear His voice. He promised to speak to us, and later He sent the Holy Spirit of God to live in us and speak for Him.

Spirit and Word: The One-Two Punch

I am counting on hearing Jesus through the Holy Spirit. How about you? I am in a mess here with all the voices that crowd Him out. I am counting on His voice to lead me out of the world's noise and doubt and misdirection and into safe pastures – places where I can hear Him clearly and consistently.

Today God speaks through His Holy Spirit. Do you believe that? Are you willing to take the risk and believe Him? Are you willing to be quiet enough to hear Him?

God's Word is also one of His primary means of communicating with His children. In his book, *The Anointing*, R. T. Kendall says:

> God's Word – the Bible – is infallible, inerrant and unchanging. And God gave us the Bible yesterday. But the Holy Spirit applies it today. And if we are open to the immediate and direct witness of the Spirit, the Bible will be doubly real to us. [12]

It was by His Word that the earth – indeed, the entire universe – was created. [13] And He tells us that He will reveal His will to use through His Word, the Holy Scriptures. But remember: God's Holy Spirit and His Word are a one-two punch, and we must be as open to the voice of the Holy Spirit as we are to reading God's Word in the Bible. We must be willing to allow the Spirit to lead us, direct us, and help us discern where God wants us to be. And when we hear His voice, we must also go to His Word and make sure that the voice and the

Word agree.

An Effective One-Two Punch Requires Both

The problem is that we are sometimes open to the Word but not the Spirit, or open to the Spirit but never delve into the Word. Sometimes we forget either the One or the Two, but both are essential if we are to make space for God in our daily lives.

I once heard something that put it all into perspective for me:

> To have the Word without the Spirit is to dry up;
> To have the Spirit without the Word is to blow up;
> To have the Word and the Spirit is to grow up

You and I need both the Word of God and the Spirit of God. Neither is exclusive. He speaks to us through both together.

Unusual for Us, Usual for Him

It may seem unusual for God to speak to me in German but He came alive that day in my preaching through that word (*Neuschwanstein: New Swan Stone palace*).

It may seem unusual for God to speak to me about an adoption but He brought life to my friend and her daughter, and He allowed me the honor of reinforcing and sealing a decision they had already made (with the Holy Spirit leading).

Reminder From A Nut Case

Think about Elijah, the nut case who experienced the undeniable power of God on Mount Carmel, then promptly forgot that the King of the Universe had recently spoken to him, shown up on the mountaintop, and proved Himself yet again. (We talked about Elijah in Chapter 3, *In The Eye of the Storm.*) If God was going to decide never to speak to us again, Elijah would have been a good reason. If you think about it, though, the Bible is full of people who over and over again give God great reasons for never speaking to us again. He just never gives up on us (thank God).

Anyway, Elijah fears for his life and runs into a cave and God asks him what he's doing in there. (Don't you love it? As if God didn't know what His prophet was doing in the cave.) Elijah has just seen God light a fire that consumed a sacrifice. God did His part, as usual. Then, not long after that wondrous example of God showing up, Elijah ran. He ran because he was afraid of the voice of one woman. It is true that woman, Jezebel, had some influence and was pretty formidable – but, come on, Elijah had just seen God at work. I'm guessing Jezebel's power was pale in comparison to God's. Still Elijah ran and ended up in a cave.

Funny thing: we do it too.

We Have Seen The Nut Case and He Is Us
Okay, time for a confession. If Elijah was a nut case … maybe I am too. How about you?

Shall we have a mass-confession? Now that I think about it, I am willing to admit to multiple cases of temporary insanity over the years. I cannot count the number of times God has proven Himself to me, provided just what I needed when I needed it … and then something or someone has come against me and I have promptly forgotten God's unfailing faithfulness and run for the nearest cave.

But God never lets me stay in the cave, and He was not going to allow Elijah to stay in his cave either. He intended to teach Elijah not to listen to any other voices but His:

> The Lord said, "Go out and stand on the mountain in the presence of the Lord, for the Lord is about to pass by. " Then a great and powerful wind tore the mountains apart and shattered the rocks before the Lord, but the Lord was not in the wind. After the wind there was an earthquake, but the Lord was not in the earthquake. After the earthquake came a fire, but the Lord was not in the fire. And after the fire came a gentle whisper. When Elijah heard it, he pulled his cloak over his face and went out and stood at the mouth of the cave. [14]

We are all like Elijah. The storms and fires (even scary, powerful people) that threaten to destroy us and try to divert our attention from the voice of God may be different, but we all experience them. Yet when we leave our caves of discouragement and disillusionment, God is speaking.

We Will Hear Him

Other voices threaten to overtake His because, even though He is a huge God, He chooses most often to speak in a still small voice. Almost a whisper. In order to hear Him, we have to quiet our souls and listen with our spiritual ears. If we do, we will hear Him.

We *will* hear Him.

Do you hear Him as you read this chapter? Do you sense God telling you to leave your cave, to make quiet space in your life to listen for His voice and ignore all the others?

Earplugs

Again and again, the Israelites hardened their hearts to the voice of God. [15] We can do that too. By our own wills, with our own agendas and our own busyness and our tenacious commitment to worldly success and (fill in the blank), we can become desensitized to His voice. Sometimes we use earplugs, and sometimes we don't even know we're doing it. These potential barriers to hearing God's voice include, but certainly are not limited to: unconfessed sin; elevating doctrine (dogma) over a relationship with God; having a form of godliness but denying God's power;[16] refusing to walk in the light that God gives us[17]; and limiting our hearing to God's Word (the Bible) only and forgetting that when He speaks directly to us (through His Holy Spirit) He will never, ever, contradict Scripture.

His Communication Methods

God's Word teaches us that in these last days – right now – we will hear and see spiritually as He pours out His Spirit on us. [18] This Word was confirmed at Pentecost. We will hear God's voice in a variety of ways, including dreams and visions, visitations of angels, and prophecy.

Dreams and Visions

We read about dreams and dream interpretation throughout the Old and New Testaments. Joseph, one of Abraham's sons, dreamed that he was in the field harvesting wheat and his brothers' bundles of wheat bowed down to his. It was not such a good decision on Joseph's part to share this dream with his brothers; he wound up in a pit, then was sold into slavery. But the dream was straight from David's heavenly Father, and it came to pass exactly as God had given it to David.

How about Nebuchadnezzar? He had several dreams that Daniel interpreted. Dreams were a common thing. Why would God stop using dreams as methods of communication?

Angels
What about angelic visitations? God spoke through His angels to Mary and Joseph, warning them to go to Egypt to protect their child. An angel spoke to John the Baptist's dad and told him that he would have a boy; and told him that the child's name was to be John; and told him that John would prepare the way for the Savior of the world. Angels as messengers for God were commonplace. Can you think of any good reason why God would stop using angels to bring His messages to us?

The Word tells us that we entertain angels at times without knowing it. [19]   How about you? Have you ever met an angel?

Prophets
Throughout the Bible, in both the Old and New Testaments, God speaks through His proph- ets. He uses these committed people to tell what is to come. Paul writes that the gift of prophecy is real but that we should be aware that it can be abused. The Corinthian church needed correction when they abused their prophetic gifts.

We know from Scripture that there were (and will be) true and false prophets. Why would God choose to stop using prophets to communicate with His people?

No Good Reason
I am convinced beyond the shadow of a doubt that God speaks today. He speaks through His Holy Spirit, and He still speaks through communication channels He has used since the beginning of Time. He gives His children dreams and visions; He sends angels to deliver messages; and He gives some of us prophetic words. He hasn't changed. Why would He?

Over the course of time we have chosen to believe that our King no longer speaks to us. Some of us have seen people badly abuse gifts they have been given and put words in God's mouth that contradict Scripture and deny the Truth. But there is no good reason to believe that God no longer speaks to us. Nothing He has said to us – in His Word or through His Son or His prophets or His Holy Spirit or His angels or dreams and visions – has ever suggested that He has given up on communicating with us. There is no reason to stop asking to hear His voice. I know that, for me, there are compelling reasons every single day to ask Him to speak.

Are you willing to leave your cave and stand on the mountain and wait for His whisper? I Am is still speaking today. He is not speaking to hear Himself talk. He is speaking into our lives so that we can know that we matter to Him and He has a plan for us and He knows what the next step is to be. The very next step, and the step after that.

My son, if you accept my words and store up my

commands within you, turning your ear to wisdom and applying your heart to understanding, and if you call out for insight and cry aloud for understanding, and if you look for it as for silver and search for it as hidden treasure then you will understand the fear of the Lord and find knowledge of God.[20]

God wants us to hear His still small voice. It is really the only one that matters.

Notes

1. John 10:3-4
2. Exodus 3:6
3. Exodus 3:13-14
4.   Dan Wakefield, How Do We Know When It's God (quoting Wendy Wright), 258
5.   1 Corinthians 13:12
6.   Hebrews 13:8
7.   Hebrews 1:1
8.   John 1:1
9. John 14:25-26
10. John 10:2-4
11.   Psalm 80:1
12. R. T.   Kendall, The Anointing: Yesterday, Today, Tomorrow, 176
13.   Genesis 1
14. 1 Kings 19:11-13
15.   Hebrews 3:7-8
16.   2 Corinthians 10
17. 1 John 1:5-7
18. Joel 2:28-30
19.   Hebrews 13:2
20.   Proverbs 2:1-5

5 LIVING THE SPIRIT-FILLED LIFE

I suspect that Mary had not heard the conversations between Jesus and His disciples. You know the ones where He said that He must go so that His Father could send the Holy Spirit. I wonder if the disciples leaned in a little closer when Jesus described what the Holy Spirit would do for them someday. At the time they did not understand, but on Pentecost it became so clear. Jesus was true to His Word and sent the Comforter to come alongside them. But Mary already knew The Comforter in her friend Jesus. When her duties could have tempted her to jump up from her front row seat with Jesus to get her work done, she simply sat at His feet. She knew comfort when she saw Him. She knew the Comforter in the person of Jesus. After Jesus left I believe that Mary, well acquainted with Jesus, flowed right in to living the Spirit filled life. I doubt she missed a beat. I feel sure she shed a tear or two, but she recognized the Holy Spirit and welcomed Him in to her home.

Who is the Holy Spirit? Doesn't it make sense that we have to meet Him and understand who He is before we can decide if or how we'll make space for Him in our lives? If we don't understand who the Holy Spirit is, how He functions, and especially why we need Him, the idea of making space for Him doesn't make much sense at all.

Who Is He?
When I was a child, and as I grew up, the Holy Spirit – who He is and what His roles are – was not often the

subject of sermons or teaching. I think that is still the case these days in many churches, and I believe that's so because many people find the Holy Spirit confusing. Baffling. John Ortberg explains:

> A lot of the people that I talk with may have a pretty concrete idea of God the Father and a vivid picture of Jesus the Son, but the Spirit seems kind of vague, often seems impersonal, like some kind of force. He is not. This is an important point. If you know Jesus, you know the Spirit. Father, Son and Spirit are three different persons, (emphasis mine) but they don't have three different personalities. It's not as if you could give them the Meyers-Briggs test (for those of you who are into that) and they would have three different temperaments, and the Holy Spirit would be the shy one. It's not that kind of deal. [1]

First and foremost, the Holy Spirit is the third person of the trinity. The Holy Spirit is a co-equal with the Father and the Son. As John Ortberg tells us, He is a distinct person with the same personality as the Father and the Son. The Holy Spirit is One and Three-in-One. Remember the Three Musketeers' motto, *All for one and one for all?* Well, with a slight re-write, that's a fairly good description of the holy trinity and the relationship of the three persons of the Godhead: All in One and One in All. God the Father, God the Son, and God the Holy Spirit are separate, distinct, and perfectly unified.

Mysterious and Knowable: The Third Person

Listen, no matter how deeply we look into the trinity – in this case, the Holy Spirit specifically – we will never 'solve' the *mystery* of God's three persons. At least on this side of eternity, let's not try to solve anything; instead, let's revel in this truly glorious mystery and learn as much as we can through what God has taught us. The Father has revealed much about His Holy Spirit – through His Son Jesus, as well as the men and women throughout history who have written down and passed along what God has made known to them.

The mystery of the Holy Spirit – who He is, and how He does what He does, how He lives and moves in us – the mystery of all that – is deeper than ever. You see, the confusion is lifted and dissolved as we press in with each prayer, each question, each Spirit-led reading of God's Word … and the gorgeous mysteriousness grows deeper.

Two analogies that attempt to reveal something of the relationship between the Father, Son and Holy Spirit have stuck with me. They don't 'solve' anything, they are not formulae and they are not comprehensive; they are simply interesting illustrations of a general theme, ways to think about the mystery.

One is the egg analogy: one complete egg has three components: shell, egg white, and yolk. The other is the three forms that water can take: solid (ice), liquid (water), and gas (steam); each is a separate and distinct form, but they are all, finally, H_2O.

The Music of the Godhead

Victoria Brooks describes the relationship – the perfect unity – between the Father, Son, and Holy Spirit this way:

> Everything Jesus did on earth was sovereignly synchronized with the music of His Father's will. *Every move He made was dependent upon the leading of the Holy Spirit. (emphasis mine)* Father, Son, and Holy

Spirit, the ancient Chord of Three, has never ceased to sound. Like God Himself, the Music has no beginning and no end. This love song that the church has been commissioned to play was written long before she was ever born. It predates her and her salvation message. Long before the earth was created, long before mankind was made. The Music of the Godhead ran throughout the great-unformed expanse that is now our universe. [2]

Mysterious and wonderful and unsolvable, isn't it? But listen: the Godhead, the Three-in-One, playing a love song over the universe, perfectly joined together in synchrony, is beckoning the church (you and me) to enter the song. The Holy Spirit calls us into the music. We are being called to minister to the Father and the Son.

Mysterious though He may be, the Holy Spirit is knowable, and as I read what Vicky Brooks says about the relationship between the Father, the Son and the Holy Spirit, a question rises and floats in my mind: "Are we willing to learn to know and love The Music?"

The Ministry of Love
Until we understand who the Father, Son, and the Holy Spirit are, we cannot enter the Music – we can't be a part of this ministry of love. Living the Spirit-filled life is about asking the third person of the Trinity to live in us so that we can enter into a relationship with the All of Him, the three-in-one.

So that we can be in the Music; so that we can love unconditionally, just as the Father, Son and Holy Spirit do.

Living the Spirit-filled life is not only about recognizing who He is, but also surrendering to His lead.

Leading and Following: Dancing with the Best

There is nothing more wonderful than dancing with someone who knows how to lead. When I was a little girl, my Father would put my feet on top of his and glide me around the room. He is still an incredibly good dancer. I felt like a professional dancer when I was with him ... because he led so well. Following was easy.

Allowing the Holy Spirit to lead and guide us is like dancing with a superstar.

I think the TV show *Dancing with the Stars* has been so successful because we all secretly wish we could dance like that. We think if we just had the right coach we could dance. I am mesmerized by the show, but what captivates me most is how the dance coach is able to teach the stars how to dance – particularly the football players and others who don't 'look the part'. Theory is one thing; doing is another.

I recently read an e-mail comparing dancing and doing God's will:

> When I meditated on *guidance*, I was drawn to *dance* at the end of the word. I reflected upon how doing God's will is a lot like dancing. When two people try to lead, nothing feels right. The movement doesn't flow with the music, and everything is quite uncomfortable and jerky.

> When one person realizes this and lets the other person lead, both bodies begin to flow with the

music.

What a beautiful picture of following the lead of the Holy Spirit, the third person of the trinity – the dance coach, the one who leads, and the dance partner. Three in one.

In the Beginning … And From Then On

In the beginning, *God* created the heavens and the earth. Now the earth was formless and empty, darkness was over the surface of the deep, and the *Spirit* of God was hovering over the waters. [3]
(*emphasis mine*)

We see God and His Spirit at the moment of creation, distinct and in perfect unity. And we also hear God refer to the Trinity:

> Then God said, let us make man in *our* image, in our likeness and let them rule over the fish of the sea and the birds of the air over the livestock over all the earth and over the livestock, over all the earth [4]
> (*emphasis mine*)

The Holy Spirit was at work throughout the Old Testament He was always near the people, though not in them. He 'came upon' them for a particular reason and a finite period of time, to accomplish a specific job (known in the Greek as *epiklisis*) For example, when the temple was being built in Jerusalem, God filled Bezalel, a skilled craftsman, with the Holy Spirit in order to divinely work through him:

> Then the Lord said to Moses. See I have chosen Bezalel son of Uri, the son of Hur, of the tribe of Judah, and I have filled him with the Spirit of God, with skill, ability and knowledge in all kinds of crafts[5]

We see the Holy Spirit on Moses, and when the Israelites complained that they were tired of the manna that God had sent them, Moses complained to God that he could not carry all of the people himself. God tells Moses to bring him 70 of Israel's elders and that He would take the same spirit that was on Moses and put it on them [6]

In Deuteronomy, before Moses died he laid hands on Joshua, his successor, and Joshua was filled with the spirit of wisdom.7 Just before Gideon defeated the Amalekites and the Midianites, who were oppressing Israel, the Spirit of the Lord came upon him [8]

The Holy Spirit Rests on Jesus

In the eleventh chapter of Isaiah, the prophet tells us that God's Spirit would rest on Jesse's descendant (David and ultimately Jesus):

> The Spirit of the Lord will rest on him – the Spirit of wisdom and of understanding, the Spirit of counsel and of power, the Spirit of knowledge and of the fear of the Lord. [9]

The Holy Spirit was upon Jesus when He was among us. He followed the will of His Father, and He stayed connected to the Godhead. There was never a time when Jesus was not connected to His Father and their Holy Spirit.

In the third chapter of Luke's gospel, when Jesus was baptized by John the Baptist, the heavens opened and the Holy Spirit descended upon Jesus in the form of a dove. Can you imagine that scene? And as the heavens opened up, God the Father looked down at His Son and spoke: *You are my Son whom I love; with you I am well pleased.* [10]

Wow.

Listen again to John Ortberg:
> You may never have thought about this, but
> everything that Jesus does, He does through the
> Spirit. Luke goes directly on from there. Jesus, full
> of the Holy Spirit, returned from the Jordan and was
> led by the Spirit in the desert. (Luke 4:1) He's filled
> with the Spirit; He's led by the Spirit. The very next
> event after He spends forty days in the desert being
> tempted, Jesus returned to Galilee in the power of
> the Spirit and news about Him spread. (Luke 4:14)[11]

No Longer On, But In
Tucked away in the book of Joel is a passage that pointed
to Pentecost, the time after Jesus' death and resurrection
when believers were filled with the Holy Spirit. No longer
would the Spirit come upon people for a period of time
to do specific works – the Spirit would indwell, stay, lead,
and direct the paths of God followers:
> And afterward, I will pour out my Spirit on all
> people. Your sons and daughters will prophesy, your
> old men will dream dreams; your young men will see
> visions. Even on my servants, both men and
> women, I will pour out my Spirit in those days. [12]

Through His prophet Joel, God was talking about us.
The prophecy spoke into the age to come when the Holy
Spirit would fill Christians. Just as the Spirit was in every
single thing that Jesus did and said when He was on the
earth, that same Holy Spirit became available to us after
Jesus ascended to His Father.
Jesus knew we would need the third person of the
Godhead in order to enter into the music.

He knew we needed *the* expert dance coach to lead us, teach us, empower us. . . and remind us of everything Jesus had said and done when He was with us.

Labor Pains and Living Water
Thirty-four years ago I had my first encounter with the third person of the trinity. Born and raised in the Greek Orthodox Church, I was in love with God the Father and yearned to stay close to His Son. I loved walking into the church sanctuary and seeing the magnificent icons depicting the story of Jesus. I memorized Scripture; I sang the beautiful worship songs. I simply loved being in the house of the Lord.

But when I left the church building, I wondered if Jesus stayed back in the church until we returned again the following Sunday. Where was His Presence? It certainly loomed large in our magnificent Byzantine church. He was *everywhere* there. But what about when I left?

After I was married and had started a family of my own, I somehow ended up attending a Bible study in another church. It was there that I began to become familiar with the Holy Spirit. Not that the church of my youth did not talk about Him – pointing out that the Holy Spirit was leading us in our faith – but He wasn't as near to me as the Father and the Son. He was more concept than person. I asked the priest at the church that held the Bible study if I could talk to him about this, and he agreed to meet with me.

The day we met, the priest prayed a simple prayer: "Lord, would you fill your servant, Joanne, with your Holy Spirit

– release a full measure of Your Presence into her life. "
He explained to me that when I became a Christian by
accepting Christ as my Lord and Savior, the Holy Spirit
was present, and he reminded me of Paul's letter to the
church in Ephesus:

> And you were included in Christ when you heard the
> word of truth, the gospel of your salvation. Having
> believed you were marked in Him with a seal, the
> promised Holy Spirit who is a deposit guaranteeing
> our inheritance until redemption…. [13]

The question was not really whether the Holy Spirit was
present in my life; He was there. What I needed to ask
myself, and wrestle with, was whether I recognized Him
and surrendered to Him. Did I desire to be fully
surrendered to His work in my life? Well, I wasn't so sure.

By the way, I was nine months pregnant at the time.
That's an important detail because that night I woke up
thinking I might be in labor. My doctor-husband was on
call at the hospital, so I phoned him to tell him that I had
a strange sensation in my veins. Okay – if you didn't yet
think I was weird, you probably do now. It's officially out:
something strange was happening to me, and I am hard-
pressed to adequately describe it. I felt as though I had
water rushing through my veins. It didn't hurt, but it was
surprising and disconcerting. I had never experienced it.
I had given birth before, but this water- rushing-in-my-
veins thing was new. If this was my 'water breaking', it
was doing it in a very different way (not to mention
location).

My husband calmly assured me this was not labor, though
he didn't have any more of a clue about what this

phenomenon was than I did. I was greatly concerned. Or maybe I was more curious than concerned.

A few days later my labor began, and after the baby was delivered, the priest whose Bible study I attended came to see me in the hospital. When I told him about my strange sci-fi rushing-water-in-veins experience, he quietly picked up his Bible, flipped to a passage in John's gospel and read:

> If anyone is thirsty, let him come to me and drink. Whoever believes in me as the Scripture has said, streams of living water will flow from within him. [14]

I had been thirsty; I had gone to the priest and talked to him about the Holy Spirit, and the priest had prayed for me to receive a 'full measure' of Him and His presence. I had said I wanted to know the Holy Spirit better, and the Holy Spirit took me at my word. The priest asked on my behalf, the third person of the trinity heard the cry of my heart and released His Spirit in me as I surrendered to Him.

The same night the priest had prayed for me to receive the Holy Spirit, His Living Water had begun to flow *within* me.

I once heard my experience compared to a house wired with electricity. Until you turn the power on, the house is still dark. Up to the day with the priest, my spiritual life had extended only to knowing about and accepting Christ (wiring my 'house' with electricity); but asking the Spirit to actively live in me, yielding to His work in me, flipped the switch and lit the entire house!

I suspect that I could have kept Him in a dusty corner of my living room space. Sure I could have. Jesus says He stands at the door and knocks,[15] but we have to choose to say Yes to Him and open the door to let Him in. If I had not asked the Holy Spirit to come live in me, I would not have discovered the full life that Christ describes:

> I have come that they may have life, and have it to the full. [16]

After that experience, the Scriptures became clearer to me and my heart seemed to be on fire, excited about the prospect of each day with the Lord – each day with the Living Water *within* me.

The Disciples Waited

Can you imagine the scene in the upper room? Jesus told His disciples to wait. He had promised that He would send His Holy Spirit. In fact Jesus told them that He had to go in order to send His Spirit:

> But I tell you the truth: It is for your good that I am going away. Unless I go away, the Counselor will not come to you; but if I go, I will send him to you. [17]

He told them not to leave Jerusalem but to wait for the gift His Father had promised.

And the day came. All of them were huddled together. Their Savior was gone. All they had to hold on to was a faint promise that He would send His Spirit. Whatever that meant. I wonder what I would have done. Would I have been among the faithful? Or would I have been sitting beside the empty tomb wondering, *What's next – what do I do now?* How about you?

The disciples knew what was next. They held onto a promise. And they were not disappointed:

> When the day of Pentecost came they were all together in one place. Suddenly a sound like the blowing of a violent wind came from heaven and filled the whole house where they were sitting. They saw what seemed to be tongues of fire that separated and came to rest on each of them. All of them were filled with the Holy Spirit and began to speak in other tongues as the Spirit enabled them. [18]

God with them: Emmanuel: His Presence made real. Jesus had not left them alone; He had not forsaken them. He had empowered them to be His witnesses throughout the earth:

> But you will receive power when the Holy Spirit comes on you; and you will be my witnesses in Jerusalem, and in all Judea and Samaria and to the ends of the earth. [19]

God demonstrated His faithfulness to His Promise. His Presence was real... and everlasting.

The Presence

Jurgen Moltman describes the Holy Spirit's unrestricted Presence:

> The Holy Spirit is more than just one of God's gifts among others; the Holy Spirit is the unrestricted Presence of God in which our life wakes up, becomes wholly and entirely living and is endowed with energies of life What the Holy Spirit begins here will be completed and perfected in the kingdom of glory [20]

Living a Spirit-filled life means acknowledging, and then yielding to, the work of the Holy Spirit in our lives; allowing the Holy Spirit to fully possess us, from the inside out   The more you surrender, the more His Presence becomes real:

> Do not get drunk on wine which leads to debauchery. Instead be filled with the Holy Spirit [21]

Your Kingdom Come
As we surrender to the Holy Spirit we co-labor with God to bring His Kingdom to earth. Jesus told us to pray that His will be done and His kingdom come to earth. The kingdom of God is advanced through our earnest prayers of faith and through our actions. And our actions must be led by the Holy Spirit. Remember: every single thing that Jesus said or did while He was here, He said or did through the Spirit.

In Us, Always Moving, Always Speaking
There are three aspects of the Holy Spirit that enable us to better understand His work on earth through us. The Holy Spirit:

- Is with us and in us
- Is never static
- Speaks

As we know, the Holy Spirit is present – here and now at work – but He is also never static, never stationary or motionless. The Holy Spirit is kinetic, always in motion. That is why His works are referred to as the 'moves of the Holy Spirit'. Those who are filled with Him, who follow Him and abide in Him, likewise are not static. Those who live the Spirit-Filled life are ever moving, going where the Spirit leads, doing as the He instructs.

The Spirit also speaks. God is The Great Communicator. A great part of the Spirit's work is to communicate to His people what is on His heart and mind. The problem is that we may not be tuned into the same station as the Spirit. We may be surfing AM and He's on FM. We need to put our spiritual antennae up and tune into *His* station. We need to take a deep breath, clear our heads and listen.

The world and self and our myriad interests cause static and make it difficult to hear His voice. But He is speaking. Always has been.

Are we listening?

Doing and Saying as Jesus Did and Said

The music of heaven could be heard now and then when the Spirit descended upon people in the Old Testament. But now, since Jesus sent His Holy Spirit to live in us, the music of heaven can be heard in our hearts *whenever* we listen for the voice of our Shepherd.

John the Baptist pointed to the music, and the Holy Spirit is the broadcaster who shares the music with the world. Jesus depended completely on His Father; He did only what His Father (through the Holy Spirit) told Him to do; He said only what His Father (through the Holy Spirit) gave Him to say.

As we yield to the voice of the Holy Spirit, as we live the Spirit-filled life, He will direct our paths. That is a promise from the One who never breaks His promises.
The Holy Spirit is the conduit for bringing life to the world – full, unhindered, everlasting life. Where the Holy

Spirit is active and present and fully acknowledged, where people are tuned in, the abundant life is visible and available.

Gifts of the Spirit

The church is confused about the gifts of the spirit – or, more accurately, the church is divided on whether or not the gifts are for today. Frequently I hear people ask if God *really* gives the gifts to those who believe in Him and ask the Holy Spirit to live in them. Here are my rhetorical questions in response:

If we believe that every good gift is from God and He does not change,[22] can we dismiss the gifts of the Spirit as "not good" or invalid in some way? Can we say that God has changed His mind and decided to eliminate the gifts or stopped giving them to those who ask the Holy Spirit to live in them? Does that make any sense?

Building The Body

Paul writes to the Corinthian church to describe the various gifts that were given to the church to build up the body of Christ:

> There are different kinds of gifts, but the same Spirit. There are different kinds of service, but the same Lord. There are different kinds of working, but the same God works all of them in all men. Now to each one the manifestation of the Spirit is given for the common good. To one there is given through the Spirit the message
> of wisdom, to another the message of knowledge by means of the same Spirit, to another faith by the same Spirit, to another gifts of healing by that one Spirit, to another miraculous powers, to another

prophecy, to another distinguishing between spirits, to another different kinds of tongues, and still another the interpretation of tongues. All these are the work of one and the same Spirit, and he gives them to each one just as he determines. [23]

Some of the gifts are more easily understood, and desired. Who doesn't wish to be filled with the gift of wisdom? Others are harder to understand, particularly in this Age of Reason in which we find ourselves. But what we do know is that the gifts Paul outlines were given for the common good of those in the body of Christ on earth – to build up the church, to advance the kingdom of God.

Administered With Love

A few years ago I received a call from a young woman who asked that I pray for her to be able to get pregnant. She had been trying for quite a while. So we prayed together, and shortly after that, I heard that she was expecting. I also prayed for my daughter to conceive after she and her husband had tried for a year without success. Within a few weeks she told me she was pregnant. These are not coincidences. The most important thing to remember about using the gift(s) the Holy Spirit has given us is that they should be administered with love:

> If I speak in the tongues of men and angels, but have not love, I am only a resounding gong or a clanging cymbal. If I have the gift of prophecy and can fathom all mysteries and all knowledge, and if I have a faith that can move mountains, but have not love, I am nothing. [24]

If we are filled with the Holy Spirit and have the gifts of

the Spirit and do not have love, we have nothing; and we *are* nothing.

Love never dies, never gives up, never fails.

Fruit of the Spirit
Most important in our living the Spirit-filled life is the development of the character of Christ in us, which is otherwise known as the fruit of the spirit:

> But the fruit of the Spirit is love, joy, peace, patience, kindness, goodness, faithfulness, gentleness, and self-control. [25]

Instructed and led by the Holy Spirit, Paul defined the gifts of the spirit, and he is the one who reminds us that life in the Spirit is based on our willingness to grow to be more Christ- like. What good is it to have the gifts if we are not like the giver of the gifts? What good is it if we rejoice in the gifts He gives us if we do not show others the love and character of Christ as we use those gifts?

Paul reminds us that living the Spirit-filled life is based on our willingness to grow into the image of Christ. The gifts of God are irrevocable – He freely gives them to us – but our purpose in being filled is to draw others to Christ. In fact, that is the Holy Spirit's purpose. The Spirit points to Jesus, not to Himself.

And our ministry must be the same as the Holy Spirit living in us: to keep drawing people back to Jesus.

God wants us to live fruitful, Spirit-filled lives, and He has given us all we need to do so. The best gift of all is His Holy Spirit. Jesus told us that He had to leave earth in order for His Spirit to come and live in us. Jesus knew that the gift He would send would be more than enough to enable us to live abundant lives.

Are you filled with His Holy Spirit? Are you living the Spirit-filled life?

If so, hallelujah! If not, are you willing to surrender and be filled?

Are you thirsty?

Ever had living water rushing through your veins?

Notes

1. John Ortberg, The Holy Spirit Adventure, Menlo Park Presbyterian Church, February 2006
2. Victoria Brooks, The Reach of the Heart, 34-35
3. Genesis 1:1-2
4. Genesis 1:26
5. Exodus 31:1-5
6. Numbers 11:16-25
7. Deuteronomy 34:9
8. Judges 6:34
9. Isaiah 11:2
10. Luke 3:22
11. John Ortberg, The Holy Spirit Adventure, Menlo Park Presbyterian Church, February 2006
12. Joel 2:28-29
13. Ephesians 1:13
14. John 7:37
15. Revelation 3:20
16. John 10:10
17. John 16:7
18. Acts 2:1-4
19. Acts 1:8
20. Jurgen Moltman, The Source of Life, 10-11
21. Ephesians 5:18
22. Hebrews 13:8
23. 1 Corinthians 12:4-11
24. 1 Corinthians 13:1-2
25. Galatians 5:22-23

6 WHO TO BELIEVE

Mary, most likely had issues to deal with in her life just like we do. When she chose Jesus over all of the other possibilities she chose life. She chose freedom. She chose Her Counselor. We have choices to make every day and often our choices are affected by whom we believe. Do we listen to what others say about us? Do we listen to our own thoughts that are not so objective? Or do we make space to seek The Counselor, Jesus Christ? Sadly we often chose to believe the lies. We get caught in the trap of our false perceptions and our thoughts that run wild. We chose the lies over the truth. The only way we can get out of this cycle is to sit at the feet of The Counselor, asking Him for wisdom, and asking Him to sort out what is true and what is not. Often it is our emotions that take us on the fast track in the wrong direction. Let me give you an example.

A few weeks ago my son-in-law left a message on my answering machine saying he was disappointed in me, surprised and hurt by the things I had said about him.

I was undone by the tone of his message and immediately began to review our recent times together, our conversations. What had I said, how had I disappointed, surprised and hurt him? I could not think of anything I had said or done to warrant his leaving this devastating message. I love him!

Why would he leave the message and not confront me

directly? Was he not going to speak to me again? I was
frantic about it. I was helpless.

Stinkin' Thinkin'

Thus began a tortuous process that I have recently
termed *stinkin' thinkin'*. It may be a new phrase for you,
but I am willing to bet that the stinkin' thinkin' process –
the destructive mind game – is familiar to most, if not all,
of us. Upon listening to my son-in-law's message, I
began to think I was a rotten mother-in-law, and although
I couldn't think of a thing I had done, I began to fabricate
things that I might have done or said ... or might have
implied by something I had done or said. Does this ring
any bells for you? Can you relate? If you're honest with
yourself, is it possible that you have engaged in stinkin'
thinkin'?

Before I knew it, I was convinced that my relationship
with my son-in-law was over, my daughter was
disappointed in me, and my grandchildren would be
upset. Exactly how this had happened was a mystery,
but I began to repent fervently for what I had done
without my knowledge. I was a wreck, my mind was a
wreck – my thinkin' was stinkin'! I picked up the phone
to call my husband because I needed to inform him that
my life was ruined. Did he know already? Would he ever
speak to me again? As I picked up the phone I saw there
was another message on my answering machine. Funny, I
hadn't noticed it before.

The second message was also from my son-in-law: "Hey,
Joanne, it's Gregg. " (chuckling) "Hey, I forgot to add
one thing to the last message: April Fools!"

Why is it that we fall prey to our thoughts running wild? Why do we believe what others tell us about ourselves – our bodies, our minds, our spirits? And not just loved ones and close friends; I don't know about you, but I've allowed the opinions of complete strangers to rattle me and lead me deep into the sinkhole of stinkin' thinkin'. Often with no validity whatsoever, we allow what is said or suggested to us to overshadow and outweigh the real truth. When we give our stinkin' thinkin' room to live and breathe, it can consume us.

I had said and done nothing wrong to my beloved son-in-law, but at his suggestion my thoughts got away from me, and before I listened to the second message I had come up with a train wreck of conclusions. Conclusions about me.

I Think, Therefore I Am What I Think

In Proverbs, King Solomon tells us, *As a man thinketh in his heart, so is he.*[1] In other words, the way that you think will determine the way that you feel and the actions you take in reaction to those thoughts and feelings. Our thoughts are extraordinarily powerful – for good or ill. Stinkin' thinkin' can kill.

If spiritual warfare is the life-and-death struggle in which we *demolish arguments and every pretension that sets itself up against the knowledge of God, and we take captive every thought to make it obedient to Christ* [2], then the first and last field of conflict in spiritual warfare is our mind.

Remember where Jesus was crucified? It was a hill called *Golgotha,* which means *the place of the skull.* The territory of our uncrucified thought life is the place of assault in our lives, and to defeat the assaults of stinkin' thinkin' we must be crucified in the place of the skull.

The Battle Is Raging

In our minds we fight on three fronts: the flesh, the devil, and the influence of the world. Each of these fronts represents a battleground, a place of assault where our mind is susceptible to stinkin' thinkin'.

The battle of the flesh rages when we allow our thought life to be out of control. Often our thoughts are irrational and based on emotion rather than knowledge or intuition. Sometimes we are our own worst enemy in allowing faulty thinking to weasel its way into our lives.

Cardinals are territorial birds and will fight off intruders, including other cardinals; if they see a mirror on a car they will attack the mirror thinking that their own reflection is another bird. The cardinal's enemy in this case is merely a reflection of himself. Many of our perceived enemies are uncanny reflections of ourselves and our own ungodly stinkin' thinkin'.

On the other hand, the devil's attacks are craftier than even our own flesh assaults. The enemy will gladly use our own stinkin' thinkin' against us by encouraging us to agree with it. Jesus was very clear that the battle we fight is between the kingdom of God and the kingdom of the enemy. If the enemy can get us to agree with our irrational un-Christ-like thinking, he finds a platform from which to oppress our thoughts even further and cause us to prove out Solomon's proverb: as a man thinketh in his heart, so is he.

Our agreement with the enemy's lies and the lies of the world in which the enemy prowls will deter- mine the way we feel and the actions we take. The enemy is the Father of Lies. He is not creative, he is an opportunist; he has no new strategies, only new opportunities: the openings we offer him when we agree with his lies.

The influence of the world is the third front or battlefield of our minds. God's Word is the sword we use to combat the influence of the world. The world belongs to God, but when and where His Word is disregarded we fall prey to the counterfeit.

Strongholds

The apostle Paul uses the word *stronghold* to define spiritual fortresses where Satan and his legions are sheltered. The stronghold in this sense is a place into which the Devil and his demons are invited and allowed living space: a place of protection for the enemy; a place in our thought life the deceiver finds to hide.

These strongholds exist in the thought patterns that govern individuals, churches and communities, and if we are to prevail in spiritual warfare we must ruthlessly pull them down.

The Old Testament *stronghold* is a Godly counterpart, referring to a place of protection from the enemy. King David hid from King Saul in the wilderness strongholds at Horesh. These were mountainside caves, very difficult to assault. As David explains, the kingdom use of stronghold is a place of agreement with God's Word: *He who dwells in the shelter of the Most High will rest in the shadow of the Almighty; I will say of the Lord, He is my refuge and my stronghold.* [3]

The enemy's strongholds are where we allow him to hide in our thoughts and build a dark fortress and feed our thought life with lies. The enemy cannot create; he takes what is good and right and true and

counterfeits its use for his own purposes. The kingdom use of stronghold is a place of our protection, a place of agreement with God's Word.

God intends for us to hide our thoughts in the stronghold of His Word, and the enemy intends for us to agree with his lies, to pass his counterfeits and disregard God's truth.

Who to believe?

Last April Fools day, I believed the counterfeiter. My son-in-law played a good-natured joke, the enemy got me to agree with my own stinkin' thinkin' – things that never happened – and before it was all over I was convinced that my relationship with my family was ruined.

Beloved fellow Christians, we must begin to recognize that the battle for our minds is raging. The warfare is all around us; the battlefields are where we are, in the now-here, every day. The world tells us lies and the enemy gets us to agree; or he throws counterfeits and lies – situations, stresses, inconveniences, hardships – into our paths as roadblocks. He hides in the dark-thought strongholds we have allowed in our lives, and then at the right opportunity he jumps out to divert us, mislead us, cause us to stumble. He loves our stinkin' thinkin' because when we are engaged in it we are in agreement with him.

The enemy is the father of lies. Some lies have been embedded in the womb of our thoughts since birth. Some are hidden until the enemy draws them out at the time he chooses.

Rats, Lies and Liberation

Recently my clothes dryer smelled really bad – like the motor had burned out. It stunk. When the repair technician took a look, he found a rat's nest in the motor. The nest was so huge it had wrapped itself completely around the inside of the dryer. Rats build nests in our thought life until the space we've allowed them is so large that the motor of our lives burns out. Stinkin' thinkin' destroys. The lies consume us and can lead us to do things that reflect the lies we believe.

Think back to a time when you believed a lie. Consider how your buying into that lie affected your behavior. Isn't it remarkable how even the smallest "nest" in our thoughts can cause us to react in ways we later regret?

The enemy's mission is to rob, steal and destroy. God's mission is to set the captives free. When we agree with the enemy's lies we are headed for destruction. Agreement with God's Truth sets us free.

Who to believe?

Consider this: a mother dies and the young daughter feels abandoned, believing that she is unwanted and rejected. She lives out her life oppressed by a spirit of rejection. Or maybe a friend, even a parent, told you that you were stupid or silly or unattractive or would never amount to anything. So often we live out our lives in the center of those deceptions, making choices based on the stinkin' thinkin' that has resulted from terrible untruths. And we never fully achieve God's highest and best for our lives because we do not believe in ourselves as He believes in us.

What about you? Can you think of a lie you have believed that has influenced the way you have lived your life?

Who to believe?

In his second letter to the church in Corinth, Paul described stinkin' thinkin' as any thinking that exalts itself above God's truth and gives the devil a foothold, a place of influence in an individual's thought life. [4] The image is one of wrestling our stinking thoughts to the ground. Any area of our heart or mind that is not surrendered to Jesus Christ is an area vulnerable to attack. It is here in the uncrucified thought life of a believer's mind that the pulling down of the enemy's strongholds is of vital life-and-death importance.

Lately I have been reading through II Kings, and it seems as though every chapter begins by stating that the king of Israel at the time did what was evil in the sight of God – that he refused to bring down the high places of pagan worship. As I have read through the book, I've felt the Lord reminding me that I still have uncrucified high places in my thought life, places that need to be surrendered to God's truth.

I had healing that brought relief from symptoms of rejection, but I had never allowed myself to get to Golgotha, the place of the skull. I continued to feed the lie, to allow it space in my living room. I continued to give in to stinkin' thinkin'. The lie caused me to push myself to please others and to become a perfectionist in order to avoid rejection. Can you relate to this? You know, perfectionism really is the counterfeit of excellence. Perfectionism is about our plan for our life, not God's plan; it drives us away from His design and intention for us. On the other hand, excellence is driven by our love for God and our deep desire to please Him and be approved by Him. Truly, He is the only One whose approval matters.

If our thoughts are of God and for God, it is absolutely impossible for stinkin' thinkin' to take control.

The Route to the Root
Examine the fruit of your life. Can you see the fruit of a lie believed? Golgotha is the place of getting to the root of the lie. It is the place where we begin the process of healing by agreeing with God at the root. Finally I realized the truth: I am not perfect and never will be; I will disappoint others, and they will disappoint me.

The word *perfect* in God's dictionary means mature, growing to be more like Jesus. It doesn't mean getting everything right.

Getting to the root of the lie and agreeing with God's truth has set me free from the bondage of striving to be perfect to avoid rejection. What about you? What lies have you in bondage? Who do you believe?

One clue to getting to the root of a life-killing lie is to look for where the emotion is. Where there is excessive and/or irrational emotion, a lie is often embedded. Emotions like anger, stress, anxiety, fear, and sadness are often the tip of the iceberg; a stinkin' lie may be embedded at the iceberg's base.

Underneath the surface, sometimes down very deep, is the root of the lie, the reason, the initial misdirection or wound. And we must work from the emotion on the outside to the inside where the lies are embedded and a stronghold has been built. The process of deliverance begins in a place of internal conflict, which escalates as we look at the emotions and uncover the lies. The closer we get to the root, the more the internal conflict escalates and we look for an escape route to avoid the pain. We go back to the cave of stinkin' thinkin' because it has become a safe place for us, a familiar and comfortable place. It is here the enemy has made his home.

The mind is an incredibly powerful thing. God made it so. He created it to be a gatekeeper for His activities on earth. Paul reminds us that our minds must be renewed. Renewing your mind means learning to recognize the lies, taking them captive, and agreeing with God's Word. This renewal is something we must do all the time, every day.

The battlegrounds of the flesh, the influence of the world and the enemy work away on us and beat us down. We have to be prepared to offer God our thought life at Golgotha, surrendering the lies, renewing our minds, so that we can bring kingdom reality to earth:

> Therefore, I urge you, brothers, in view of God's mercy, to offer your bodies as living sacrifices holy and pleasing to God – this is your spiritual act of worship. Do not be conformed any longer to the

pattern of this world, but be transformed by the renewing of your mind. Then you will be able to approve what God's will is; his good, pleasing and perfect will. [5]

Often our thoughts conflict with the mind of Christ. That is natural, the way of the world. But though we are in the world we do not need to be of it, and our thoughts must be submitted to Christ so that we can know His will and be the agents who bring His kingdom to earth. We are His Plan A, and there is no Plan B.

This explains why there is such intense warfare in our thought life. The enemy knows very well that we are God's plan, and he wants us to be defeated in our thoughts so that our minds, filled with lies and stinkin' thinkin', will block the truth of God's Word. If the enemy is effective in his mission, our agreement with his lies will prevent us from working as agents advancing God's kingdom.

There are several practical steps to freedom when your thought life is destructive; steps that have enabled me to get free from my own stinkin' thinkin':

1. Look for your emotional trigger points (stress, anxiety, fear, sadness).
2. Repent; renewing your mind begins with repentance.
3. Take your thoughts captive (wrestle them to the ground).
4. Renew your thoughts by focusing on the truth (Philippians 4).
5. Be grateful; gratitude creates space for God and

gratitude keeps your mind tuned to the right channel. We can be on FM with our stinkin' thinkin' and God is on AM with His truth. Tune in to His Word and agree with it. It will set you free.

My son-in-law and I are closer than ever. Next April 1st I'll be ready for him. In fact, I'm working on a few ideas myself – I may beat him to the punch and call him first. His April Fools joke was a great example of how quickly I allow my thoughts to get out of control. With no basis in truth, absolutely unfounded, the lies I invited into my living room crowded out the God thoughts and wrecked me.

Who to believe? Make space for God thoughts and let His truth wreck your stinkin' thinkin'.

Notes

1. Proverbs 23:7, King James Version
2. 2 Corinthians 10:5
3. Psalm 91:1-2
4. 2 Corinthians 10:5: ...we demolish arguments and every pretension that sets itself up against the true knowledge of God, and we take captive every thought to make it obedient to Christ.
5. Romans 12:1-2

7 IS LIFE IN THE FAST LANE REALLY LIVING?

We all know that life in the fast lane is not often fulfilling. We go so hard that we can hardly catch our breath let alone spend time on ourselves or spend time nurturing our relationships with family and friends. We all dream about a time when we are not so busy. But then when we have a quiet moment we don't know what to do with ourselves. We have been programmed to stay on the hamster wheel and have believed a lie that one day it will all be worth it. Martha was doing what any of us would have done. She was preparing the best meal for her guest of honor. After all, this was the Messiah, the Miracle Worker, the one who brought her brother Lazarus back from the dead. There was nothing she could do that would be enough to adequately express her love and thanksgiving to her friend. So she cooked, and she busied herself with the details of the dinner party. Now here is the thing. Martha was right. She had things to do and she needed to do them but when she complained to Jesus about Mary not helping He did not rush to her defense. No. Instead He said: "Martha, Martha, you are worried and upset about many things, but only one thing is needed. Mary has chosen what is better…" Martha had work to do but Jesus wanted her to prioritize her work; first Jesus, then work. The work will flow much easier from a place of rest. Perhaps Jesus could have said this to Martha: "If you want to be a better Martha, you must first be a better Mary and learn to work from a place of rest. "Sounds counter intuitive, but I would put my bet on Jesus knowing the best and most efficient way of doing things.

Why is it that when people ask me how I'm doing my most common response is "I'm busy"? Maybe you don't say that, but I do – all the time it seems – and I hear a lot of other people saying the same thing. I have one friend who has a different answer to that question. He says, "I'm blessed. " I like that reply better, yet more often than I care to admit the *I'm-busy* one jumps out of my mouth before I've given it any thought.

Wearing The Busy Badge
It makes me think of the Scripture that says the mouth speaks what the heart is full of. [1] Am I really

that busy, or do I just want others to think I am? Does it make me feel more productive or valued if people think I am busy?

The truth is, I am busy. Who isn't? But why would I want to wear busyness like a badge? I think next time someone asks me how I'm doing I am going to say, "I'm fruitful. " No – that sounds worse, doesn't it? Prideful and pretentious. But that's exactly what I want to investigate right now: what is the difference between being busy and being fruitful? How can we make space in our lives for the things that God is calling us to and remove those things that we do to satisfy only ourselves or others?

Busyness vs. Fruitfulness
On the way to the grocery store I came up with a list of things that keep us busy for busy's sake; things that keep us living in the fast lane as if that were some sort of badge

of honor. This list is a work in progress and certainly not exhaustive, but it's a start. Some of the things that keep us focused on busyness and not fruitfulness are:

- The *I-can-do-all-things* syndrome
- Keeping up with the Joneses
- The issue of self worth
- Running from problems
- The lies we believe
- Running without purpose

Life In the Fast Lane

Is life in the fast lane really living or is there a better way? Do you remember where we left off with our discussion of Martha and Mary in Chapter 2, *The One Needed Thing*? Martha was running around their house, aggravated with her sister and asking Jesus to have words with Mary. Martha asked Jesus if He even cared that she was working while her sister Mary lazily sat at His feet. Jesus responded:

> "Martha, Martha, ... you are worried and upset about many things, but only one thing is needed (emphasis mine). Mary has chosen what is better and it will not be taken from her. "[2]

Mary made a choice to worship Jesus. She chose to seize the opportunity to spend time with the Lord. She knew her priorities, and life in the fast lane was nowhere near the top of the list. What Martha was doing was important – they had to eat – but Mary had chosen the better thing, the one needed thing: worship.

In that chapter we discussed the crucial importance of making worship a priority; and now we'll look at some of the things – the spirit-less activities, the distractions – that keep us from putting Jesus first.

Life in the fast lane is not really living; it is merely existing. Only putting Him first – seizing every opportunity to be with Him, to seek Him, to sit at His feet – is real life. Busyness is the enemy's way of keeping us from doing the one needed thing.

B-U-S-Y ... With A Little Help From The Enemy

As I mentioned in the chapter called *Connecting*, I have heard it said that *busy* stands for *being under Satan's yoke*. Jesus was clear when He told us to take His yoke (and no other yoke) because His is easy, and His burden light.[3] Satan has a plan, and so far it has worked pretty well: if he can keep God's people busy, then they will not have time to develop their relationship with God. Can we sit at His feet like Mary if we are busy, worried and upset like Martha? No way. The enemy will keep us so busy that we won't have time for our Lord, or we'll be too tired to invest in a relationship with Him.

Sometimes Satan is very subtle. In fact the closer you are to God, and the more you are intentionally making space for God, the more the enemy will use the good things to get in the way of the best. Know what I mean? Does this sound familiar? Listen, I know I may be preaching to the choir. I should probably be looking in the mirror right now. I know I want to do good things for God, but I allow my schedule to get so packed that when the time comes to do the best thing – spending an extra hour with Him or going on a silent retreat or going to prayer group – I don't have time.

Like it or not, this is a choice I have made. Often I allow

myself to be so busy that I don't have time to notice what I've done!

Which One Is Better – Good or Best?

My mother used to say, "Don't let the good get in the way of the best." Oh, how true. And someone else once said to me, "Good, better, best, don't let it rest, until your good gets better and your best is best." Though that may sound a little peculiar, it seems to me it's the same thing my Mom was saying.

As far as we know, Jesus didn't tell Martha that she was doing something good; He simply said that Mary was doing something better. So let's look a bit closer at our list of things that keep us so busy we can't do the best.

The I-Can-Do-All-Things-Myself Syndrome

In his letter to the Philippians, Paul writes that he is content in every situation, whether he is hungry or well fed, living in plenty or in want. He tells them that it is because he has learned that he can do all things through Christ who strengthens him. [4]

Paul had a lot to be dissatisfied about: he was beaten so many times he may have lost count. I know I have. He was thrown into jail on numerous occasions. He gave up his favored position as a Pharisee, having studied under the famous Gamaliel. He was a respected scholar before he was a Christian missionary, then was debased by those who had formerly appreciated him. He had lived a privileged life and now he counted it as nothing compared to his relationship with Christ.

The trouble is that we haven't found the secret to

contentment because we are independent, self-sufficient and in need of no one. Or are we? The truth is that we all need help from God. It's just that for some of us it is more difficult to ask for help. Paul knew that his strength came from God and not from his scholarship or his life of privilege.

What about you? Have you learned the secret of dependency on God?

The Keeping-Up-With-the-Joneses Syndrome

We can all relate to this to one degree or another, can't we? Your neighbor gets a flat-screen TV and invites you over to watch the football game, and the next thing you know you can't live without one. That was I. The mystery of the ages: How had I lived all these years without that large TV hanging on my wall? How had my family survived?

If you can't relate to a TV, how about something for your kids? My friend's daughter wanted a pair of Ugg® boots. I think they call them Uggs because they are soooo ugly, but that's just my opinion. Anyway, my friend took her to buy a look-alike boot, but that is not what this pre-teen wanted. She wanted the real thing with the official Ugg® label and double the cost. Can you imagine paying double for ugly?

My husband never cared for labels growing up. Still doesn't. He makes me look really bad.

When he was a little boy he used to tear the alligator emblem off his socks. I didn't ask his mother if he did that to his shirts. That could have been a mess, leaving a hole or something – but my husband would not have cared in the least. He simply didn't and doesn't care about labels.

There will always be bigger and better. I remember watching one of the Veggie Tale videos with my granddaughter. The story was called Madame Blueberry. Madame Blueberry was never satisfied, she wanted more and more things. My favorite line in the story was: "How many things are there?" Madame Blueberry definitely intended to keep acquiring things, and she was simply checking to see how much more stuff was out there.

Whenever I buy something that I don't need, Mr. No-label Practical (you know who) uses that line. It was obviously his favorite line in the Madame Blueberry story too. He'll ask me, "How many things are there?" It sort of takes the thrill out of the purchase, if you know what I mean.

How many more things are there? How many more Joneses are there to keep up with? We can do all things through Christ who gives us strength … but is buying flat screens, Uggs and you-name-the- label(s) what we really want to do?

Self Worth
Now this is a big issue for some of us. Staying in the fast lane assures us of our worth and value. Right? As long as we work harder, faster and more efficiently than everyone else we are affirmed and feel good about ourselves. Right? Heaven forbid if you are unproductive; people suddenly forget the good stuff. Right?

Perfectionism drives some of this. For some of us, striving to be the best can force us to live life in the fast lane. But is it really living?

I had a friend who was a gourmet cook. I don't particularly like to cook so I was in awe. One day when our children were little she decided she and I should cook a meal together. She was going to teach me how, show me the culinary ropes. She whipped out her gourmet magazine and began to prepare a soufflé. I had never made one before and kept silent. She worked as if she were painting a beautiful picture: her hands deftly folded the egg whites; her focus and dedication were intense. The problem is that I am a people person, and this seemed like nonsense to me; I wanted to enjoy being with her but our conversation was extremely limited because she was single-mindedly focused on her project.

The day was rough. I felt like the student who just didn't get it. I went home and decided to try out my newfound talents. My first soufflé failed miserably. Never fear, I thought; I had been taught that *if at first you don't succeed, try, try, again.* And I did – again and again. I was a failure. My husband so wanted to live with Martha Stewart, or at least have her prepare his meals. Unfortunately he was stuck with me. Now, I am a perfectionist, so it took a lot for me to get over my failure. These days my husband cooks, and that works much better for us.

Everyone wants to be successful, but when our success – or lack thereof – determines our self worth, we are in deep trouble. Jesus told us not to fret about the basics:

Therefore I tell you, do not worry about your life, what you will eat or drink or about your body, what you will wear.

> Is not life more important than food and the body more important than clothes? Look at the birds of the air; they do not sow or reap or store away in barns and yet your heavenly Father feeds them. Are you not much more valuable than they?[5]

Jesus wants us to know that we are valuable to Him. One translation of this passage in Matthew's gospel tells us *not to toil or spin*. That is what we do when we think that "doing" makes us valuable. We worry about whether or not we have done enough or if we have done it perfectly. We store up what we don't need. And we do it all to make us feel valuable and valued. But it is not *doing* that makes us valuable; it is *being*. Being His.

And Jesus tells us we are already of great value. We don't need to do all that. A good friend told me that her theme for the year is: "Don't try and prove yourself; be yourself." I have adopted it as my own for this year, and my husband is wishing I would adopt something else.

Being myself has become my excuse for everything. Like when I don't want to do something. "I don't need to prove myself, honey."

Okay, maybe I need to check my motives.

Living in the fast lane is not going to give us the value and affirmation we seek. Living in His lane is really living – living abundantly – and our self worth can only come from God.

Running From Problems

This is something we all get caught up with every now and then. This one really keeps us in the fast lane. Do you know how fast you need to run to get away from your problems?

Here is the thinking: if we keep running we won't have to deal with the problems. The problem with that is ... our problems always have a way of finding us no matter how fast we run. If we don't deal with them, they keep coming back. The real truth is that they never leave.

My grandson told me the other day that he could fly. When I asked him to demonstrate he decided he couldn't fly that day. That's what we do. We think we can fly away, we figure we can get up above our problems. But we weren't made to fly. We weren't made to live in the fast lane either.

Driving in the Fast Lane

I am not a great driver and I have a tendency to drive too fast. These personal driving facts became clear to me when I lived in Germany years ago. Have you ever driven on the Autobahn?

The Autobahn is made for fast drivers. Actually *fast* is not really, uh, fast enough to describe how people drive on the Autobahn. So what's the big deal – I was a fast driver driving on a highway where fast drivers drive fast, right? Well, yes and no. The problem was that I was scared to death as I drove on the Autobahn. What I thought was flying was really slow for the Germans in their rocket-powered cars. I couldn't tell the difference between the fast/passing lane and the slower/90- miles-per-hour lane. Maybe there wasn't any difference. I don't think I closed my eyes as I drove, but I cannot swear to it.

Running (and sometimes driving) in the fast lane keeps us from slowing down enough to deal with the issues of life. It may begin as a strategy for some of us, but it never ends well. We all have problems, and they are often uncomfortable things that we would rather not deal with. I know indefinitely postponing the addressing of my problems is a strategy that has occurred to me on more than one occasion. But that's like postponing tomorrow; we can only do that for a few hours ... until today becomes tomorrow. Right?

Sometimes we run with our tongue. Jesus' brother James tells us that the tongue is like a restless evil, full of deadly poison.[6] He says that the tongue is like a spark that can set a forest on fire.[7] But we keep on talking. Not about meaningful things but about anything that will keep us from addressing head-on the real issues of our lives, the things that have hurt us, depressed us, frustrated us, made us feel alone and weak and worthless.

Or we use our tongue as a weapon to ensure that no one gets close enough to us to recognize our problems and ask us about them.

Living in the fast lane keeps us from facing our problems.

The Lies We Believe

Often we keep running because we have believed a lie. It is a lie that is common in the secular world. It's the lie that tells us if we don't keep charging ahead someone else will take our place. Someone who can run faster, drive faster, think faster, talk smoother.

So we get on the hamster wheel and start to run ... and spin. Though we may feel like we are getting somewhere, we aren't really. We're spinning. If we are fast runners, we are spinning faster than those who aren't as fast. Around and around we go, never realizing that we are not actually going anywhere. We're not arriving. We're not even leaving. There is an old phrase you may remember: *We're going nowhere fast.*

The lie that we believe is that faster, busier, more productive is the somewhere we are going. But the truth is our goal should be *the one needed thing.*

Merry Hampster Wheel

I got on my hampster wheel this Christmas and started spinning. I began to shop the first of December; I decorated my house; I baked; I shopped some more; I had people over; I went over to peoples' houses; I shopped some more; and then I collapsed when it was all over. Christmas-life in the fast lane.

Why do we do this to ourselves? Because we believe a lie. We have to have the perfect Christmas, whatever that is. We have to keep up, run faster, get it all done, whatever it is. And for what? Because we believe that we have to, that's why.

There are other lies we believe. What about the lie that we have to be skinny? What is up with that? How busy do you keep yourself trying to be skinny? It is plastered all over the magazines. Poor movie stars who gain a little weight; they might as well never leave their houses. You know what's really fat? The lies we listen to. Big fat lies.

We run faster to look perfect; we run faster to keep up with traditions in our head that say we have to bake, decorate, shop and visit hundreds of people all in the month of December. Jesus told Martha she was distracted and He speaks to us through the ages: "Slow down. Just be. Spend time with me. "

Not Fast, But With Purpose

Did you know Paul told us to run. He did. He did not say to run fast, but he most definitely told us to run and run well. He instructed us to run until the race was finished. He told us to run with a purpose:

> Not that I have already obtained all this, or have already been made perfect, but I press on to take hold of that for which Christ Jesus took hold of me. Brother, I do not consider myself yet to have taken hold of it. But one thing I do; forgetting what is behind and straining toward what is ahead. I press on toward the goal to win the prize for which God has called me heavenward in Christ Jesus.[8]

Paul tells us to press on – to run toward the prize, which is Jesus. If we are going to insist on life in the fast lane, then the only legitimate pursuit is *the one needed thing*. The winner of the Greek races received a wreath when he won. Our reward is life *with* Christ and in Christ. He is our great reward. Life with Him is the prize.

Taca the Climber

My husband and I love to climb mountains. I don't mean like real climbers with ropes and all – just simple climbing. Or so I thought. One year in Canada, I decided that I wanted to prove myself. Those who know me at all can see trouble looming already. Well, here's some unsolicited advice: never try to prove yourself to your spouse.

I chose a difficult hike. As we were waiting to cross over to the place we would begin our climb, the game warden told us to beware of bears. The more he talked, the more fearful I became. But then I noticed that there was one Japanese man who seemed extremely calm and collected. I saw that he had on a backpack and wore a belt with a bell; and he wore a demeanor that declared he had done this before. So when it came time to climb, I raced up to the front of the line where this master climber was and left my husband in the dust.

As we proceeded up the mountain, the man with the bell on his belt began to cry out in Japanese every few minutes. After he cried out, he would ring his bell. I found his screams and bell ringing slightly disconcerting, so I asked him why he was doing that. He said that it would keep the bears away. "Ah," I said knowingly. I felt secure behind him. We got to talking and he told me his name was Taca. He said that he had been doing this for years in this part of Canada. "You really have to be careful," Taca told me. "Ahh," I said knowingly. I believed him.

At one point we had to climb on our hands and knees in a tunnel and then scale our way around a narrow part of the mountain. Where Taca went, I followed. I stayed close to him.

I felt very secure climbing with Taca because he was well equipped and well trained; he had the right gear and he was an experienced hiker.

Training Tips

In his instructions to the Philippians Paul does not mention my friend Taca, but what he says reminds me of the man with the backpack and the bell. Paul tells us to press on running like a trained athlete. As we run the race God has planned for us, training is the key. Let's look at some tips.

Tip 1: A Schedule

1. A trained athlete must have a schedule – a plan to get in shape and to prepare for the race. As Christians we need a plan to get in shape spiritually. Living a life that is purposeful is what we are after. If we are intent on knowing God intimately and in sharing the good news about Jesus Christ with others we will be plenty busy – wonderfully busy – and our *business* will yield a great harvest.

Tips 2 and 3 (from Philippians 3:12[9])

2. Acknowledge that your life is out of control. In humility recognize that you are not perfect.
3. Press on to take hold of Christ's goal for you. Surrender daily to God's will and stay in touch with God through prayer daily to accomplish His will. Listen for His instruction, then follow it.

Tip 4 (from Philippians 3:13[10])

4. Forget what lies behind; don't look back. If your life has been out of control and filled with stress and disappointments, look forward. Paul actually says to

strain toward what is ahead. That is a picture of stretching yourself forward. It may be a stretch to look ahead when life in the fast lane keeps calling you back.

Tip 5 (from Philippians 3:14[11])
5. Never give up. Keep pressing on to the goal that Christ has for you. Purposeless life in the fast lane is not really living; life pressing into God's plan for you is the goal.

Tip 6
6. Have a plan to spend time each day in the word and in prayer. Keep paper and pen close by and journal what you sense God is saying. Surrender your day to Him, and you will never regret it. Good athletes have a plan of exercise and diet. Time with God exercises your spiritual muscle and reading His Word is the bread of life.[12]

Jesus Did What His Father Said

Jesus did only what His Father told Him to do. He wasn't influenced by the crowds that came out to see Him, and His actions were not dependent on what others said about Him. He wasn't a people pleaser, or a politician. He was not wishy-washy. Jesus knew what to do because His Dad told Him. He trusted His Father in heaven completely.

What if we lived our lives like that? Wouldn't it simplify things?

Life in the fast lane is often connected to how we want others to perceive us. As I said in the beginning of this chapter, everyone wants to be perceived as busy. No one wants to be a slacker. But is that really a badge we want to wear? What if our badge said: *Unabashed Follower of the One and Only God*? What would our lives look like if we did only what the Father told us to do?

The only way we will know what He's saying to us is if we spend time with Him, sitting at His feet like Mary, focused on the one needed thing.

I am convinced that life is not meant to be complicated – life in Christ that is. Imagine with me for a moment: Jesus goes up to the mountainside to pray. He has left his disciples and the enormous crowds to have some "down time" with His Dad. Imagine Jesus saying: "Dad, this was a great day. The demoniac was delivered, the man at the pool of Siloam was healed, we had the wonderful meal you provided on the hillside for 5,000. " Or maybe He would tell His Dad how great it was to have the conversation at the well with the Samaritan woman. Then He might say, "Hey, Dad, what's on the schedule for tomorrow? No, never mind – surprise me tomorrow!"

Jesus did only what His Father told him:
> I tell you the truth, the Son can do nothing by himself; he can do only what he sees his Father doing, because whatever the Father does the Son also does. For the Father loves the Son and shows him all he does.[13]

That is the key to purposeful living: slowing down to be with Jesus; and just as Jesus did what His Dad showed Him, so we can do as the Holy Spirit instructs and guides us.

Jesus Was Not Held Hostage by the Demands of the World

Jesus really needed faster transportation. He could have strapped on those tennis shoes with wheels and zipped through his day a lot faster. Have you ever thought about all the walking he had to do in His sandals? I suspect they were pretty worn out. Here's the thing though: I doubt He was running from place to place. He walked; He stopped and looked around; He had conversations with anyone who wanted to talk with him; He had an ongoing conversation with His Dad, with His disciples. His days were full, but they were intentional and purposeful. The crowds were at one moment praising Him, and the next moment cursing Him. The Pharisees were condemning Him, and some of the lepers he healed forgot to thank Him.

But nothing kept Him from His purpose to heal and set the captives free and proclaim the good news. The demands of the world, the tyranny of the urgent, did not hold his heart captive. He was free to do what His Dad told Him to do, and there were always enough hours in the day to do what had to be done.

How About You?

Do you ever end your day saying, "I wish there were more hours in each day"? I have said that plenty of times. There never seems to be enough time. But on those days when I surrender my calendar, those days I press on toward the goal of following God's plan, I have ample time to do what needs to be done. The problem is the demand of the urgent gets in the way. Good intentions give way to the squeaky wheel that demands the grease.

I have good news. There is another way to live. I can't

say that I live this way every day but I have found the secret to not allowing the tyranny of the urgent to disrupt God's plans. It is a Scripture we looked at in Chapter 2:

Be still and know that I am God.[14]

I stop and ask God: "Is this interruption from you?" I stop and pray and ask Him for assistance. Fast- lane mode doesn't afford me the time to stop. Seeking-God mode does.

What's On Your Plate

Years ago a speaker at a conference told us that she had taken a year off from ministry. She had been burned out. During that year off she looked at all the things she was doing and took each one of them to the Lord. I was in a season of running like crazy and wondering if I was in God's will with some of the things I was doing, so I decided to do the same thing the conference speaker had done.

I imagined a big plate with all my activities and commitments on it; and during my quiet time I prayed and questioned God about each thing on my plate. One by one, things were removed until all that was left was a huge gold plate – the one needed thing. From that point He and I began to add only those things that I sensed I was called to do. Being a wife, mother and daughter were things that remained, and I realized that my plate was half full with just those. They were necessary and blessed, and they required a lot of my time. Carefully and prayerfully, with the leading of the Holy Spirit, I added a few other things. Once I had made Jesus my priority, and only He remained on my plate, the other things I needed to be doing became very clear.

Jesus told us the same thing when He said, "… seek first his kingdom and his righteousness, and all these things will be given to you as well. "[15]

What things? The things He has called you to do. The things you were created for!

Stewarding Our Gifts

In his book *Little House on the Freeway*, Tim Kimmel talks about stewarding our capabilities:

> Well-managed talents, on the other hand, give a person a strong sense of purpose and value. They help us to counter the overwhelming pressure from the culture to make us feel insecure. Insecure people are never static with their insecurity…. Every Christian has spiritual gifts. These were given by God in order to round out the church…. Poorly maintained talents can become overtaxed. In many people's lives, their weaknesses are nothing more than strengths pushed to the limit. If we push our spiritual gifts to an extreme we burn out. If we push our emotional gifts to an extreme we get depressed. If we push our physical gifts to an extreme we get sick. [16]

We all have talent, gifts from God, and if we don't steward them well, which involves managing our time well, we will end up in the fast lane. We have already determined that life in the fast lane is not really living.

The best way to handle our God-given gifts is to manage our time. Be realistic. Prioritize what has to be done and approximately how long it will take. Fill in your calendar leaving margins for the unexpected. I used to have something scheduled every two hours. I was always running from place to place, never having time to sit down, reflect, be creative. Now I schedule fewer things and leave a margin in my days. It is in those margins where (and when) God seems to be most active.

He fills in the blanks. He creates. He refreshes and renews and restores. God allows my day to be interrupted by *His* design.

An Audience of One
Sometimes we get tripped up by thinking that our lives are played out like performances. The people we come in contact with are the audience and we are on stage. Once we learn that life is all about an audience of One, things change. Racing around to prove ourselves isn't necessary, and searching for significance does not play a role in our lives because we know our significance lies in the One who created us.

Our identity is in Him and searching for another identity becomes unnecessary. In the book *Running on Empty*, Fil Anderson tells the following story:

> I recall reading many years ago an interview of a member of the Boston Philharmonic Symphony Orchestra. In it the interviewer asked how it feels to get a standing ovation after a performance or a negative review the morning after. I was initially puzzled by the classical musician's response as she explained how she used to be greatly affected by the crowd's reception, however, over time, had learned to look only for the approval of her conductor. Her logic was simple; her conductor was the only person in the crowd who really knew how she was supposed

to perform.[17]

Here is the question we must all answer: "Is life in the fast lane really living"? Jesus told His disciples in John 15 that apart from Him they could do nothing; that fruit was expected but could only be produced if they clung to Him, the Vine. He was telling them that as long as we keep running – as long as we are distracted by so many things and disconnected from Him – we will not find success or rest.

Are you running? Are you distracted by many things in life? Are you in the fast lane and not even certain how you got there? Stop and talk to Jesus about it. Take the time for Him. He says:

> Here I am! I stand at the door and knock. If anyone hears my voice and opens the door, I will come in and eat with him and he with me. [18]

Jesus is knocking. Can you hear Him? Do you believe He wants to come in? Will you open the door and make space for the meal of a lifetime?

Notes

1. Luke 6:45: For out of the overflow of his heart his mouth speaks.
2. Luke 10:41-44
3. Matthew 11:30
4. Philippians 4:12-13
5. Matthew 6:25-27
6. James 3:8
7. James 3:5
8. Philippians 3:12-14
9. Not that I have already obtained all this, or have already been made perfect, but I press on to take hold of that for which Christ Jesus took hold of me.
10. Brothers, I do not consider myself yet to have taken hold of it. But one thing I do: Forgetting what is behind and straining toward what is ahead....
11. I press on toward the goal to win the prize for which God has called me heavenward in Christ Jesus.
12. I am the bread of life. He who comes to me will never go hungry, and he who believes in me will never be thirsty. (John 6:35)
13. John 5:19-20
14. Psalm 46:10
15. Matthew 6:33
16. Tim Kimmel, Little House on the Freeway, 141
17. Fil Anderson, Running On Empty, 66
18. Revelation 3:20

8 DYING TO LIES, REVEALING HIS DREAMS

Mary had a winsome way about her. I believe that she was drawn to Jesus because she knew He was Truth. She instinctively knew that she needed to sit and listen to what He had to say about her. Her head was probably filled with all of her dreams but she wondered if she was capable of fulfilling them. What about the way she felt about being a woman? In her day, women were considered beneath men and yet she was able to sit at the feet of a man and feel important and loved because she knew He was no ordinary man. He was consuming Love. He made her feel safe and secure while at the same time challenging her to fulfill her destiny. His words brought her life. She needed to know her identity was not in what she did but in who she was—a child of the King Messiah. She needed to know that the God of all creation fashioned her with a unique purpose.

Do you believe that The God of all creation formed and fashioned you? Isn't that astonishing? You are unique: there has been, is, and will be <u>no other exactly like you</u>, ever. You are like a snowflake, except much much better: you were made to last … forever.

Knitted By The Original Knitter
You were 'knit in your mother's womb'[1] with a purpose and destiny for your life.

I just watched a video to see how complicated the process of knitting is. Wow. For all you knitters, I am very impressed. The knit-and-perl stitch seemed so intricate, yet the expert doing the demonstration in the video made it look so easy.

David writes that God, our Creator, intricately knit you in your mother's womb, one stitch at a time: knit, perl ... knit, perl ... knit, perl ... you! When the One Who created knitting planned your birth, He must have had a twinkle in his eye. *Ah, yes ... this one will be one of a kind, exceptional, called and prepared for the work I have for her/him:*

> For it is by grace you have been saved, through faith – not by works, so that no one can boast. For we are God's workmanship, created in Christ Jesus to do good works, which God prepared in advance for us to do. [2]

A Purpose Only You Can Fulfill

God created you with a purpose in mind; a purpose only you can fulfill. You and you alone. I do not mean *by yourself.* I mean with God, by God and through God you have a purpose. Now if that doesn't make you want to get up and shout, I don't know what will.

We are not supposed to be wandering aimlessly around wondering what our purpose is or what purpose there is to living. We are called to find our purpose by seeking Our Creator. When we know Him, He shares His secrets with us. [3] He deposits His vision for each of us deep within our hearts – a vision that we alone can accomplish. Imagine with me ... God knitting you in your mother's womb, God knowing you before you are made; God having you formed whole in His mind before the knitting has even begun. Imagine. Linger with those images of God and who He is, what He is capable of, and how well He knows you.... Does that exercise stretch your imagination like it does mine?

The History of Your Knitting
He leans down and whispers into you – into your ear and your heart and your soul – into your very blood and bones – the destiny-vision He has for your life; and He plants the seed of that vision deep in the soil of your heart and soul: "Let me see what color your eyes will be; brown like your mother's or blue like your dad's? Let's (meaning let us – *Father, Son, Spirit*) put in your genetic code and stich- perl in beautiful skin and curly hair and the slender fingers of a pianist or baseball pitcher or writer
... and your destiny... yes: I can see your destiny. Now let's plant the seed. I long for you to water it and to walk with me and relate to me even as my one and only Son, Jesus, and our Holy Spirit did ... and do ... and will.

Your Free Will Is My Will
"Free will is a two-edged sword, isn't it? I gave you full authority to choose, just as I gave it to Adam and Eve and every single human being ever created. I want loving children, committed Kingdom partners – not robots. I am the author of Kingdom Reality, not Science Fiction. I am the Real Truth, the Whole Truth, and nothing but The Truth.

I gave you the ability to choose to love and be loved by me – to serve me and allow me to guide your every step; and I also freely gave you the ability to choose to turn away from me, to say *No* to my invitation and my myriad promises.

"Knit, perl.... Did you know I invented knitting? Did you know I am the King of Knitting?"

No Need for Stage Fright ... Or Fright of Any Kind

"There should be no excuses for not fulfilling your destiny. But there are sometimes. Moses gave me a hard time when I called him to lead my people. 'Me?' he said. 'How can I be a leader when I can hardly speak?'

"Moses had stage fright. But listen: didn't he know that I had given him all he needed to accomplish the dream – our dream of leading our people out of Egypt? My dream eventually became Moses' dream because he loved me so much. And because, again and again, I made good on my promises. He learned that when you allow me to lead, there is no need for stage fright or any kind of fright.

"I have never, ever broken a promise. Not once. Listen: if I ceased being love, if I ceased keeping my promises, I would cease being God. Do you understand that? Really?

"Child, you are unique, set apart to do good works. I knitted you that way. Don't listen to the world – listen to me; don't look at yourself through the world's eyes – see yourself through mine. My vision is perfect. You are a masterpiece. You are creative like your Creator; you have the ability and talent to do great things. "

Remember to Seek Me

"Now remember to seek me because I hold the secrets of the only kingdom that will last forever.

"You will need to seek me to pursue your God-given talents, and I shall be your biggest fan. I shall never leave your side; I shall coach you like no other coach you have ever had; and I shall cheer you on as you accomplish great things.

"Knit, perl.... Did you know I invented knitting? Did you know that I knit you in your mother's womb? Did you know that you are a masterpiece?"

Living Into Your Destiny: Finding Your Wings, Planting Your Seeds

There is a song by Mark Harris that beautifully describes the challenge of living into our God-knit destiny:

> I pray that God would fill your heart with dreams
> and that faith gives you the courage
> to dare to do great things...
>
> It's not living if you don't reach for the sky I'll have tears as you take off
> But I'll cheer you as you fly....[4]

My son-in-law, Gregg, is a hopeless romantic. Wait a second – you know, that's just not right. It's an old oft-used phrase – hopeless romantic – but it really does not describe my son-in-law. Gregg is a hopeful romantic – there is nothing hopeless about him. For example, when he proposed to my daughter, Gregg rode up to our house on a horse holding 100 roses in his arms. He – Gregg, not the horse – was wearing armor; he had a helmet (visor up), a sheathed sword, a shield, and chain-male gloves. He looked like he had just finished a jousting tournament. Now, you have to understand that Gregg was and is not a proficient horseman, so the approach he

143

had chosen – on horseback, with an armful of roses – was risky from the start. I honestly don't remember if he was holding onto the reins at all. But Gregg was undaunted. He was on a mission of love. Sir Galahad had nothing on my future son-in-law.

Well, he dismounted his gallant steed, dropped to one knee and proposed to my daughter. She said *Yes* by the way. Wouldn't you?

I have told this story countless times –and every time I relate the Gregg-Proposes story, the women who hear it sigh ... and the men most often look a little disgusted. After all, it makes them look bad. Who the heck *is* this Gregg character? And ... who could ever measure up to that?

Funny thing is ... it got to be a thing with the men in my life. My other son-in-law planned a romantic surprise dinner out on the dock behind our house, complete with music and white wedding bell decorations. And my son planned an elaborate proposal that included hundreds of candles and rose petals leading the way to the engagement ring.

Gregg didn't stop with his romantic ventures. The following spring he planted rye grass on the overpasses of our city in such a way that when winter came and everything else was dead, the hearty rye remained and said: *I love my wife*.

God plants His seed in our hearts. It's a seed He designed with us in mind, and it says, "I love you ... and I have great plans for you. " It's a seed that when watered

144

will begin to reveal the Father's heart for us, His vision.

And each of us is uniquely able to fulfill His dream. He made us that way.

God Calls Jeremiah

In the thirteenth year of the reign of Josiah, the king of Judah, God spoke to Jeremiah:

> Before I formed you in the womb I knew you, before you were born I set you apart; I appointed you as a prophet to the nations. [5]

Now Jeremiah wasn't so sure about this call 'to the nations'. He told God that he really wasn't a good speaker and that he was only a child. And the Lord responded:

> "Do not say 'I am only a child'. You must go to everyone I send you to and say whatever I command you. Do not be afraid of them, for I am with you, and will rescue you," declares the Lord. [6]

Guess God has heard Jeremiah's brand of excuses a lot – the *I-am-scared-to-death-of-the-call* kind of excuses. He was ready with His answer to Jeremiah. He would be with him and rescue him when mission impossible seemed overwhelming.

God created us to be dreamers and to co-labor with Him to see that the dream comes true. Everyone has a dream planted deep, and the fulfillment of that dream is our destiny.

Joseph's Dream ... And Ours

Joseph had a dream that seemed a bit far out. He

dreamed that he was in the fields with his brothers binding sheaves of grain when all of a sudden his sheaf rose and stood upright. All his brothers' sheaves gathered around Joseph's sheaf and bowed down to it. Wow – pretty cool dream, Joseph. He thought so too, but he should have kept it to himself.

Joseph's brothers were already jealous of the preferential treatment their dad gave him – and now this? Bowing down to him? His brothers were older than he, and they thought he was a spoiled, arrogant kid. They had had enough of the dreamer ... so they threw him into a pit, then sold him into slavery.

That happens now too, doesn't it? Maybe not with quite as dire results, but ... we pridefully share our dreams, thinking probably that those we share them with are going to be happy for us – and we get thrown into the pit.

Mary figured this dream thing out. Remember? After the shepherds worshipped her son and the wise men visited, Mary simply pondered these things in her heart. [7] She had a dream planted in her heart, but her humility kept her dream in seed form waiting for God's fulfillment. How wise for a small- town teenaged girl.

So Joseph got excited and shared his dream. Ponder? Young Joseph? Not hardly. He was thrilled at the dream God had given him and his pride landed him in the pit. You know the end of the story though, right? We talked about Joseph in another chapter, but it fits here too. Joseph's pride was dealt with in the pit and in prison. He needed to develop the character of God, Christ-likeness, in order to fulfill his dream God's way.

So sometimes we have a great vision of what God is calling us to do, but God waits until we grow in our character to enable us to fulfill the dream. The Original Knitter gives us a dream-vision to reach for, to grow toward. God says, "This is your dream, and you *can* fulfill it ... in *my* time. "

Joseph's faith and integrity and steadfastness enabled him to end up in a key position of influence in Egypt – second only to the Pharaoh himself – and in this position of authority and trust, he was able to save the nation of Israel and his entire family.

God knows what He is doing. Like Joseph, we sometimes get in the way of the fulfillment of our destiny, and the One who knit us in our mother's womb allows a few trips to the pit to ensure that we will be prepared to carry out the call.

Dreamers ... And The One Who Leads The Way

We are all given dreams. Each of us. In a wonderful variety of ways, God plants pictures in our hearts, souls and minds of what He has called us to do. At the same time He creates us, He imagines the works He has prepared for us. But we need to seek The Dreamer in order to fulfill the dream. Apart from Him, we are nothing.

Some of us dream of being great athletes; others, successful business people, mothers, fathers, artists, pastors, poets. What is your dream? Are you close enough to your Creator, have you made enough space inside you to hear Him whisper: "This is the way; walk in it. "[8]

In that *walk-in-it* passage in Isaiah, God promises His people abundance purified of idols. He knows the perfect way to achieve His purpose ... and the perfect time to go into action. [9] And He knows the perfect way for you to achieve your purpose. Sometimes an awakening process is brought about by our rebellion or resistance; and God uses the circumstances we get ourselves into in order to discipline us and set us on the right course. The course toward the fulfillment of our destiny.

He is our Teacher, the One who leads the way. [10]

Friendship Enables Destiny: Abiding in the Vision Maker

Jesus told His disciples that if they stayed close to Him – really close, like a branch to the vine, a branch dependent on the vine – they would bear fruit that was lasting. [11] Our close and growing friendship with Jesus is what enables us to dream His dreams, to receive from him the dreams that only we can fulfill. The dreams he made for us.

Our friendship with Jesus calls forth in us the secrets of the kingdom, those things God wants to accomplish on this earth. So here we are again: circling around, circling back to the vision planted in the heart of this book: making space for God. We must make room at the center of our lives for staying *connected* to Him, *abiding in* Him, *remaining with* Him.

Abide means to *stay close, fixed, or attached*, and the Vine – the dream weaver, the vision maker, Jesus– offers us the sap of life that the natural vine offers the branch. The sap nourishes the branch and enables the branch to bear fruit. The fruit we bear is dependent on our connection to the vine. When we remove the excess junk from our lives and connect to the life source in Christ, creative ideas and energy flow.

God's plan and purpose on this earth is to expand His kingdom. And we are the agents He has appointed to fulfill His plan.

Thy Kingdom Come

Jesus taught us to pray:

> Our Father in heaven, hallowed be your name, your kingdom come, your will be done on earth as it is in heaven. [12]

Jesus' destiny was to come to earth and make a way for us to return to the Father through forgiveness of our sins. Our destiny is to advance His kingdom on earth by proclaiming the good news of Jesus Christ – that He came to set the captives (us) free. So when we pray for God's kingdom to come on earth, we are in essence praying that we will be faithful to follow God's plan of expanding His kingdom on earth. We are committing to being the hands and feet of Christ on earth; His friends who listen to His secrets; His ambassadors who represent Him on earth; His people who are willing to fulfill His purposes on earth. That really puts this dream thing into perspective, don't you think?

We Are The Design

We are His dreamers, dreaming His dreams as we draw close to Him. Each of us has a unique calling, a unique contribution in making our Lord's dream come true. Have you ever stopped to think of it that way? If God is going to accomplish His will on earth, we are the ways He is going to do it. He is the way and the Truth and the life[13] ... and we are His way on Earth. It is true that He could easily reach down and zap things to turn out the way He wants, but that is not His design. We are at the heart of the Creator's design.

We *are* His design.

Bill Johnson says:
> While much of the church is waiting for the next word from God, He is waiting to hear the dream of His people. He longs for us to take our role, not because He needs us but because He loves us. [14]

God has given us liberty in Him to be creative, to dream big dreams, because He is the Dream Giver. He makes our dreams, and He makes them 'come true'. He wants us to step out and take a risk to help fulfill our dreams because when we are close to Him, His dreams become our dreams.

The Dream Giver
In *The Dream Giver*, Bruce Wilkinson tells the story of Ordinary, a Nobody, who leaves the land of Familiar to pursue his Big Dream. The Dream Giver persuades Ordinary to leave his place of comfort and begin the journey of life. He must overcome the Border Bullies, make his way through a wasteland and battle fierce giants – and he succeeds. With God (the Dream Giver) going before him, walking beside him, and watching his back, Ordinary succeeds. The obstacles are removed as Ordinary pursues his dream and lives into his destiny.

Border Bullies, There and Here

Once Ordinary breaks through his comfort zone and takes a risk to leave the land of Familiar, the Border Bullies appear. These are people who once loved him and begged him not to leave Familiar, not to take a risk, not to pursue his dream but to go back to his comfort zone. Wilkinson has given us a great metaphor in this story of Ordinary and The Dream Giver. We break free of our traditional place of comfort to follow a God-given dream, and the naysayers, though perhaps well meaning, stand in our way. They give us all the reasons not to live into our destiny. Their voices plead for us to stay, and there is a great temptation for us to go no further.

Years ago, I decided to go for a dream that the Lord had planted in my heart. Once I began to establish the *Drawing Near to God* ministry, the obstacles began popping up. The voices of the crowd narrowed down to the voices of those who loved me most, those in my 'inner circle' who did not understand my passion to pursue a dream that seemed implausible, if not downright impossible.

The problem was that, unlike Mary, I did not ponder in my heart what I sensed God was telling me to do. Much more like Joseph, I trumpeted the dream, which at the time seemed a bit "out there". Over the course of the first few years I realized that the voices became louder than the dream and I began to wonder if it was worth it to pursue the vision I had been sure God gave me.

Like Joseph, I ended up in the pit, in prison, wondering if I had even heard from God at all. Little by little, though, encouragement came even as I backed off from my purpose. God kept sending support, sometimes from unlikely places; people put courage back into me. And then, like Ordinary, as I grew to trust the Dream Giver, I pressed on. The truth is that the voices I heard in my head (and still do on occasion) declare that I am too ordinary to have such a big dream. But I have a choice here – in fact, we all have the same choice: follow our dream or listen to the lies.

Dying to Lies, Revealing His Dream

If we are going to be successful in following our destiny, step number one is to abide, staying close to The Vine. Step number two is allowing God to free us from the untruths that oppose His vision. In the chapter called *Who to Believe?*, we discussed stinkin' thinkin' and how easy it is to believe the lies the enemy uses to stop us from pressing into God's call. Remember? What lies have you believed that have caused you to turn back from your sense of call? What lies have tried to kill your dream, derail your destiny?

Maybe you don't think you have the skill – the right degree, or any degree at all. Perhaps you think you don't have the necessary time or that maybe you didn't hear God correctly. Perhaps no one believes that you can do it and you are beginning to believe the same thing. Maybe you have been praying for a breakthrough for so long with no apparent result, you have given up. The enemy is determined that you join forces with him and agree with his lies. He doesn't want to see God's kingdom grow, and if you fulfill your destiny in God then it thwarts his purposes. The enemy plants seeds of lies, but God's truth always prevails. Always.

When my stinkin' thinkin' threatens to derail my destiny, I have to fight the lies with God's Word. It is really helpful to remember that we are in great company; there are lots of friends who went before us who never saw the fulfillment of their dream, but they stuck with it:

> By faith Abel offered God a better sacrifice than Cain....
>
> By faith Enoch was taken from life so that he did not experience death....
>
> By faith Noah, when warned about things not seen, in holy fear built an ark....
>
> By faith Abraham, when called to go to a place he would later receive as his inheritance, obeyed and went....
>
> By faith, Abraham, even though he was past age – and Sarah herself was barren – was enabled to become a father....
>
> All these people were still living by faith when they died. They did not receive the things promised; they only saw them and welcomed them from a distance.[15]

Faith is the key that unlocks our dreams. Without faith it is absolutely impossible to seek God, and He rewards those who seek Him[16] and keep on seeking. Faith opens doors to our impossible dreams; faith lights the way and dispels the lies. Faith communicates truth and brings the breakthrough we need.

God's Word will grow in the heart of any surrendered

believer. His Word is our anchor when the waves of doubt and unbelief threaten to overtake our dreams. His Word promises that He will never leave us or forsake us.

So start dreaming with God. He knit you in your mother's womb and every stitch-and-perl was filled with destiny – your destiny, uniquely yours to fulfill.

Passion for Excellence

Sometimes in the pursuit of our dream(s) we get tripped up by the world's definition of *perfection*. We think we must strive to be perfect, right? After all, Jesus tells us we are to be perfect ... as our heavenly Father is perfect. [17] Well, the Greek word for *perfect* means to be mature, so Jesus is telling us that we must grow to be more like our heavenly Father, more like Him, more Christ-like. So, our spiritual journey should always involve making more room for the King of Excellence to move in and through our lives. We all have various ideas of, translations of, what the world means by *perfect*, but the kind of perfection our Lord wants for us and from us is the kind that comes when we continue to grow in Him, when we continue to dream the dreams He makes for us and shares with us.

If we use *perfection* in the secular sense (trying to get things 100% right), we are driven by performance; but if we understand that perfection means being more like Jesus, then we'll strive for grace-filled maturity, for *excellence*. As we pursue our God-given dreams, it is critical that we understand the difference.

We must be driven by our passion for excellence and creativity in making Christ known to a broken world. We are not called to live passive lives; we are called to live abundant, passionate lives. If we are determined to live for Christ and pursue our dreams, He will give us what we need to fulfill them. He promises that. We do not have to toil or spin. Our Father knows what we need to accomplish His will.

Weapons of the Wise

In *The Traveler's Gift* by Andy Andrews, David Ponder is a man who has given up on life. When David visits with the angel Gabriel, Gabriel asks him a telling question:

> "What is the difference in people, David Ponder," the angel began, "when they hit despair? Why does one person take his own life while another moves to greatness?" David shrugged. "I don't know. Maybe it's a difference in circumstances. " "Circumstance are rulers of the weak," Gabriel said, "but they are weapons of the wise. Must you be bent and flayed by every situation you encounter?"[18]

Here is the key. The lies we believe will influence our destiny; if we believe those lies rather than God's promises, we will not fulfill our dreams. We can leave our place of comfort, take a risk, and begin the bold pursuit of our dreams, but when we listen to the lies and believe that circumstances – good or bad – will rule the day, we will fail.

Only when we trust the Dream Giver will we follow our dreams to their successful completion. Only then can we partner with God and see His kingdom established on the earth.

Notes

1. Psalm 139
2. Ephesians 2:8-9
3. Mark 4:11
4. Mark Harris, Find Your Wings
5. Jeremiah 1:5
6. Jeremiah 1:7-8
7. Luke 2:19
8. Isaiah 30:21
9. From English Standard Version commentary on Isaiah 30:21
10. Isaiah 30: 20
11. John 15:7-16
12. Matthew 6:9-10
13. John 14:6
14. Bill Johnson, Dreaming With God, 28
15. excerpts from Hebrews 11
16. Hebrews 11:6
17. Matthew 5:48
18. Andy Andrews, The Traveler's Gift, 145-155

9 WALKING ON WATER

Have you ever thought of what courage it must have taken for Mary to sit at the feet of Jesus? She had to risk shame and embarrassment for her outward display of affection for Jesus. She must have feared the wrath of her sister after Jesus left. But I think what she may feared the most was the rejection of others as they shunned her for worshipping Him. Fear can be gripping but fear can be overcome. In the shadow of the love of Jesus, fear doesn't stand a chance. Mary may not have known that it was the love of Christ that drew her to sit at His feet and that it was the love of God that would cast out her fear. Fear can paralyze us and keep us from making space to worship Jesus with great abandonment. Fear has been around a long time and fear is not interested in being dethroned.

In his first inaugural speech in March 1933, referring to the Great Depression and the dire economic crisis in which Americans then found themselves, Franklin D. Roosevelt told his fellow citizens: "The only thing we have to fear is fear itself." He was offering hope for America's future and expressing confidence that the U.S. economy would turn around. Today, 77 years later, we find ourselves in similarly fearful times, and we would do well to recall and ponder what President Roosevelt said back then.

Fear Paralyzes ... Or Empowers

Actually Roosevelt was likely borrowing from Francis Bacon when he spoke about fear. About 400 years ago, referring specifically to changes in personal fortune, Bacon wrote: "Nothing is to be feared but fear itself. Nothing grievous but to yield to grief. " Bacon was also urging people to be courageous, faithful, hopeful.

Fear can paralyze or empower. It depends entirely on how we respond to it, what we do with it. If we invite it in and offer it a place to live in us, fear crowds out space for God. When we say *Absolutely not* in response to fear's knock on our door – when we give it no breathing space – there is more room for God to bring His peace, His creativity and His power into our lives.

The choice is ours. The King of the Universe designed us that way.

The Runaway Train

The other day my granddaughter and I were leaving the stable after her riding lesson. We passed a terrible wreck, but even before we reached the scene of the accident Mary Catherine became exceedingly fearful. Her friend had left the stable before we had, and when Mary Catherine saw the line of traffic and knew that there had been a wreck up ahead, she was worried that her friend had been involved in the accident. It took us 20 minutes to make our way to the scene, and by then my granddaughter was convinced that something terrible had happened to her friend.

Sometimes our fear has no basis in fact; and sometimes we are willing to forego details and allow fear to enter and misdirect our thoughts as quickly and unexpectedly as a runaway train. If we allow it, fear can ride in on our irrational thinking, ignite our emotions and paralyze us.

Faith and Love = Train Brakes

Have you ever heard Casting Crowns' popular song, *Voice of Truth*? The first part of the song says:

Oh, what I would do to have the kind of faith it takes
to climb out of this boat I'm in onto the crashing waves
to step out of my comfort zone into the realm of the unknown where Jesus is,
and he's holding out his hand

But the waves are calling out my name and they laugh at me
reminding me of all the times I've tried before and failed
the waves they keep on telling me time and time again
"Boy, you'll never win, you'll never win. "

But the Voice of truth tells me a different story
the Voice of truth says "do not be afraid!"
and the Voice of truth says "this is for My glory" out of all the voices calling out to me
I will choose to listen and believe the Voice of truth[1]

The song goes on to talk about David and Goliath and the kind of faith and courage it took for the pre-teen boy armed with a slingshot and a few stones to stand up to the ferocious giant: the same faith and courage it took for Peter to step out of the boat and "onto the crashing waves."

The voice of truth says, "Do not be afraid. " Faith and courage and God's perfect love can deal a death-blow to fear and stop that runaway train in its tracks.

Peter's Focus

Peter understood facing fear. He may have been a bit impetuous at times but he sure was courageous. At three in the morning Jesus walked out to the disciples who were in the middle of the lake in a wind- and wave-tossed boat:

> When the disciples saw him walking on the lake, they were terrified. "It's a ghost," they said, and cried out in fear. But Jesus immediately said to them: "Take courage! It is I. Don't be afraid. " "Lord, if it is you," Peter replied, "tell me to come to you on the water. " "Come," he said. Then Peter got down out of the boat,
> walked on water and came toward Jesus. But when he saw the wind, he was afraid and beginning to sink, cried out, "Lord, save me!"[2]

Peter heard the Master's voice, but at first he was tentative. Was it really Jesus? Was it really his friend and Savior? "'Lord, if it is you,' Peter replied, 'tell me to come to you on the water.'"

Good move, Peter. Always wise to make sure it is Jesus calling and encouraging and not some dare-devil so-called friend.

After making sure the guy walking across the lake could be trusted, Peter's next step was to get out of the boat.

Then he had to walk on the water. At first his eyes were on Jesus and he was doing fine. He was walking on the water! Can you imagine the thrill of that? If I'm going to be absolutely honest, I can't quite imagine it. I can be awestruck by the concept, but I cannot imagine the sensation. I wonder if Peter had ever been that focused, that single-minded before in his life.

Can you imagine how delighted Jesus was that His friend had trusted Him enough to step out of that boat in faith?

But then Peter's focus shifted a little and he noticed the whipping wind and the roaring waves – and maybe even the shouts (or awed silence) of the other disciples behind him, safe in the boat – and he was afraid. In that moment he took his eyes off Jesus and forgot what his Lord had said only a minute or two ago about taking courage and fearing not, and he was seized by fear. Courageous Peter was paralyzed. Fear will stop a good walk on water every time.

Peter began to sink and needed Jesus to save him. Then Jesus asked him why he had doubted. Doubted what – that Jesus was there? Even Peter could not have missed that. Doubted what then – that Jesus' battery pack could maintain the power it took to keep Peter upright on water? No, that's not the uncertainty Jesus was referring to.

The Lord of the wind and waves was questioning Peter's faith. It was Peter's battery pack that had gone dead. In the midst of walking on the water – in the very moment of faith-in-action – Peter suddenly heard the waves crashing around him, and the fearful voices in his head drained the faith right out of him.

Your Boat

But the voice of Truth had told Peter a different story. The voice of truth had said, Take courage, don't be afraid. And the voice of Truth says the very same thing to us here and now.

In *If You Want to Walk on Water, You've Got to Get Out of the Boat*, John Ortberg asks, "What is your boat?"

> Your boat is whatever represents safety and security to you apart from God himself. Your boat is whatever you are tempted to put your trust in, especially when life gets a little stormy. Your boat is whatever keeps you so comfortable that you don't want to give it up even if it's keeping you from joining Jesus on the waves. Your boat is whatever pulls you away from the high adventure of extreme discipleship. [3]

What is your boat?

A Recent Boat of Mine Was a ... Boat

A few years ago, my husband and I went snorkeling offshore. We went on a large boat with the specific objective of seeing manta rays, the largest species of ray. The water was rough that day and my mask quickly filled with water. I gasped for air – fear gripped me – and suddenly I was paralyzed. I knew that in order to see and appreciate these amazing sea creatures I was going to have to get a grip. But I couldn't. I panicked. And I jumped back in the boat.

My husband, as well as others on the boat with us, kept

coaxing me to get back in the water, but that was it for me. I made up my mind – I was not getting out of that boat again! My 'boat' that day was literally a boat. It was safe and secure, and that's what I wanted more than anything.

Well, okay, I remained safe that day, but the truth is that the boat and my desperate need for the safety it represented kept me from seeing the magnificent manta rays. I was no longer interested in high adventure; I was more interested in my own comfort and safety than seeing an incredibly beautiful sight.

Isn't that what happens? The boat we choose may be safe and secure, but if we want to experience all that God has for us, we need to get out of the boat and trust Him.

Recognizing Fear and Not Being Afraid

As a shepherd boy, David must have been fearful at times. There were so many predators that wanted to kill his sheep. He was a good shepherd who protected his sheep, and it is from his understanding of fear and God's assurance to care for him that David wrote what is probably his best-known Psalm:

The Lord is my Shepherd, I shall not be in want.
He makes me to lie down in green pastures, He leads me beside quiet waters,
He restores my soul.
He guides me in paths of righteousness For his name's sake
Even though I walk through the valley of the shadow of death I will fear no evil,
For you are with me; Your rod and your staff They comfort me. [4]

David knew the secret of being at peace and not fearing evil. He knew that God would always be with him. He stood on that promise more than once in his life.

Good shepherds take their sheep up the mountain in the summertime. When autumn approaches and the early snow falls on the high ridges, shepherds lead their sheep to lower elevations. Finally, at the end of the year, the sheep are taken back home, back to the ranch or farm or wherever their enclosed, protected pens are located. During all that time away from home, out in open country, the sheep are alone with the shepherd. He is the one who protects them from predators, rushing rivers, disasters, or wandering away from the flock and becoming lost.

David knew firsthand the danger his sheep faced, and as a shepherd he penned the words in the twenty-third Psalm from a place of knowing the danger that lurked for his sheep: *I will fear no evil, for you are with me.* David knew his sheep felt secure in the care of the good shepherd.

We all want to get to the mountaintops of intimacy with God, but we must almost always go through the valley(s) of the shadow(s) to get there. [5]

Fear Not
God spoke to the Israelites when they were fearful:
> But now, this is what the Lord says – he who created you, O Jacob, he who formed you, O Israel: "Fear not, for I have redeemed you; I have summoned you by name, you are mine. When you pass through the waters, I will be with you; and when you pass through the rivers they will not sweep over you.

When you walk through the fire, you will not be burned; the flames will not set you ablaze. [6]

Since I am writing this chapter at the beginning of a new year, I decided to talk with the Lord about what He wanted for me this year. I asked Him how I could serve Him, what changes I needed to make, how I could best be who He created me to be. As I listened for His voice, I sensed Him telling me that I needed to praise more and pray less. My focus has always been on prayer – telling God what I need, asking Him to intervene in the lives of my children and friends, detailing a long list of things that I take to Him on a daily basis.

More Praise, Fewer Prayers

But what I heard Him saying clearly was that He wants me to stop praying my list all the time and begin thanking Him regularly for what He has done, what He is doing, what He will do. He was asking me to step up my faith and trust that He has been, is now, and forever will be at work in all my requests.

For the last two weeks that is exactly what I have been doing: praising and thanking God as if He had already answered all my prayers. I do not know when and how He will respond to the things that I have been diligently praying this last year, but I do know that my practice of praise has increased my faith. My grateful heart is remembering what He has *already done,* and my trust is growing.

Why Is It So Hard to Trust?

The Israelites went in and out of trusting God. One minute they remembered Him and offered sacrifices and

praise, and the next minute they seemed to forget everything God had
ever said or done.

More than once, God had told them, *"Fear not"*. He told them to remember that although they strayed from Him, He would never abandon them; that He had redeemed them; and that raging waters and burning flames would not consume them.

God was telling His people that they could trust Him. And that's what He said to me two weeks ago. It is what He is saying to anyone willing to listen and willing to remember what the One true God has already done, what He is doing right this minute, and what He will do.

Why is it so hard to trust? Are we afraid that if we 'let go and let God' we will fall into the raging sea and be drowned? Are we afraid our masks will fill with water and we'll panic and there will be no one to save us? Do we think He will forget the promises He has made. Why is it so hard to believe the One true God who made us and has never once broken His promises to us?

Peter trusted Jesus enough to get out of the boat; then with another leap of faith he was up on the water – walking on the lake! And then his attention wandered and the waves scared him. Why?

What Makes It Difficult for You?
What are you facing that provokes fear in you? Health issues? Financial fears? Generic uncertainty about the future fueled by the way the world *looks* and what the headlines say?

I know that the world in which we find ourselves these days is fraught with waves and flames and stone walls and broken bridges and 'natural disasters' that threaten to overtake us. Isn't it? And yet, in the midst of the crashing waves and raging firestorms and earthquakes and floods – even in the midst of war and rumors of war – God is speaking. Can you hear Him? Listen: *Take courage.*

Fear not. I am with you.

What waves are so high and harsh and unrelenting that God cannot calm them? What fire rages so fiercely, so hot and uncontainable that the Creator of the universe cannot put it out?

The Key: Roots Reaching Deep Into Him

One of my favorite Biblical passages is in the seventeenth chapter of Jeremiah. The prophet describes a person who trusts God, and he uses the metaphor of a tree that is planted by water:

> "But blessed is the man who trusts in the Lord, whose confidence is in him. He will be like a tree planted by the water that sends out its roots by the stream. It does not fear when heat comes; its leaves are always green. It has no worries in a year of drought and never fails to bear fruit. "[7]

Jesus told us repeatedly that He is the Living Water and that we are to put our spiritual roots deep into His Living reality. That is the key to abundant Life, the key to fearless, adventurous, spirit-led living: roots that reach down deep into the Living Water of Jesus.

Now what I really love about the passage from Jeremiah is the next line:

The heart is deceitful above all things, and beyond cure. Who can understand it?[8]

It's true, isn't it? Our hearts are deceitful. Our hearts betray us again and again, taking the bait, swallowing the world's version, accepting the counterfeit, listening to the enemy's propaganda, giving in to fear.

Who can understand it? Why is it so hard for us to trust our King?

The heart is the wellspring of life, and we must not allow wickedness to take root there. In times of stress we have to be certain that our spiritual roots go deep down and search for the Living Water. Fear stands at the well where we go to drink, but God's love lies deep in the place where our spiritual roots will find the kind of water that never evaporates and never fails to satisfy.

We do not have to fear when the stresses of life come; we need fear neither flood nor drought, neither fire nor ice. Even and especially when we find ourselves in the desert, we can bear the fruit of praise and thanksgiving as we trust our Creator.

How do we do that? How do we deal with the fears we encounter?
How does God deliver us from our fears?

Unbelief Fuels Fear
In his wonderful book, *Dreaming with God*, Bill Johnson points to unbelief as a main cause of fear:

> But the massive effort to protect ourselves from being fooled is more a sign of unbelief than it is of

our wisdom keeping us from deception. Such a fear only exists where unbelief has reigned for a long time.

However, 'Love believes all things' (I Corinthians 13:7 NASB). A deeper encounter with the love of God frees a person from the tendency to protect themselves out of fear through unreasonable caution. And considering that 'faith works through love' (Galatians 5:6), it is reasonable to say that even the faith to believe God for miracles can come by experiencing His love. Overwhelming encounters with the extravagant love of our heavenly Father will do much to dismantle unbelief. "[9]

Fear is fueled by unbelief. Walking on water toward his Lord, Peter suddenly saw the wind-swept waves, his faith wavered, and he began to sink. You and I are really no different – walking in faith one minute, then suddenly allowing unbelief to creep in as a wave comes 'out of nowhere' and hits us. We say, "Where are you God?" even though we knew He was 'there' a minute ago.

Funny thing about God: He allows the waves in order to strengthen our faith. He knows there are times when we will choose to look away from Him and sink. He wants to use these trials of fear for our good, but we often sink into the sea of despair.

Is that where you are right now? Is fear prowling around, whispering lies, making you take your eyes off Jesus? Turn your eyes back to Him then, and listen: "Take courage!"

God's Perfect Love Casts Out Fear

God promises us that His perfect love drives out fear. Jesus' disciple John writes:

> God is love. Whoever lives in love lives in God, and God in him. In this way, love is made complete among us so that we will have confidence on the day of judgment because in this world we are like him. There is no fear in love. But perfect love drives out fear because fear has to do with punishment. The one who fears is not made perfect in love. [10]

God's love is perfect, and it is His perfect love that packs fear's suitcase and sends it on the road. Fear is silenced by God's love. So that begs the question: do we know His love? Has His love, demonstrated on the cross, really sunk in? Has the perfect love of our God cast out our fear of punishment?

Justice: The Cost of Bed-Breaking

I remember jumping on my bed as a child. Of course I was not allowed to jump on my bed, but I was a pretty free spirit and I sometimes used my four-poster like a trampoline. It was fun; I enjoyed it very much. That is, until ... I broke the bed. My poor mother. I'll never forget her face as she came into my room that day. I was on the floor, looking quite surprised, with the bedpost beside me and the broken supporting slats lying nearby. I wished she had lost it – you know, yelled at me or banned me from the family. Anything would have been easier than the punishment she gave. My sentence was to pay the cost of having the bed fixed.

I was scared to death. I was only 10 years old after all – too young to work. What was my mother thinking? I was just a free spirit in dire need of a trampoline. How was I going to earn the money to fix my broken bed?

But here's the thing: my mother swiftly rendered the verdict and the sentence, but neither she nor my daddy treated me any differently. Their love was unconditional and obvious, and their discipline was just and to the point. And they were quite willing to help me figure out how to make the money to pay my debt.

A Perfect Conversation

Our Father in heaven sent His Son to accomplish something we could not. We were quite a mess when Jesus' dad sent Him to earth. Can you imagine the conversation between Father and Son prior to Jesus' arrival here? Lately I've been giving it some thought. Here's my version:

"Son, the people you and I created in our image – the ones we love so much – cannot get close to me. You know what I'm talking about: they are rebellious and their sin gets in the way of our relationship. Son, this is hard for me ... but I want you to go to earth and pour out your life for them. It's really the only way. You are the only way. You are the only way, the only truth and the only life ... and I need for our people to know once and for all that perfect love will cover their sin. I want you to show them that perfect love will cast out all their fears. "

I guess it's not exactly a conversation, is it? At least not the kind of conversation we are used to. For one thing, the Father does all the talking; it doesn't seem much like a two-way exchange. And when the Father is done explaining and instructing, He doesn't ask Jesus if He's

171

okay with the plan, does He?

In my imagined conversation, Jesus knows what His Father is going to say before He actually says it – maybe *while* He is saying it – but the son does not interrupt His dad. He listens closely; maybe He nods from time to time to indicate that He is 'getting it'. And when His Father is finished, I imagine Jesus smiles and nods and hugs His dad. Maybe He looks into His dad's eyes and says, "Perfect plan, Dad."

The punishment we deserved – the wrath of God – was taken on by God's one and only Son. It was a plan they came up with together. And it was a strategy, a promise, a gift as perfect as the One(s) who created it.

A Perfect Gift: Hinds' Feet on High Places

As a child, my favorite book was *Hinds' Feet on High Places*, an allegory by Hannah Hurnard. I loved the story of how Much-Afraid escaped her relatives (the Fearings) and her cousin (Craven Fear) and made the journey to the High Places of God's perfect love. The Shepherd told her to step out in faith and He led her out of the valley of Fear and Humiliation and onto the mountain of His Love. The Shepherd told Much-Afraid that He would take her to His Father's kingdom, the Realm of Love. No fears were able to live there because God's perfect love casts out all fear. The Shepherd told Much-Afraid that He would make her feet like hinds' (female deer) feet so that she could climb the high mountains.

That is what Our Shepherd has given us. He has given us a perfect gift: the ability to climb the mountain of His Presence and receive His love. Our part is to accept the gift without guilt or fear or second-guessing, and to seek Him.

Seek the Lord

Did you know that the shepherd goes ahead of his sheep to prepare the place where they will graze? He looks for the best place for his sheep, and he leads them there. The shepherd makes sure that his sheep have food to eat and water to drink.

> I sought the Lord, and he answered me; he delivered me from all my fears. Those who look to the Lord are radiant; their faces are never covered with shame…. [11]

As we seek Him, the promise is that we will find Him.[12] When we live our lives pursuing and seeking the Lord, our Good Shepherd leads us to safe pastures.

Two Kinds

> The angel of the Lord encamps around those who fear him, and he delivers them. [13]

There are two kinds of fear:
1. fear of the Lord
2. fear of circumstance(s) or of man

The fear of the Lord is mentioned throughout the Bible and refers to our devotion to and reverence of God:

> Fear the Lord your God, serve him only and take your oaths in his name. Do not follow other gods, the god of the peoples around you…. [14]

And again:

> And now, O Israel, what does the Lord God ask of

you but to fear the Lord your God, to walk in all his ways, to love him, to serve the Lord your God with all your heart and with all your soul, and to observe the Lord's commands and decrees that I am giving you today for your own good. [15]

The fear of God brings us life. As we revere, worship, praise, thank and honor Him through obedience, we find our life hidden in Him: that is, our true life, not the counterfeit.

The counterfeit life surfaces when we fear man:
> Fear of man will prove to be a snare, but whoever trusts in the Lord is kept safe. [16]

Our fear of man and fear of what people think can be a substitute, an idol, if we allow it to take the place of fear of the Lord. Interesting that we all desire to have wisdom and yet God's holy Word tells us that it is the *fear of the Lord* that brings wisdom:
> The fear of the Lord is the beginning of knowledge, but fools despise wisdom and discipline. [17]

Maybe when we lose our fear of God we also lose wisdom. It is worth considering, isn't it?

Crushing Lies That Instill Fear

Do you ever pay attention to the negative things you say? I do. I know that when I give credence to lies they grow. I have seen it happen. It's sort of like water that gets under or in wood and begins to rot it from the inside-out. The enemy wants us to agree with his lies. It's simple: if Satan can get us to agree with him, then we have no room in us for the truth; our spiritual living room is filled with rot. We talked about this in the chapter called *Who to*

Believe, so I will not belabor it here. But it is one of those truths that bears repetition: the enemy is a liar and God's Word is Truth. Choose wisely what you make room for.

The enemy wants us dead. God wants us to be secure in the certain knowledge that He is always leading us to a place where we "will fear no evil. "

Increase Faith Through God's Word

God's Word probes the depths of our hearts, dislodging our false selves and revealing who we were created to be. The Word is alive, now and always, and it transforms. If we read it for information only, we will never get to the place where our hurts are healed and our fears are dealt with. Listen to this regarding our need to be transformed:

> When God puts a "finger" on those things in our lives that are inconsistent with God's will for our wholeness, it is not simply to point them out. It is not just to say that they must go or must be changed. That finger has a hand attached that offers us the nurture into wholeness that we need at that point. This concern for our whole being is the essential nature of God's knock upon the closed door of our lives. [18]

The Word of God knocks on the doors that have been slammed shut by our fears – the same fears that divide our soul (mind, will, and emotion) from our spirit. 19 If you are going to be set free from the prison of your fears, the Word must penetrate your soul. Meditating on Scripture, letting the truth of God's Word saturate your being, releases you from the bondage of fear.

Seeking the Lord, breaking agreement with the lies we believe, and meditating on God's Word are all ways to dispel fear in our lives. Another practical way is to face fear head-on.

How Low Can You Go?

My sister-in-law stayed with us this Christmas. Mary is a psychologist and a wonderful woman. On Christmas day, two hours before our planned Christmas meal, the electricity went out. We had not cooked a thing yet, and I hit the wall of panic. I had 15 people coming to eat and nothing prepared! But the thing that caused me the greatest concern was that my parents would not have Christmas dinner.

Mary is an astute observer, and she recognized that my mother and father were the focus of my anxiety. Mary reminded me that I have always been the one in the family who doesn't let things like this bother her. She pointed out that if things don't go as planned, I am the one who makes a quick transition to plan B. She told me that when she and her friends get frazzled they say, "Let's do *The Joanne* and laugh it off!"

"So what's different this time?" my sister-in-law asked.

I think I was just so concerned about pleasing my parents. It doesn't matter how old we are; we still want to bless or please our parents. Right?

Apparently I was a good case study in facing fear or whatever it was that caused me to panic. We packed up the car and drove over to my niece's house to cook over there, and on the way Mary began using her professional skill of piercing inquiry:

"What would happen if we didn't have Christmas dinner today?" she asked me.

"Are you kidding?"

"No, really. What would happen?"

"I guess I'd be extremely upset. "

"Why?"

"I wouldn't be perfect. "

"Ok, so you aren't perfect. Now what?"

"Death, just take me. Not perfect?"

"Answer the question," she said.

"I guess I'd go lie in a pit somewhere. "

"Okay, then what?"

How could she be so cold? "Well, I might grovel in the dirt because I am such a loser. "

"Then what?"

"What?" My sister-in-law wasn't flinching. I guess she'd seen this before. I probably sounded just like one of her patients. "I might just stay in the dirt awhile and enjoy my failure," I told her.

You get the point. When we boil down our irrational thinking, when we take our thoughts for a soul-searching drive down Reality Road, we are faced with the truth, the whole truth and nothing but the truth. And fear is the enemy of truth. The truth was that fear of not being perfect, of not meeting my parent's expectations, paralyzed me. It was good old fear, pure and simple, and this little exercise, as absurd as it may seem, helped me to see the crazy path I was on.

Next time you are faced with your own fears, try this: see how low you can go; follow your irrational thinking to the lowest possible point ... and then look up and see where your fears have brought you and who you have allowed yourself to become on the journey.

The Truth is named Jesus, and the Truth will set you free.

What Fear Does
As I was thinking about fear this morning, I realized that it is essentially an enemy attack against our relationship with God. Think about what fear does. Put simply, it:
1. causes us to do things we would not otherwise do
2. robs, steals, and destroys relationship with God and with others
3. steals our joy
4. makes us unwilling to take a faith risk
5. makes us retreat from God's higher purposes for us

Can you relate to any of these? Has your own fear done any/all of these things to you?

The Answer for Each of Us
One of the reasons I admire King David so much is that he was so courageous. I'm not saying he was perfect – there is no doubt he did some pretty low things. But he was a man who conquered his fear.

What was it about David that made him so brave, so willing to 'risk it all'?

Tucked in the pages of 1 Samuel are the stories that describe how David spent the "wilderness time" of his life. We all have to, don't we? But David's time in the wilderness grew his faith and his courage. His time 'out there', alone, running for his life, depending on God, gave him some invaluable tools that he would use for the rest of his days.

David spent the decade of his twenties in the wilderness. And he spent some courage-building time in the South, in Negev, on the run from King Saul. He found refuge with King Achish, the Philistine ruler who was also an avowed enemy of Saul and the Israelites. In the wilderness, David found himself in daily relationship with a mixed group of devoted followers. In his *Leap Over A Wall*, Eugene Peterson describes the people who made up David's community:

> Those who came to him are described as "every one who was in distress, and every one who was in debt, and every one who was discontented." This is the sociological profile of David's congregation; people whose lives were characterized by debt, distress, and discontent. It isn't what we would call the cream of the crop of Israelite society. More like dregs from the barrel. Misfits all, it appears. The people who couldn't make it in regular society. Rejects. Losers. Dropouts.[20]

Yet David courageously led this ragtag army to success. One day, however, while David and his band of misfits were out on a looting mission, the Amalekites raided the Negev and burned Ziklag, the city where David and his army had been living. The Amalekites took captive all who were in the city, so when David and his men returned to Ziklag they found it destroyed and their wives and families gone. David and his men wept. But here is what catches my attention in the story, what allows us to see the secret of David's strength:

> David was greatly distressed because the men were talking of stoning him; each one was bitter in spirit

because of his sons and daughters. But David found strength in the Lord his God. [21]

David should have been fearful. He had every right to fear for his life. The "dregs from the barrel of misfits" turned on him because they were so upset that their families had been taken. They were considering stoning him, and what did David do? He found *strength in the Lord*.

And that is the answer for each one of us.

Give Fear No Room

Fear could not find a place in David because he would not allow it. He made space for the love, power, and strength that His Lord God could give him, and there was no room left for fear.

Let's follow David's example. Let's resolve together to give fear no room. Let's crush it when it rears its ugly head and let's make space instead for God's love and strength. Sometimes we open the door to fear and then offer him a seat in our living room space. Then we give him a soft pillow to get comfortable. And pretty soon fear has the best seat in the house. My friends, next time fear comes knocking on your door don't open it! Once you let him in he finds ways of making himself way too comfortable.

And let's remind each other when we forget: the King who created us for greatness has promised: His perfect love casts out all fear.

Notes

1. Casting Crowns, Voice of Truth from Casting Crowns (debut album), 2003
2. Matthew 14:26-30
3. John Ortberg, If You Want to Walk on Water, You've Got to Get Out of the Boat, 17
4. Psalm 23:1-4
5. Philip Keller, A Shepherd Looks at the 23rd Psalm, 82
6. Isaiah 43:1-2
7. Jeremiah 17:7-8
8. Jeremiah 17:9
9. Bill Johnson, Dreaming With God, 69
10. 1 John 4:16-18
11. Psalm 34:4-5
12. Jeremiah 29:13-14
13. Psalm 34:7
14. Deuteronomy 6:13-14
15. Deuteronomy 10:12-13
16. Proverbs 29:25
17. Proverbs 1:7
18. M. Robert Mulholland, Jr. , Shaped by the Word, 17
19. Hebrews 4:12
20. Eugene H. Peterson, Leap Over A Wall, 94
21. 1 Samuel 30:6

10 MOVING MOUNTAINS

I have been wondering about something. Do you think that while Mary sat at the feet of Jesus she gave him her list of prayer requests? I just wonder. It would have been tempting wouldn't it? Here she was at the feet of the Savior, not just some charlatan or magic wielding man, but the One person who could answer every one of her prayer requests. Mary must have had her share of mountains in her life; those things that were obstacles, blocks--- things that we all have to face. As a woman I know about the mountains that today's woman faces; the daily juggling act balancing work and family and the guilt for never having enough time for significant relationships. We wear the guilt badge when we think we are superwomen and then fall down on the job. So what about Mary? Do you think that she poured out her heart to Jesus about all of her responsibilities as a woman; the obstacles, her fears, the stresses she faced? Here is what I think. I think that when Mary sat at the feet of Jesus her prayer request list went out the window with the breath of fresh wind that came from being so close to Jesus. I think that in that moment she took a deep sigh of relief and breathed in the life of Christ. That is what I think. But don't trust what I say or think. Try it yourself. Carve out time daily (early in the morning I find is best) and just sit and worship Jesus. This book is filled with practical ways to worship but for now just sit and reflect on His goodness, His awesome power and the truth of His Word. I promise that will not be a waste of your time.

What thoughts and images come to mind when you think of mountains? I think of the Blue Ridge Mountains of

North Carolina where my husband and I spend a great
deal of time hiking and enjoying the magnificent views. I
think of the crisp air, the extravagant beauty of nature,
and the breathtaking world God has created. When I
think about mountains I am also reminded of the
mountaintop experiences in my life – like the day I was
married; and the days I gave birth to each of my children;
and the days I attended my children's weddings. All
those mountaintop memories are engraved on my heart.

Peaks and Valleys
But mountains can bring negative images too. They can
remind us, and represent for us, those things in our lives
that can overwhelm us and seem insurmountable: loss of
health, loss of loved ones, job struggles, mountains of
debt, broken relationships.

Jesus understood all about mountains – the good peaks
and the bad valleys. He knew the beauty of creation, and
He saw the devastation of human sin and suffering.
Using the metaphor of the mountain to stand for those
things in our lives that seem impossible or
insurmountable, He taught His disciples:

> I tell you the truth, if you have faith as small as a
> mustard seed you can say to this mountain, "move
> from here to there" and it will move.
> Nothing will be impossible for you. [1]

Jesus' disciples could not heal the young boy who was
possessed by a demon. Jesus rebuked the demon and the
boy was healed. He then told His followers that they
needed to rely on God for the impossible – that
mountains could be moved by faith. Moving mountains
was a common metaphor in Jewish literature for doing

what appeared to be impossible. In another teaching moment, Jesus demonstrated the possibilities of mountain-moving faith.

> In the morning, as he was returning to the city, he became hungry. And seeing a fig tree by the wayside, he went to it and found nothing on it but only leaves. And he said to it, "May no fruit ever come from you again!" And the fig tree withered at once. When the disciples saw it, they marveled saying, "How did the fig tree wither at once?" And Jesus answered them, "Truly, I say to you, if you have faith and do not doubt, you will not only do what has been done to the fig tree but even if you say to the mountain, 'Be taken up and thrown into the sea,' it will happen. And whatever you ask in prayer you will receive, if you have faith. "[2]

Jesus understood the mountains we face, and He demonstrated time and time again that prayers offered in faith could move them. There is something so intriguing to me about what Jesus said. He was giving us a key to prayer; He was saying that prayers must have power behind them, and that that power is faith. So this begs the question: "How can we increase our faith?"

The Question of Faith
Faith ignites the power of God, and prayers powered by faith move mountains. So it stands to reason that we would all like to have more faith in order to have victory over the struggles in our lives. Right? How about you?

The Scriptures show us ways to activate our faith; faith comes:
- from hearing, and hearing comes from the Word

of God (Romans 10:17)
- from spending time with God and asking Him to open our spiritual eyes and ears (Ephesians 1:18)
- from choosing to depend on God
- from expecting to see God move in our lives
- from putting our trust completely in God and not in ourselves

Obstacles to Prayer

On our quest to move the mountains in our lives through prayer, we may find that there are equally large mountains barring the path to effective prayer. Let's take a look at some of our notions about prayer:

- *I'm just too busy to pray....*
  Do you find yourself saying that? If so, remember: if you have time to eat, bathe, sleep and do whatever else you do regularly, then you have time to pray. Are you waiting to increase your prayer life after you have studied more about prayer?

- *I don't know how to pray....*
  What is the correct way to pray? Do we need to follow a formula? Jesus knew that we would ask that question so he did give us a model to pray – The Lord's Prayer. The truth is that prayer is simply conversation with God. *Conversation*, as in *talking* and *listening*.

- *What's the relationship between faith and prayer? If the disciples had trouble with faith and they were with Jesus, why should I think I have enough faith for my prayers to be answered?*

Remember: Jesus commended faith, but He told us to pray – not to wait until we had enough faith.

Time Well Spent

Our prayer life is dependent on our willingness to make space in our lives for prayer. It's simple and logical, but it is not always easy. It is not that we must add prayer to our life; it is that prayer must become the song of our life – the words we speak, the breaths we take, the lives we live – day in and day out. Prayer is in essence the development and deepening of our relationship with Our Creator, the One who knows us best and who yearns to commune with us.

So often we think that developing our prayer life requires adding something on, but what we really need is to take some thing(s) away. Developing our prayer life requires removing the stress of performance and replacing it with a genuine thirst for intimacy with God. Richard Foster dispels the myth that we have to work at praying:

> Some people work at the business of praying with such intensity that they get spiritual indigestion. There is a principle of progression in the spiritual life. We do not take occasional joggers and put them in a marathon race, and we must not do that with prayer either. The desert mothers and fathers spoke of the sin of "spiritual greed," that is, wanting more of God than can be properly digested. [3]

Rise and Shine

In the morning when I first wake up, my thoughts are on visiting with God. I can hardly wait to get up, get my coffee and spend some time with Him sharing yesterday's events – the good, the bad and the in-between – and then looking forward to the new day with Him.

He is my best friend. He is the One who understands me and loves me just as I am, warts and all. My conversations with Him are sometimes funny, sometimes sad, sometimes stunningly revelatory, but always filled with the expectancy that He is listening patiently and waiting for me to listen in return.

Listening Prayer
Listening prayer? Huh? Yep. Listening prayer can move the mountains in your life. When I am so busy talking to God that I don't stop to listen, I have missed the whole point. When it is all about me, I have missed the point … because He is the point! I cannot recommend talking *at* God or around God or in spite of God. Good friends converse; they give and take. Good friends listen. I listen through my Scripture reading for the day and sometimes through a song of worship. Sometimes I am still like Samuel, saying: "Speak, for your servant is listening. "[4]

Sometimes I don't want to hear what God has to say. Do you ever feel that way? But God is persistent. He quietly offers me opportunities throughout the day to hear His still small voice. In order to hear Him, we must be available; we must be *listening.*

Mountain-Moving Prayers
There are so many different kinds of prayer that can move the mountains in our lives. And there are countless examples in the Bible of men and women who fervently prayed different types of prayers – at different hours, in

different circumstances, different languages, different ways.

It doesn't really matter that you have a name for the kind of prayer you pray, but it is helpful to know that at different times we may find ourselves praying in different ways.

Intercessory Prayer: Warriors and Watchmen

Intercessors are sometimes called Prayer Warriors. They fight the battles of life through prayer. They plead on behalf of others. They 'stand in the gap'[5] for people who need others to pray for them. Intercessors are also often called watchmen. In the Old Testament watchmen stood on the walls of the city and kept watch in case an enemy approached. We are all called to intercede for others; when someone says to you, even casually, "Please keep me in your prayers," you are being asked to intercede for them. Don't hesitate: pray then and there, either with the person or silently. The person may have been the one to make the prayer request, but the Holy Spirit of God is the One who prompts us to make these requests. Doesn't that make perfect sense?

Some people feel a sense of call to be on prayer alert 24/7. Francis Frangipane writes that God's desires are born – made real – through intercessors:

> The reality God has planned will always manifest first in the prayer life of his intercessors. When you hear from God and then pray His Word, you are impacting the unformed essence of life with the Spirit of God Himself. Thus God calls us not only to know His Word but also to pray His Word. We must go from intellectualizing God's Word to being

impregnated by it. (emphasis mine) I know churches have special areas where intercessors can pray or meditate. But maybe we ought to change the name from "prayer room" to "prayer womb". For everything good and holy that we see manifested in people, in churches and in life is first conceived, and then birthed, in the womb of prayer.[6]

The womb of prayer transforms impossibilities into possibilities, birthing God's will on the earth. I remember the first time I was in labor with my eldest daughter – how I was amazed that life was growing in me. Life inside me! The whole process of growth, labor, and delivery is illustrated and understood as we pray in faith for mountains to be moved, for God to intervene, for His will to be done on earth.

Prayers of Repentance
Prayers of repentance, sometimes called prayers of confession, are prayers that ask for forgiveness. Repentance in essence means changing our mind and changing our direction – turning away from sin and back to God. This kind of prayer must have been very important to Jesus because one of the first things He did when He began His earthly ministry was declare that the Kingdom of God was at hand and would be seen through repentance. [7]

Healing Prayer
Prayers for healing are described in the book of James:
>   Is anyone of you in trouble? He should pray. Is anyone happy? Let him sing songs of praise. Is any one of you sick? He should call the elders of the church to pray over him and anoint him with oil in

the name of the Lord. And the prayer offered in faith will make the sick person well; the Lord will raise him up. If he has sinned, he will be forgiven. Therefore confess your sins to each other and pray for each other so you may be healed. The prayer of a righteous man is powerful and effective. [8]

There is much discussion these days about whether or not God still heals. Is that a question for you? If so, consider these facts:

- Jesus Christ is the same yesterday, today, and tomorrow (Hebrews 13:8); God healed in the past so if He is the same now as He was then, He still heals today
- There is nothing in the Scriptures that teaches us God has stopped healing
- The most important healing is that of the broken soul who turns to Christ and His free gift of salvation

Miracles Happen When (and Where) Expected

I have two friends who are missionaries. They have traveled often to Third World countries and prayed for the sick, and they have many stories to tell about sick people being healed. One young girl had been deaf since childhood; my friends prayed for her hearing to be restored, and God responded. Even her teachers were amazed. This is just one testimony about healing prayers being answered; there are many.

Of course God still heals today. Why in the world would He decide to stop? If God stopped loving and listening and healing, He would stop being God.

I think that in Third World countries people are more desperate for God. Their faith is in Him alone because so often they have no other hope, they see no other 'way out'. It is clear to them that the earthly resources at their disposal are limited, maybe nonexistent. It is clear to them that they need a Savior. Remember, Third World countries represent the majority of national powers on the planet. But I don't think the Western world is as desperate for the hope that Jesus brings. It is not as clear to a lot of us – not yet anyway – that we are in need of a Savior. We think we are 'better off' than our Third World neighbors, at least in terms of the world's definition of 'better off'. This obvious discrepancy between the *desperation quotients* of the West and the Third World may well explain why more healing-miracle stories come to us from the Third World. You see, miracles – of every kind, not just the healing variety – happen when and where believers who are desperate for Jesus expect them to.

When you pray, do you pray with desperate expectancy? When you pray, do you expect God to respond?

Thanksgiving and Praise Prayers

I discovered something that has transformed my prayer life. My New Year's resolution this year was to worship more, and in the context of worship I have been thanking God for all He has done, is doing and will do in the areas of concern to me. Scripture tells us that God inhabits the praise of His people – He draws near to us, His Holy Spirit rises and is revitalized in us when we praise Him. Take a peek in the throne room and see what I mean:

> At once I was in the Spirit, and there before me was a throne in heaven with someone sitting on it. And

the one who sat there had the appearance of jasper and carnelian. A rainbow, resembling an emerald, encircled the throne. Surrounding the throne were twenty-four elders. They were dressed in white and had crowns of gold on their heads. From the throne came flashes of lightning, rumblings and peals of thunder.

Before the throne seven lamps were blazing. These are the seven spirits of God. Also before the throne there was what looked like a sea of glass, clear as crystal. In the center, around the throne, were four living creatures…. Day and night they never stopped saying: "Holy, Holy, is the Lord God Almighty, who was and is, and is to come."[9]

We have access to God's throne room! We can enter into the Father's Presence because of what Jesus did:
Therefore, since we have a great high priest who has gone through the heavens, Jesus the Son of God, let us hold firmly to the faith we profess. For we do not have a high priest who is unable to sympathize with our weaknesses, but we have one who has been tempted in every way, just as we are – yet was without sin. Let us approach the throne of grace with confidence, so that we may receive mercy and find grace to help us in our time of need. [10]

We are encouraged to enter the throne room boldly and to approach our heavenly Father with confidence. And it is on the wings of gratitude and praise that we do this.

Our Lord Jesus made it possible. He understands us. He has been where we are, felt what we feel. He made the way for us – He *is* the way for us – to enter His Father's Presence and to receive the grace and mercy God so freely gives.

Our prayers of thanksgiving and praise usher us into the throne room of God. Isn't that amazing?

Transforming Prayers

Speaking of amazing, consider this: as we commune with God in prayer, we behold the One in whose image we are made; we begin to see, to comprehend, what the King of the Universe has imagined; we become more like Him, and becoming more like Him becomes our mission. Amazing, wonderful, and mysterious, too, isn't it?

As we become more like Him we will know His will; we will think like Him, we will have the mind of Christ and be empowered to do His will. He will transform us. His will is to transform us.

He gives us what we need to be and do what He made us for. Amazing, wonderful and mysterious.

Doing Flows From Being

Our *doing* will flow from our *being* in His Presence. Communicating with God through prayer helps us to draw near to Him. As we communicate with Him, we are changed:

> The impulse that drives the life of the believer isn't the need to perform for God but to commune with Him. (emphasis mine) Only when we perceive the face of the One in whose image we were made do we come to know who we are and the One for whom we were made.

And because of who He is, to behold Him and
remain unchanged is impossible. As He infects us
with His Presence, we are drawn into an ongoing
mission by the One who longs for us. This mission
is simply the mission to become more and more fit
to see Him in His fullness.[11]

Are You A House of Prayer?

God spoke to His people and told them they were to
worship Him and to maintain a house of prayer. In the
gospel of Mark, Jesus cleanses the temple where the court
of the Gentiles (non-Jews) could worship God and gather
for prayer. The court of the Gentiles had become a place
to buy and sell animals for sacrifice; it had become a noisy
smelly marketplace, instead of a house of prayer:

> On reaching Jerusalem, Jesus entered the temple area
> and began driving out those who were buying and
> selling there. He overturned the tables of the
> moneychangers and the benches of those selling
> doves, and would not allow anyone to carry
> merchandise through the temple courts. And as he
> taught them, he said, "Is it not written: 'My house
> will be called a house of prayer for all nations'? But
> you made it a den of robbers. "[12]

What is keeping your temple (where God lives) from
being a house of prayer? Is the space you've made
available in your life for God a place where prayer is a
priority? If not, what crowds it out? Worry? Busyness?
Sin?

Cleaning House

I was reading an article in a magazine today about how to
un-clutter your house. These days it seems as though

194

everyone is interested in simplifying. The woman in the article was seeking professional help to clean out her junk, but before they could begin the project, the person she hired said they had to get to the root reason her client had spent years filling up all the space in her house with things. The Unclutter Guru said that in order to make space in her client's house – to unstuff it and keep it unstuffed – she first had to sort out what drove the woman to fill her house with stuff in the first place. Why unclutter and free up space if we are just going to fill it again with more stuff?

What is the root cause of the clutter in your house of prayer?

Jesus drove the money changers out of the temple, His Father's House of Prayer, and He longs to see us drive out anything that keeps us from praying – anything: worries, worthless agenda items and to-do's, any stuff that gets in the way of our becoming an agent who helps transform God's desires into realities.

Jesus Prayed on Earth
Scripture is full of passages that demonstrate the value Jesus placed on prayer. Throughout the gospels, we see Him getting alone with His Father to pray. Do you ever wonder what Jesus said? I find myself imagining His side of the conversation a lot.

"Dad, we had a good day today. Thank you for your faithfulness. Thank you showing me who you are and what you want every step of the way. I'm nothing without you. Thank you, too, for reminding me that nothing is impossible for you.

"The demoniac was delivered; the man by the pool of Siloam was healed. Another bad day with the Pharisees, though. I just don't fit into their religious box, do I, Dad? They got mad at me today because I healed on the Sabbath. But you told me that you are Lord of the Sabbath, right? I just tell them what you tell me.

"I am dog-tired today. Dad, give me strength to carry on. Thank you. "

I imagine Jesus' conversations with His Dad were filled with thanksgiving, mixed with sorrow and compassion. He saw and talked to so many helpless people; He knew they were like sheep without a shepherd. [13] When He prayed in the Garden of Gethsemane on the night He was arrested, His soul was overwhelmed with dread and sorrow,[14] and He shared with His Father all of what was on His heart. He held nothing back. And He calls us to do the same. He is not a far-away deity we cannot approach. He is Love and Hope and Promise. He came *to* us and sacrificed Himself *for* us.

Jesus, fully human, fully divine, taught us how to pray. He drew near to the only One who could give Him strength and hope, and He poured His heart out.

Jesus taught His disciples how to pray. I wonder if He gave them a model for prayer because they had asked Him how to pray. Did He know that some day future disciples would follow His model but that it would become rote, prayer from the mouth but not the heart? Did Jesus know that the meaning behind the prayer – *inside* the words – would be lost? I wonder. Here is what He taught His followers to pray:

Our Father in heaven,
Hallowed be your name,
Your kingdom come,
Your will be done
On earth as it is in heaven.
Give us today our daily bread.
Forgive us our debts,
As we also have forgiven our debtors.
And lead us not into temptation
But deliver us from the evil one. [15]

He taught us to hallow, praise, and honor the name of
God Our Father; to ask for His kingdom to come to
earth and His will to be done here and now; to ask for
our daily provision physically and spiritually; to forgive
others; and to ask for deliverance from the enemy.

And we pray that prayer, don't we? But sometimes it gets
lost in the sea of familiarity – words spoken, requests
routinely made, the meaning misplaced. I think Jesus
knew that would happen, but He gave us the model
anyway. How come? Did He know that some of His
followers would press into the real meaning, desperate to
rediscover it each time they prayed, unwilling to substitute
repetition for heart-felt petition?

I think our Lord took a chance that there would be some
people for whom His prayer was, and would remain,
fresh and real and alive.

Devoted
The First Century church was devoted to the Word, to
fellowship with other Christians and to prayer. The effect
was like striking a match that ignited miracles.

197

> They devoted themselves to the apostle's teachings
> and to the fellowship, to the breaking of bread and
> to prayer. Everyone was filled with awe, and many
> wonders and miraculous signs were done by the
> apostles. [16]

'They' lived expectantly, didn't they? They devoted themselves to, which is to say they *invested* themselves *in*. They talked the talk; they walked the walk; they lived the life.

We all want to see God perform miracles, heal the sick, deliver the oppressed, and set the captives free, don't we? Of course we do. After all, Jesus said that was His mission on earth. And yet we pray and nothing happens; we hope and are disappointed. But the early church was filled with awe, and the apostles did many wonders and miracles. How come? What's different now?

See, they were *devoted to prayer*. They were invested in it. It wasn't something they fit into their schedule when it was convenient; it was the way they lived their lives. They expected God would show up. They knew prayer mattered.

The trouble with us is that we often go to the phone before we go to the throne. We rush to our friends to tell them what is going on in our lives and leave God on call waiting. We dial Him up with a quick prayer, put Him on hold, then go to our friends to solve the problem. Don't get me wrong. We need our friends. The same God we often leave on hold made us for friendship and fellowship. And we need our friends to pray for us. But somewhere along the line we forget that it is God who has the solution.

Persistence in Prayer

One time Jesus told a story about a man who asked his friend to lend him three loaves of bread. The only problem was that it was midnight when the request was made:

> "Suppose one of you has a friend and he goes to him at midnight and says, 'Friend, lend me three loaves of bread, because a friend of mine on a journey has come to me, and I have nothing to set before him.' Then the one inside answers, "Don't bother me. The door is already locked, and my children are with me in bed. I can't get up and give you anything. I tell you, though he will not get up and give him the bread because he is his friend, yet because of the man's boldness he will get up and give him as much as he needs. So I say to you: Ask and it will be given to you; seek and you will find; knock and the door will be opened to you. For everyone who asks receives; he who seeks find; and to him who knocks, the door will be opened. [17]

Jesus wanted to be sure we understood: persistence and boldness in prayer are what open doors. He told that story so we would persistently ask, seek, and knock *until* it is given, *until* it is found, *until* the door opens.

And it is through prayer that we persist. I don't know about you, but it motivates me to keep knocking. There must be something about our persistence that makes its way into the heavenly chorus – a sound that reaches the Father's heart; the sound of a heart crying out, an expectant heart seeking the only One who can and will open the door and meet our deepest needs.

One of Prayer's Enemies Is Business

Another thing which commonly stifles prayer is men's business. The days become so full that prayer gets crowded out. Sometimes when that happens, the plea is urged in extenuation that work itself is prayer, that honest work is indeed one of the highest kinds of prayer which can ever be offered, and that, therefore, the crowding out of the devotional hour does not really matter much. But look at Jesus. Busy and crowded as our days are, his were emphatically more so. [18]

We read in the gospel of Mark about the busy days that Jesus had. People pulled on him to heal, to deliver, to cast out; his time was not His own. His life with and among us was a three-year series of interruptions, unscheduled appointments and command performances. He was always busy, even far into the night. He must have been exhausted. Yet, if we are paying attention, we notice: the busier He was, the more He found time to pray.

So Be It

The Hebrew word translated *amen* means *truly* or *so be it*. *Amen* is also found in the New Testament and has the same meaning. Nearly half of the Old Testament uses of *amen* are found in the book of Deuteronomy, and in each case the people are responding to curses pronounced by God on various sins. Each pronouncement is followed by: "And all the people shall say Amen". [19]

Many of the Old Testament references link *amen* with praise. The New Testament writers all used *amen* at the end of their letters. The apostle John uses it at the end of his gospel, his three letters and the Book of Revelation, and each time it is connected with praising and glorifying God. Paul says amen to the blessings he pronounces on the churches in his letters, as do Peter, John and Jude. In essence they all were asking God to bless them.

When we pray we are asking for the will of God, praising Him and sealing the prayer with *let it be done according to your will.*

Mary, a young woman chosen to be the mother of the Savior, was a woman of prayer. We know this because when the events that had been foretold began to unfold, she pondered all these things in her heart. I think that means that she went to her heavenly Father in prayer. When the angel Gabriel came to tell her that she would be with child, Mary was troubled and, I suspect, a bit anxious. But her response tells us that she was so much more. She was a woman centered on God, and she was able to respond: "Let it be done according to your word." She responded to God's call with an *amen* – an assurance that God's will would be done.

Prayer is the way we move the mountains of unbelief, confusion and fear in our lives.

What mountains are you facing today? Turn and seek God in prayer. He waits to hear your amen. He waits for you to turn your mountains over to Him, trusting that His answer is the perfect one.

So be it.

Notes

1. Matthew 17:14-21
2. Matthew 21:18-22
3. Richard Foster, Prayer: Finding the Heart's True Home, 13
4. 1 Samuel 3:10
5. Ezekiel 22:30
6. Frances Frangipane, In Christ's Image Training – Prayer, 118
7. Matthew 4:17
8. James 5:13-16
9. Revelation 4:2-8
10. Hebrews 4:14-16
11. Bill Johnson, Face to Face, 3
12. Mark 11:15-17
13. Matthew 9:36
14. Matthew 26:38
15. Matthew 6:9-13
16. Acts 2:42
17. Luke 11:5-10
18. Bob Benson, Sr. and Michael W. Benson, Disciplines for the Inner Life, 212
19. Deuteronomy 27:15-26

11 TEARING DOWN THE FENCES OF OFFENSES

Mary could have been utterly offended by her sister Martha. After all Martha complained to Jesus about her. Nothing worse than being chastised by your sister in front of an honored guest.   Maybe it would have been easier to take if it had been a friend complaining, but her sister? Why should I be surprised? Siblings take liberties that others don't. So Mary took the rebuke sitting down—yes sitting down at the feet of Jesus. How strange was that? Scripture doesn't tell us if she got up and bopped her sister over the head but I don't think she had to. Jesus did the bopping for her. Offenses come at us every daily, but it's always better when Jesus deals with them. I imagine that Martha was offended by Jesus when he did not take her side. But my hope is that Martha's heart was prepared to receive the tender rebuke of Jesus. If our hearts have made space for God, offenses will not find a place to land. How about you? Do you find that you are easily offended? I am hoping that after you read this chapter you will have some take home tools to help you find Mary peace when the arrows come your way and you and I both know that they will.

This week I am in my post-Christmas clean-up mode, decluttering all the rooms in my house and attempting to eliminate the mess that has accumulated throughout the past year.   As I go through this yearly ritual, I am recognizing two things:

    1. Clutter happens …

2. And often it is due to my being too busy to stay on top of things or too willing to buy things I don't need.

Can you relate? Okay, so maybe my Clutter-Happens Theory is not exactly original.

How Much Is Enough?

Regardless, I am now on duty, making space for … what? More clutter? A new pile of rarely-or-never-to-be-used stuff? My annual Declutter Routine begs at least two questions: *How much is enough?* and *What impact does clutter have on my life?*

As I consider these questions, one thing is crystal clear: clutter makes me less efficient: it takes up space that could be used for more meaningful things, more worthy pursuits.

Clutter As Metaphor

What a metaphor for our spiritual lives! As I declutter the physical space around me I am also thinking through my inventory of spiritual clutter, and I'm discovering that a great deal of space in my life, in me, which could be made available to God, is being filled with unnecessary junk. In other words, I am allowing intrinsically valuable space to be wasted space. It is a choice I've made, though perhaps inadvertently. It's a choice we all make, isn't it?

I know I've used the room analogy liberally in this book. It just seems to fit again and again. There are so many ways we can clutter our spiritual room(s) – that is, the space in our hearts and lives where the Spirit of God can live if we invite and allow Him. If our living rooms are so cluttered with stinkin' thinkin' or busyness or meaningless

ritual or the million shallow passions and pursuits the
world and the enemy urge us to invest in, we've left no
space for the honored guest. And He wants to be a
permanent resident, not just a sometime visitor.

If our spiritual house is filled with our stuff and not His,
where will God stay – where will He rest – when He is
invited in?

The Clutter of Offense: Jesus' Response ... and Ours

One kind of junk that God has been pointing out to me,
and inviting me to throw out of my spiritual house, is
offense. He is challenging me to strictly avoid taking the
bait of insult, and He is showing me that in so doing I will
make room for more of Him. He is showing me that this
is a choice I can make.

Jesus was insulted on a regular basis, and He always
responded with love – though sometimes 'tough love' –
and often with practical instruction. Upon receiving the
greatest insult of them all, while hanging on the cross,
Jesus said, "Father forgive them, for they do not know
what they are doing. "[1]

What about you? Are you easily offended? Do you take
the bait of insult and end up cluttering your heart with
bitterness or unforgiveness? God has a better way.

The Definition of Offense

The Oxford Dictionary defines *offense* as a legal term: a
breach of law or rule; an illegal act; a thing that
constitutes a violation of what is judged to be right or
natural. It also means *annoyance* or *resentment* brought about
by a perceived insult or disregard for oneself or one's

standards or principles; also, the action of attacking – in war or in sports the team or players who are attempting to score or advance the ball.

Offense comes from the late middle English and Old French, *offens*, meaning mislead; and from the Latin *offensus*, which means *annoyance* or *striking against* or *hurt*.

Another Deadly Trap

Another truth we have considered again and again in this book: Satan sets deadly traps for us, both hidden and baited. The enemy loves to confuse, mislead and misdirect us. He loves to whisper lies in our ears. He first deployed this strategy in the Garden of Eden, and he has used it every single day since. One of the most deceptive kinds of bait Satan uses is offense.

When I discovered a rat lived in my house, I had to set a trap and put some poisonous bait in it that the rat liked. If the rat had known the bait was deadly, he would not have eaten it. Likewise, offense is not fatal in itself: if it stays in the trap – if we leave it alone – no big deal; but if we pick it up and feed on it, it becomes deadly.

The Fruit of Offense

Offended people produce the fruit of jealousy, resentment, strife, bitterness – even hatred. And the consequences of picking up an offense, inviting it into our heart, are wounding, division, and broken relationships.

The Greek word for *offend* is *skandalon*, which originally referred to the part of the trap to which the bait is attached. [2] So when it is used in the Old Testament, *offend* signifies laying a trap in someone's way. In the New Testament it often describes an entrapment used by the enemy. *Offense* is a tool the enemy employs to bring people into captivity. When we offend or are offended, we are separated from one another.

Good News for Bait-Takers

The good news is that Jesus said that his mission was to set the captives free:

> The Spirit of the Lord is on me, because he has anointed me to preach good news to the poor. He has sent me to proclaim freedom for the prisoners (emphasis mine) and recovery of sight for the blind, to release the oppressed, to proclaim the year of the Lord's favor. [3]

Our Lord also told us that it is impossible to live this life and not be offended. [4] Have you been offended by someone recently? Have you offended anyone?

A Recent Fence-Building Project

Someone offended me recently. She didn't mean anything by it, but I took the bait. She said that she does not call me because I am too busy. I guessed she meant that I was too busy for her. I am most definitely a 'people-person', so her telling me this was like an arrow in my heart. One of the things I value most in genuine friendships is being available; I strive to 'be there' for my friends. Yes, it is true that I have an army of a family and my time for friendships is limited, but what I heard this friend say was: "You are never available for me."

So her words hurt; she offended me without meaning to. I took the bait. I ate it and allowed it to poison my outlook. I started building a fence between my friend and me out of the perceived offense. I thought to myself, *What about all the times I dropped everything and was there for her?*

Now all of this may seem silly to you, but trust me: the enemy knows how to hook us; he knows our weak spots and he will take advantage at every opportunity. If he can just get you to take the bait....

But we know the good news that Jesus proclaimed. Like everything Jesus told us, it was true then, and it is true now. All we have to do is *remember*! He came to set the captives free, and turning to His Word discloses the enemy's lies and gives us a fresh perspective – Christ's perspective.

That was all I needed to get back on track again. I spit the bait out and used my Lord's Word to dynamite the latest fence of offense the enemy had suggested I build.

The Tearing-Down Process
Offenses are common but, unfortunately, tearing down the fences of offenses is not as ordinary. It's not so easy. That positive tearing-down process requires our recognition of the fence(s), our understanding of the serious negative consequences of offense, and our willingness and commitment to do what it takes to destroy the fence(s) that offenses create.

It takes courage to deal with our hurts when we have been offended. It takes guts to make amends when we have offended others.

An Offended Brother and The Healing God

Did you know that when you offend someone old "Red Legs" starts helping build fences?

Satan would like nothing more than to destroy your relationships, isolate you and harden your heart.

> An offended brother is more unyielding than a
> fortified city, and disputes are like the barred gates of
> a citadel. [5]

We build walls of protection (fences) around our offended hearts – it is our nature, it's in our DNA – and it is crucial that as Christians we allow the Lord to deal with the offenses in our lives. We must permit God to tear down the fences of offenses so that we can live as His free people, just as He intended.

And we need to make space for God to do this.

A Sign of His Return

Jesus said that one of the signs of His return is that *many will be offended.*[6] The church needs to be different from the world. Wouldn't it be great if the church (we) were a lighthouse to the world and that when offenses increase we will be prepared to lead others to freedom? The truth is that we must be free ourselves if we are to be like Jesus and help lead others out of captivity.

The Offended: Some Biblical Examples

When Jesus went to His hometown of Nazareth and began teaching in the synagogue, the locals were amazed … and offended:

> Where did this man get this wisdom and these
> miraculous powers? they asked. "Isn't this the

carpenter's son? Isn't his mother's name Mary, and his brothers James, Joseph, Simon and Judas? Aren't all his sisters with us? Where then did this man get all these things?" And they took offense at him. [7]

Essentially they were saying, "Who in the world does Jesus think He is – He's just a carpenter's son after all. What does *he* know that we don't know?" Jesus' demonstration of power without credentials offended them because He did not talk or act or teach according to their narrow standards of righteousness and propriety. Jesus was so far 'outside the box', and so confident and assured – He probably scared them as much as He offended them.

David Offended Everyone In Sight

David's brothers were offended when he chose to confront Goliath; the Philistine giant was offended when young David confidently walked onto the battlefield in his street clothes to fight him; King Saul was offended when it became obvious that David was God's choice to be the new king. David seemed to offend everyone in sight. But David knew God would defend him and preserve him and lead him, and that is the key to tearing down the fences of offenses. [8]

God uses the foolish things of the world – young shepherd boys, for example – to confound the wise.

And then there was David's wife, Michal, who was offended when he "danced before the Lord with all his might"[9] (wearing only a linen ephod!) as the ark was brought back to Jerusalem. King David's ecstatic and unselfconscious style of worship did not seem to Michal to be dignified or fitting for someone in David's lofty position. Sometimes people are offended by different or unfamiliar forms of worship. But God looks at our hearts. At that moment, David's heart was full of love and joy and celebration and righteous abandon, and he could not have cared less what anyone (except God) thought. He chose to worship his King by dancing. [10]

The Pharisees

The Pharisees were another bunch who were easily and often offended. They were especially offended by Jesus of Nazareth because He spoke the truth no matter whose heart or ego it pierced. He confronted the Pharisees' hypocrisy and pointed out that even as they adhered to the letter of the law they ignored its intent:

> And why do you break the command of God for the sake of tradition?[11]

Jesus had a lot to say about them, and He most often said it directly to them. He called them a "brood of vipers"[12]; He called them unmarked graves, whitewashed tombs:

> Now you Pharisees clean the outside of the cup and dish, but inside you are full of greed and wickedness.[13]

Offended? Yep. The Pharisees were offended and they intended to end the insults by ending Jesus' life.

Sound familiar? I know it may seem harsh, but don't we sometimes want to be rid of the offender? Don't we sometimes wish that those who offend us would *get what they deserve*? It's true, isn't it? I know I've wished that those who've offended me were 'anywhere but here'. Have you?

That is why we need a Savior. That's why we need the One whose mission is to set the captives free.

When Jesus healed on the Sabbath He offended the Pharisees. They were indignant. They had zeal for the Sabbath but they were blind to the Lord of the Sabbath.[14]

Are you offended when what you perceive as your tradition or truth or way of doing things is called into question? Am I the only one who becomes a porcupine when what I think is right is challenged? There are all sorts of reasons we become offended, but at the root of them all is self. Here I go again with another repeating theme: self is overrated; self-concern can often be a stumbling block for those who would follow Jesus; when in doubt, deny self and ask: "Will this honor God?"

Sources of Offenses in Biblical Examples
So what do the biblical passages I've cited have in common? What are some of the common sources of offenses?

- Offenses occur when God doesn't act the way we think He should: our pride
- Offenses occur whenever we see the question: "Who does he think he is?": our jealousy
- Offenses occur when God uses the foolish things of the world to confound the wise
- Offenses occur whenever we see self-righteous indignation at work: counterfeit to holiness and righteous indignation
- Offenses can occur when people are confronted with truth and do not have a teachable heart
- Offenses occur when we think we are the center of the universe: we leave no room for God to be

the center, so we are easily offended

Quick Offense Test[15]
Take a moment for this test. Answer the questions as honestly as you can to see if you have a heart that is easily offended:

- Are you offended (does it make you jealous) when someone is promoted and you are overlooked (in the work place, at home, anywhere)?
- Are you offended (do you feel slighted or misunderstood) when others don't appreciate your hard work?
- Are you offended when someone is not interested in your opinion (and you can tell because they aren't listening but constructing their own argument as you talk)?
- Are you offended when someone lies to you?
- Although it is certainly wrong for someone to lie to you, you will know you have been offended/wounded if you turn inward and allow the wound to fester.

The Sound of An Offended Heart
Wolfgang Amadeus Mozart was a child prodigy, a genius as a musician and composer. Already competent on keyboard and violin, he composed from the age of five and performed before European royalty; at 17 he was engaged as a court musician in Salzburg. His contemporary, Antonio Salieri, was five years older and established as the Court Composer of the Italian Opera in Vienna before Mozart moved there.

In *Waking the Dead*, John Eldredge refers to *Amadeus*,

Peter Shaffer's film about Mozart, and discusses how
Shaffer fictionalizes the relationship between Salieri and
Mozart for dramatic effect. Eldredge says that Shaffer
"creates a villain worthy of the devil himself in the
character of the court composer Salieri. "[16] Once Mozart
came to Vienna, Salieri began to see the younger
composer as his chief rival, and his envy of Mozart
poisoned his heart.

Listen to the sound of Salieri's offended heart in these
lines from the film. Mozart's wife has brought some of
her husband's music to Salieri, hoping to get Mozart a
job; the young couple was very poor and desperately
needed money. In this scene Salieri looks at the sheets of
music and narrates:

> These were first, and *only* drafts of music. But they
> showed no correction of any kind. Not one. He had
> simply written down music already finished...in his
> *head*.... And music...finished like no music is ever
> finished....

Later Salieri addresses God:

> From now on we are enemies, You and I. Because
> You choose for Your instrument a boastful, lustful,
> smutty, infantile boy ... and give me only the ability
> to recognize the Incarnation. Because You are
> *unjust...unfair...unkind*! I will block You. I swear it. I
> will hinder and harm Your creature here on earth as
> far as I am able. (*Shaking his fist in the air*) I will ruin
> Your incarnation.

Salieri was offended with Mozart's incredible gift, but
even more, he was offended by the God who bestowed
that gift on Mozart and not on him. Salieri did not

214

believe that God had acted as He should. Salieri did not believe that Mozart deserved the gift he had.

Offended by God

Have you ever been offended by God? I was once. God offended me when He allowed two of my husband's sisters to die. I could not understand any bit of it. For a time, I could not accept it – I could not wrap my heart around a God who took both of these women I loved at such an early age.

But I watched my mother-in-law, the dead women's mother. And I saw very clearly that she was not offended. She was broken, and she grieved deeply, but she was not offended by God. Not at all. In her sorrow and grief she clung to Him more than ever. And her response to my doubt and desperate questions was to have faith and to remember that God is good *all the time*. God is sovereign.

My mother-in-law did not take the bait; she did not build a fence of offense. But I did.

Thankfully, Jesus' mission impossible found possibility in me. He came and set me free from the offense by showing me His undying, unfailing love for my sisters-in-law, and their mother, and my husband ... and me. The bait is always tempting; and it is always poisonous.

Jealousy

Did you know that the source of offense is often jealousy and that jealousy manifests itself through those closest to you – family, friends, co-workers?

The hurt from friends and relatives is the most difficult offense to deal with:

> For it is not an enemy who reproaches me; then I could bear it. Nor is it one who hates me who has exalted himself against me; then I could hide from him. But it was you, a man of my equal, my companion and my acquaintance. We took sweet counsel together, and walked to the house of God in the throng. [17]

It makes sense that the closer the relationship, the more severe the offense. The truth is only those you care about can hurt you. The higher the expectations you have of someone the greater the fall when they hurt you (or you hurt them).

Offender Offended: Joseph

Joseph was Jacob's eleventh son. He was despised by his older brothers because their father favored him and set him apart by giving Joseph a very cool robe, well known today as the coat of many colors. Problem number one: jealousy:

> This is the account of Jacob. Joseph, a young man of seventeen, was tending the flocks with his brothers, the sons of Bilhah and the sons of Zilpah, his father's wives, and he brought their father a bad report about them. Now Israel loved Joseph more than any of his other sons because he had been born to him in his old age and he made a richly ornamented robe for him. When his brothers saw their father loved him more than any of them, they hated him and could not speak a kind word to him. [18]

After that Joseph had a dream and set himself up for big

trouble by the way he spoke about the dream with his brothers. Problem number two: pride:

> Joseph had a dream, and when he told it to his
> brothers, they hated him all the more. He said to
> them, "Listen to this dream I had:
> we were binding sheaves of grain out in the field
> when suddenly my sheaf rose and stood upright,
> while your sheaves gathered around mine and bowed
> down to it. " His brothers said to him,
>
> "Do you intend to reign over us? Will you actually
> rule us?" And they hated him all the more because of
> his dream and what he had said. [19]

Joseph set himself up for a fall by handing the bait to his brothers. Pride and jealousy were the enticing poison, and they ate it without reservation. Joseph offended his brothers and they threw him into a pit. They were planning to kill him, but they decided to sell him into slavery instead and then tell his doting father that he had been killed by a wild animal.

But God...

But God took Joseph out of the pit and into an Egyptian palace. Don't you just love it? There is always a *but God* isn't there? And as you probably know very well, there is a lot more to this story. Joseph offended Potiphar's wife when he refused to sleep with her, and his integrity landed him in jail. In Joseph's story, offenses are put out like bait waiting for the taker. The brothers took it; Potiphar's wife took it. They threw him into the pit; she had him thrown into jail. People do ugly things when they are offended.

Magnets for Offense

Joseph had to deal with his own pride. It had to be rooted out so that the fulfillment of Joseph's prophetic dream could come true. Dealing with jealousy and self-righteousness and pride, rooting out our "magnets" for offense, often necessitates our being tossed into the pit for some period of time. God was preparing Joseph to rule.

What are your magnets for offense? What makes you prone to offend, even if you do not intend to? What is God preparing for you to do? How are offenses, or being easily offended, standing in the way of your calling?

The Key to the Jailhouse Door

Forgiveness is the key to the jailhouse door. Forgiveness renders our magnets for offense powerless and tears down the fences of offenses. Forgiveness is the thing that stops the enemy in his tracks and negates the bait he sets for us.

Remember, the word *skandalon* refers to the part of the trap where the bait is attached; it often describes an entrapment used by the enemy. Offense is a tool the enemy uses again and again to entrap us, to put us in jail.

Satan sets deadly traps for us; some are hidden and some are baited with offense. Offense is not deadly as long as it we leave it in the trap.

Truths in Joseph's Story

There are some amazing, life-changing truths we can learn from Joseph's story, including:

- When we are in the pit, our humility grows and

God never forsakes us

- When we follow God's principles the rewards are beyond our wildest dreams; Joseph ended up blessing those who cursed him and doing good to those who hated him, and when he did he fulfilled Jesus' commands in Matthew 5:44[20]
- If we grasp and live out the truth that no one can stop the plans of God, we will surely grow in humility and faithfulness
- If we yield to God's work in us, if we say Yes and wait on Him, he will take us from the prison to the palace

Finally Freedom

We have all offended others, and we have all been offended. Jesus was offense personified because of the radical claims of truth that He made. He said clearly that He was the Son of God and that it was through Him – not the law – that the Jews would be saved. The Pharisees – almost all the religious leaders of the day – were offended when the carpenter from Nazareth made these claims. How could he even call himself a rabbi, a teacher? They were offended by His claim that He would replace their religious system and all they believed in. How dare he suggest that he could tear down the religious walls that they had built?

They were so offended, they killed Him.

The gospel message through the ages has offended people: it exposes lies, it demands a verdict – it cannot be ignored.

Offenses occur when pride is at work.

We must allow the Lord to purify our hearts like gold.
Let's resolve to remember next time: leave the bait in the
trap. Let's practice tearing down the fences of offenses as
soon as we begin building them.

Let's remember that forgiveness is the key to the jailhouse
door and that as we gain our freedom from the offense
trap we will be able to partner with our Lord in setting
captives free, once and for all.

Notes

1. Luke 23:34
2. John Bevere, The Bait of Satan, 7
3. Luke 4:18-19
4. Luke 17:1
5. Proverbs 18:19
6. Matthew 24:10, King James
7. Matthew 13:53-58
8. 1 Samuel 17
9. 2 Samuel 6:14
10. 2 Samuel 6:16-23
11. Matthew 15:1-14
12. Matthew 3:7
13. Luke 11: 39
14. Luke 13:17
15. The essence of this 'offense test' was taken from The Bait of Satan by John Bevere
16. John Eldredge, Waking the Dead, 148
17. Psalm 55:12-14
18. Genesis 37:2-4
19. Genesis 37:5-8
20. But I tell you: Love your enemies and pray for those who persecute you....

12 COSMIC FORCES

The devil will try anything he can to keep you from
making space for God. How do I know? Try it for a
week and you will know exactly what I am talking about.
The last thing he wants you to do is worship Jesus
because he knows that when you make worship space
available for Jesus, He will communicate His Presence to
you. And when that happens, watch out world. A world
filled with people who have spent time in the Presence of
God are something to contend with. The devil doesn't
stand a chance. I have a theory that when Mary sat at the
feet of Jesus her sister Martha left the kitchen and peeked
around at the two of them sitting and talking. I bet that
she wanted to join them but she was so distracted with
her preparations she simply would not stop—not even
for a moment. I bet that she was in the kitchen
grumbling about the unfairness of it all: " Well, someone
has to be task oriented. Someone has to bear get this
stuff done. " Have you ever said that before? Have you
ever wished you could just stop the world long enough so
you could get off and sit at the feet of Jesus? Well, you
don't have to stop the world, you only have to stop
yourself. And the truth is you don't have to stop long—
just long enough to hear The Shepherd's voice--- long
enough to enjoy His Presence. Then you can roll up your
sleeves and get back to work. It is a lot more fun that
way. When you make space for Jesus, work will easily

flow from the place of rest. Remember the enemy's plan is for you to work first and then if there is time give it to Jesus. He knows that there will never be time; that unless you make space for Jesus first, you will simply get on your hamster wheel and never get off.

Today's sophisticated, skeptical, often cynical postmodern society leaves very little room for believing that the enemy not only exists but is a formidable power that can oppress us and influence our thinking.

Do You Believe the Devil Exists?
I grew up in a world in which the presence of evil was always acknowledged but was not to be feared. I grew up in an America that believed in the goodness of God and the evil of Satan. Pure and simple.

My grandmother (*Yiayia* in Greek) came over from Greece as a child bride who had been selected by my grandfather's parents. My grandfather was already living in America, Yiayia was in Greece. He went back to Greece to marry her without ever having met her. That was the way it was done.

My Yiayia came to this country with a simple faith and a no-nonsense approach to life. She believed that God is good, that His Son conquered Satan and death, and that the devil still prowls around, intent on causing trouble for God's people. When it was apparent to my Yiayia that the devil was at work, her response was to kick him out. I can remember her very matter-of-factly commanding, "Get out!" I don't think he ever hesitated to run away from her. Sometimes she would spit at him.

The enemy and his evil intentions were as real to my grandmother as the clock on the wall or the room she was standing in. I have to admit that every now and then she may have been referring to me – I was a regular trouble-maker myself. I cannot tell you for sure if it was the devil, but I can tell you that it worked. If my Yiayia told him to leave, he did – and I straightened up too! You didn't cross my grandmother.

Heavy Darkness, Fear and Psalm 23

As a little girl I encountered something that changed my life. I knew for sure from that time on that there was a force – an intelligent and resourceful evil – that wanted to influence me, to paralyze me with fear. I would go to bed at night and within a short time I would sense an evil presence. I know it may sound weird to you (unless you have experienced something like this), but it was a matter of fact to me as a child. I'll never forget it. I was afraid, and there was this thick, midnight-dark feeling that engulfed me.

One night when the darkness tried to overwhelm me I began to recite the 23rd Psalm. We memorized Bible verses in Sunday School, and the psalm came to me as I felt the unnameable fear creeping in. So I spoke the words young David the giant slayer had written thousands of years ago, and as I did, the heavy soul-less feeling left me. It was as if my yia yia had commanded it to *Get away from here!*

Coincidence? No way. I got a chance to command the darkness the next night too. The same thing happened: fear tried to smother me in my bed, and using the memorized words of the psalm, I spoke to God in the midst of it, expressing my confidence in Him and His authority, and the heavy darkness didn't have a prayer.

It was not long before the dark presence gave up and left me alone. The beautiful irony is that I was 'left alone' – that is, not attacked anymore – because the dark presence knew very well that I had acquired a powerful not-so-secret weapon; and we both knew I was not alone at all.

I was encouraged and protected by God's Word – that is, by the Presence of God dwelling in His Living Word – and the enemy doesn't have a chance against that.

The Enemy Versus The Sword

Years later, as I read about Jesus in the wilderness and how He used scripture to defeat the devil, I knew that my childhood experience had been authentic. I had made space for God, called to Him for help, and I had wielded the sword of His Word. The light of God's Truth burned away the darkness, and I believe to this day that this is why I have such affection for the Word of God. It is powerful and alive, and though it was written down for us thousands of years ago, it was and is custom-made for the now-here: "For the word of God is living and active. Sharper than any double-edged sword, it penetrates even to dividing soul and spirit, joints and marrow....."[1]

Scriptures are very clear: the devil is real, and he is on the prowl: "Your enemy the devil prowls around like a roaring lion looking for someone to devour. Resist him, standing firm in the faith..."[2] Also, in his letter to the church at Ephesus, Paul warned the people: "...do not give the devil a foothold. "[3] So for now, for me, if my yia

yia, Peter, Jesus and Paul all confirmed that there is a devil, a thief who comes to steal and kill and destroy, that's good enough for me. It does not matter that it seems unsophisticated or unbelievable.

In fact, I am certain the devil – *the enemy, the father of lies* – loves it when the world pays attention to his whispered suggestions and assertions and then helps to deflect attention from him and his motives by scoffing at the idea of an intelligent evil force with malevolent objectives and by ridiculing belief in the devil's existence as unsophisticated and unbelievable.

And something else: my Sunday School teachers did not tell us to be sure and recite Psalm 23 when we were attacked at night by fear and the heavy-dark. They didn't prepare us kids for bedroom spiritual warfare. I don't think it occurred to them. So, who was it that brought David's words of peace and protection and promise to me when I needed them? Who or what made me think that speaking to and about the Lord, my shepherd, in the presence of my enemies would help?

In The Beginning: God's Cosmos and Angels
Cosmos, from the Greek 'kosmos', means "an orderly harmonious systematic universe; the opposite of chaos. " God created the world, the cosmos. He brought order to chaos, spoke light into the empty darkness. He created a harmonious universe, beautiful, perfectly balanced: "And God said let there be light and there was light. God saw that the light was good, and he separated light from the darkness. "[4]

In the very beginning of time, God created the earth by

226

separating the light from the darkness, and He is still doing that today. Our heavenly Father's creation continues. Everywhere He sends forth His Word, light is poured onto and into dark places. His Word is still bringing order into places that are chaotic. His Word is still putting the devil in His place.

God's order includes angels that play many roles. There are angels sent to serve people, to give assistance, to bring messages from God. There are warrior angels dispatched in response to our prayers for help. [5] There are angels like Gabriel who told Mary she would be with child[6] and The Angel of the Lord who told the shepherds where to find the newborn Savior.[7] There are ministering angels[8] and 24X7 worshipping angels who worship at the King's throne endlessly. [9] There are angels who take us to heaven[10] and archangels, seraphim and cherubim.

Angels are a part of His created order, an integral component of the cosmos. They are in the unseen realm of God's kingdom and they break into our natural circumstances to bring supernatural intervention. They are kept very busy!

Isaiah gives us a picture of the throne room where angelic beings are worshipping God:

> In the year that King Uzziah died, I saw the Lord seated on a throne and the train of his robe filled the temple. Above him were the seraphs each with six wings; with two wings they covered their faces, with two they covered their feet and with two they were flying. And they were calling to one another: "Holy, holy, holy is the Lord Almighty; the whole earth is

full of his glory. [11]

There are more than 300 accounts of angels recorded in the Bible. They have voices and personalities and they serve at the pleasure of the King of the Universe. Sometimes they appear as humans. Remember when Peter was thrown into jail and an angel appeared, told Peter to get dressed and released him from his cell?[12]

One of the many names of God that describes His character is *Captain of the Host*. He is the leader of the angelic armies:

God! Let the cosmos praise your wonderful ways, the choir of angels sing anthems to your faithful ways! Search high and low, scan skies and land, you'll find nothing and no one quite like God. The holy angels are in awe before him; he looms immense and august over everyone around him. God of the Angel Armies, who is like you, powerful and faithful from every angle?[13]

Today it is trendy to believe in angels, especially in the New Age movement. It is not cool to talk about Jesus, but angels are safe for conversation and speculation. Although angels are indeed part of God's created cosmos, we are not to venerate, worship or pray to them. We are to follow the angels' example
and praise and worship the only One Who deserves it: our King, the One and Only Almighty God.

Why am I talking so much about angels? When we look at God's cosmos and His harmonious plan for earth, we must recognize both good and evil. God created angels to help us. He considers us to be His masterpiece,[14] and

He dispatches His angels to give us assistance, bring us messages, keep us from harm.

The Fall: The Beginning of Spiritual Warfare

But there was a world-changing mishap along the way. Lucifer, also known as Satan, the one who "… masquerades as an angel of light,"[15] rebelled against God and took a third of the angels down with him. God had given Lucifer as many gifts as any other angel, but he became proud and wickedly ambitious, and his rebellion set the stage for all-out war.

The fallen angels who followed Lucifer became known as demons. And the once-beautiful Lucifer became known as Satan, God's sworn enemy. Ezekiel describes what happened:

> You were the model of perfection, full of wisdom and perfect in beauty.
>
> You were in Eden, the garden of God; every precious stone adorned you: ruby, topaz and emerald, chrysolite, onyx and jasper, sapphire, turquoise and beryl. Your settings and mountings were made of gold; on the day you were created they were prepared.
>
> You were anointed as a guardian cherub, for so I ordained you. You were on the holy mount of God; you walked among the fiery stones. You were blameless in your ways from the day you were created till wickedness was found in you. Through your widespread trade you were filled with violence, and you sinned. So I drove you in disgrace from the mount of God, and I expelled you, O guardian

cherub, from among the fiery stones.[16]

Lucifer was perfectly made, just as his Creator intended; he had a rank similar to Gabriel (chief messenger angel) and Michael (chief warring angel); he was chief musician and then he became chief of the fallen angels, chief of the demons. Lucifer was beautiful and an instrument of worship. He had access to God, but he rebelled and was cast out of heaven.

The sixth chapter of Jude says that Lucifer and his gang of fallen angels lost their place of authority. This was when the conflict between cosmic forces began. This was the beginning of spiritual warfare.

We Are At War …

There was (and is still) a clash of two kingdoms: the Kingdom of God and the kingdom of Satan. The Kingdom of God is the rule and reign over the earth; the kingdom of Satan is the *desired* rule and reign of the fallen Lucifer, the thief who prowls, who seeks to steal, kill and destroy.

Make no mistake, there is a battle raging all around us. It is a battle with the highest stakes imaginable. In his book, *Waking The Dead*, John Eldredge quotes Jesus talking to His followers: "The thief comes only to steal and kill and destroy; I have come that they may have life, and have it to the full. "[17] Eldredge says:

> Have you ever wondered why Jesus married those two statements? Did you even know he spoke them at the same time? I mean, he says them in one breath. And he has his reasons. By all means, God intends life for you. But right now that life is *opposed*.

It doesn't just roll in on a tray. There is a thief. He comes to steal and kill and destroy. In other words, yes, the offer is life, but you're going to have to fight for it because there's an Enemy in your life with a different agenda.... There is something set against us.... We are at war.... A bitter clash of kingdoms, a bitter struggle unto death.... [18]

... And We Know Who Wins

We are at war, a bitter struggle is in progress, but there is another absolute fact about which Christ-followers must be crystal clear and confident: In His life on earth, and through His death and resurrection, Jesus conquered Satan. The war on our time-bound earth is not yet over, the battle rages all around us – but though we do not know the timetable, the how's or the when's, we know who wins. We must have no doubt. God's final victory is no more a *maybe* than Jesus' resurrection was.

God's final victory over evil is guaranteed. It is a done deal.

Satan is under the dominion of God. He is God's enemy, but he is by no means God's equal. God created him, then he rebelled against God, said he wanted to be the same as God. Unchecked pride and immense self-deception. From that moment forward, the devil's days have been numbered. We do not know that number, but God does.

Then how come we fall prey to the enemy's roar? It's simple really: we have a case of repetitive amnesia. We forget what we know; then we recall it and repent having forgotten it; then we forget it again. The world and the enemy twist and blur the truth on a daily, if not hourly, basis. The everyday struggles we face cause us to forget eternal truths.

We forget that Jesus is in us and that He is greater than Satan ever was or ever will be. We forget our King's promises, we forget that He *is* Love, and we forget that Love conquers death. We forget that when He willingly hung on the cross for us, Jesus crushed Satan for all time.

We have authority over the enemy because of what Jesus has already done – but we forget. And then we fall prey to Satan's tactics of fear, torment, and lies; with our amnesia we allow ourselves to be accessible to the detached, chaotic thinking the enemy brings.

Remember when Jesus was baptized by John the Baptist in the Jordan River? Immediately following His baptism, He was led into the wilderness to be tempted by the devil. Jesus' heavenly Father allowed that. Do you know why?

Jesus came to earth fully God and fully human. He stood for us against the assaults of the devil. He sent Satan flying that day when He used scripture to counter the devil's assault. The enemy used lies and deception, and our Lord countered with His Father's Word. Talk about an unfair fight! And Jesus continued to assault the devil everywhere He went in His three-year ministry, even and especially as He walked to the cross.

Our Lord's final battle was won on the hill called Golgotha. There He defied evil and death and bought our freedom with His own precious blood. At the end He said quietly, *It is finished.*[18] If we remember that, if we

232

do not forget what Jesus has already done and what He promises to those who believe in Him, we no longer need fear death. And we should no longer fear evil either. Our King has conquered them both, once and for all. It is finished.

I meet two kinds of people: those who fear the devil and those who fear God. Those two fears cannot coexist in a person. It's one or the other. Jesus took the claws out of the roaring lion, so even though it is true that the beast still prowls and roars, he cannot harm us if we stand with Jesus and rely on His Father's Word. The prowling lion is toothless and clawless as long as we remember what our Lord has already done. As long as we remember and remind one another who wins the war.

God wants us to be on the offensive, not the defensive. Christ gives us the authority to trample on the enemy.

Battle Training Up Close and Personal
Years ago, I was in a huge spiritual battle. My beautiful, bright daughter was a rebellious teen. She knew Jesus, but the enemy wanted to separate and distance her from her love for God. She made some bad choices, some unintelligent decisions, and the enemy used each failure to pull my daughter closer to him. The battle began.

I would wait until she went to sleep each night, and then I'd go into her room and pray for her as she slept. I put Christian music on, inviting God into her room, battling for her life.

I had a circle of Christian friends and family whom I would call to intercede for her. There were days when I'd call someone and not even be able to speak through my tears. Whoever I had phoned knew exactly why I was calling without having to hear it from me; they would pray, covering me and my daughter with Christ's love and protection and promises. Through their passionate prayers, they would remind me who wins in the end. I would hang up never having spoken a word.

We were in a life-and-death battle – and you know what? Jesus never loses. This I know from personal experience. This I know beyond the shadow of a doubt.

Do you know how the battles against the enemy are won? Every battle against Satan and his evil forces is won on our faces before God. We take the battle to Him, on our faces, on our knees, with humility and honesty and petition and confident thanksgiving. We trust the King of the Cosmos, our Almighty God. What is impossible for us is nothing for Him. He never leaves us, never fails us.

God wants us to show up on the battlefield. He wants us to actively enlist in His army; he wants our agreement and our vigorous participation. He expects us to bring what we have, and He promises to do the rest. We have His authority, His say-so, and we need neither fear nor retreat ever again.

Every battle we fight sends the enemy further away.

Today my daughter is the most amazing woman you could ever meet. She loves God. She has seven children she is raising as recruits for the King's army!

Spiritual Warfare Biblical Case Study #1: Job

Look at the battle between cosmic forces – spiritual
warfare – in the book of Job. Job shows us the conflict
between God's sovereignty and Satan's horrific
harassments with crystal clarity.

Job is an incredible example of a godly man who faces
torment, loss and utter destitution and yet says
of God:

> I know that my Redeemer lives, and that in the end
> he will stand upon the earth. And after my skin has
> been destroyed yet in the flesh I will see God.[20]

In the beginning of the Book of Job Satan asks God if
there is any man who is righteous and blameless in God's
sight. God chooses Job and allows Satan to test him
severely. God will not allow Satan to kill Job, but the
enemy is permitted to do everything else.

God allowed illness, as well as the loss of Job's children,
livestock and home. Even Job's friends and wife turned
against him. But in the end everything he lost – his
fortune, his home and his sons and daughters – were
restored to him. Job's faith was redoubled. God's
faithfulness was really never in question.

Job was tested during the warfare, and he passed. By his
enduring faith – refusing to give up on a God Who had
apparently given up on him – Job proved God's
faithfulness and was assured that his King would not fail
him: "But he knows the way that I take; when he has
tested me, I will come forth as gold. "[21]

Job knew that his time of intense, seemingly unbearable

testing and warfare would refine him, make him better.
He did not know how, but he knew that God would not
abandon him. The suffering that God allowed in his life
became the way for Job to go deeper into an intimate and
trusting relationship with his heavenly Father. God and
Job believed in each other.

Through thick and extremely thin, Job fought off amnesia
and kept his eyes on the Captain of the Host. He never
forgot who wins in the end.

The Enemy's Traps

How does spiritual warfare affect us personally and what
can we do about it? Satan and his gang set traps for us.
The traps the deceivers set are both hidden and baited.
Skandelon is the Greek word that refers to the part of the
trap to which the bait is attached; in the New Testament,
it often describes an entrapment used by the enemy.

When I was fighting the enemy for my daughter's heart,
there were two traps that Satan set: one for her, one for
me. The father of lies wanted to trick my daughter down
the wrong path and cause her to keep making rebellious
choices; and he wanted me to become hopeless and
fearful and feel like a failure. He was defeated.

But you can be sure that it was not easy. I did feel for
much of this period in our lives like a parent who had
failed miserably. In the chapter titled *Who To Believe*, I
wrote about how we can fall into the *stinkin' thinkin'* trap,
believing the enemy's lies and deception, and how our
minds are the primary battlefront of spiritual warfare. Our
minds are where the devil sets up his first assault. If he
can deceive us into believing his lies, our actions will

236

follow. Well, he worked overtime on my daughter and me, trying to poison our minds with stinkin' thinkin'.

My most challenging battle in prayer was to trust and believe God's reassurances to me, and to believe what He thought about me. I had to believe that as a parent I would not fail my daughter. And my most powerful weapon in this spiritual warfare was prayer.

Satan and his cohorts are working overtime setting traps. They are baiting the traps with anything they think will cause you and me to fail or to fall. They want to crush our hope and trample our trust in God.

The key is not to take the bait. And until the war is finally won, the bait will always be there. We must recognize the traps and prayer-walk through them.

The Armor of the Lord
The enemy's mission in spiritual warfare is to bring chaos – to rob, steal, and destroy; to confuse our minds; to introduce fear and hopelessness and isolation. Jesus' mission statement is to set the captives free and to destroy the works of the devil. [22]

The war continues. What can be done?

Paul provided the answer in the sixth chapter of his letter to the Ephesians. Paul teaches us how to prepare for battle, and he begins by telling us to be strong in the Lord. He acknowledges that relying on our own strength will cause defeat, but depending on the Lord's strength will defeat the schemes of the enemy. Paul then tells us how to stand against the devil's schemes:

Put on the full armor of God so that you can stand against the devil's schemes. For our struggle is not against flesh and blood, but against the rulers, against the authorities, against the powers of this dark world and against the spiritual forces of evil in the heavenly realms. [23]

Paul tells us clearly what the Lord has told him: spiritual warfare is not against people (flesh
and blood) – our battles are against the evil one and the demons he has enlisted to set the traps for us. We must not take the bait. And we must not attempt to wage the fight with our own strength. In spiritual warfare – where the battle is fought by cosmic forces – we must use the weapons and authority of God.

Paul continues regarding how to protect ourselves, using the image of a soldier arming for battle:
> Therefore put on the full armor of God, so that when the day of evil comes, you may be able to stand your ground, and after you have done everything, to stand. Stand firm then, with the belt of truth buckled around your waist, with the breastplate of righteousness in place, and with your feet fitted with the readiness that comes from the gospel of peace. In addition to all this, take up the shield of faith, with which you can extinguish all the flaming arrows of the evil one. Take the helmet of salvation and the sword of the Spirit, which is the word of God.
> And pray in the Spirit on all occasions with all kinds of prayers and requests. [24]

Stand and Fight: Victory Is Assured
Stand against the enemy's lies and fight the battle in

prayer. There may be traps set for you.

There may be powers of this dark world that threaten to overtake you, but do not be afraid – God has armed you for battle. You have His weapons, His armor, His unbreakable promises. If you are armed and stay close to him, you are prepared.

He has gone ahead to fight for you. Enlist in His army, show up on the battlefield. Do not hide; be bold and confident. Go where He leads, and when you step out in faith, wearing His armor, trusting Him absolutely, He will fight for you.

Have you ever heard the expression *the devil's beating his wife?* I was on an errand yesterday, driving my car, and that expression came to mind. It is a phrase used to describe a *sunshower,* which is an unusual meteorological phenomenon in which rain falls while the sun is shining. The term is used in the United States, Canada, Australia, New Zealand, Ireland and parts of Britain, but is rarely found in dictionaries. In the United States, particularly the South, a sunshower is said to show that "the devil is beating his wife. " He laughs and she cries.

All that to say that yesterday was one of those days when it poured rain and then the sun came out again … and again. And it made me think about the Bride of Christ and the raging spiritual warfare that we find ourselves engaged in. The devil is beating Jesus' bride – the church, us. We are weary and battle-worn – in fact the enemy is depending on our weariness; he is banking on our giving up and giving in.

But if we can sharpen our swords and stay connected to our Groom, stay centered in the calm Eye of the Storm, then He fights our battles. We have to show up, stand up and refuse the temptation to be weary and worn out, but He is the One Who leads us and conquers the enemy.

And each battle we win, each victory, changes us and makes us more like Him. When you are weary and considering throwing in the towel, remember this, cling to this: remember what we discovered in the chapter about the Eye of the Storm. We can settle for merely weathering the storm or we can become storm warriors, transformed, changed by the Presence of God to be more like God's One and Only Son.

What made me think about all this is that the last two weeks have been insane for me – but I have experienced God's Presence, peace and leadership first-hand in my life. It has been stunning to see God lift my hands and fight for me. My job was to stay close to Him, to show up on the battlefield, and that I did.

You can too. We all can, can't we?

"This is what the Lord says to you: Do not be afraid or discouraged because of this vast army. For the battle is not yours, but God's. "[25]

And we know who wins, don't we? Amen and Hallelujah!

Notes

1. Hebrews 4:12
2. I Peter 5:8-9
3. Ephesians 4:27
4. Genesis 1:3
5. Daniel 10; Revelation 12
6. Luke 1:28-38
7. Luke 2:9-12
8. Hebrews 1:14
9. Revelation 5:11,12
10. Luke 16:22
11. Isaiah 6:1-3
12. Acts 12:6-10
13. Psalm 89:5-8 (The Message)
14. God saw all that he had made, and it was very good…. (Genesis 1:31; emphasis mine)
15. 2 Corinthians 11:15
16. Ezekiel 28:12-16
17. John 10:10
18. John Eldredge, Waking The Dead, 12-13
19. John 19:30
20. Job 19:25
21. Job 23:10
22. Luke 4:18; 1 John 3:8
23. Ephesians 6:11-12
24. Ephesians 6:13-18
25. 2 Chronicles 20:15

13 LOVE'S UNBROKEN PROMISES

We do not know much about Mary from Scripture. We do know that she had a brother and a sister, Lazarus and Martha. We also know that before Jesus went to the cross she anointed him with oil in preparation for his burial. She used a very expensive perfume at the time so her devotion was costly. It was also unusual both because she poured the oil on Jesus' feet and normally it was poured on the head, and she also used her hair to wipe off the oil. In those times respectable women did not unbind their hair. What motivated Mary to pour out such extravagant devotion and love on Jesus? I think it was because in her encounter with Jesus, she was changed from the inside out. When Martha was running around the house Mary chose to be with Jesus. All the broken promises she had experienced in life melted away and all she knew was that her Messiah made good on His promises. She trusted Him completely and I wonder as she prepared him for burial by anointing His feet with oil, if she really knew that someday He would come back from the grave? I don't know that for sure, but I do know that while sitting at His feet she met the Promise Keeper and her devotion to Him was all she had to offer Him in return. In that moment she may not have known that He would keep His promise to go to the cross, but she did know that He held the key to her liberty. The cross….. the finished work of the cross was but a shadow being cast down on her act of devotion.

Have you ever seen the sign on the road that says: What part of *It is finished* do you not understand? Whoever made that sign was asking us what part of Jesus' finished work on the cross do we not believe. Our Lord's last words were, "It is finished," and He meant it. He meant that what His heavenly Father had sent Him into the world to do had been accomplished. Completely and for all time. And the person who wrote that sign was suggesting that it is at that very place, at the crossroads of unbelief, where we fail to grasp the entirety of what Jesus did for us.

The Cross and Our Crisis of Faith

From Jesus' death on the cross forward, the promises of God through His One and Only Son were fulfilled. So our crisis of faith lies at the crossroads: † : that is where we either throw caution to the wind and take God's Word for it and allow the Holy Spirit to lead us forward or we choose not to believe.

Questions At the Crossroads

Are you willing to make space for God and His promises?

Are you willing to believe that God's promises in His Word are

243

true?

Are you willing to truly believe that it is finished?

Unless the Lord Builds the House

In my quiet time the other morning I came across the
Scripture:

> Unless the Lord builds the house, its builders labor
> in vain. Unless the Lord watches over the city the
> watchmen stand guard in vain. [1]

You know how sometimes a Scripture jumps off the page
and grabs you and wrestles you to the ground? That's
what happened to me with the first two verses of Psalm
127. I sat with those words for what seemed an eternity
until I heard God's still small voice say: "Joanne, if you
will allow me to build, you will be assured of success. "

What was I building without Him? Where and when had I
mixed the bucket of cement on my own and started
constructing something apart from God?

I recognized that I was depending on my *I-can-do* attitude
rather than doing all things in *God's* It-is- finished *strength*.
[2]   When I read the verses they penetrated my heart and
mind, and I was found out; I heard His Spirit and realized
that I could no longer continue building on my own.
God had searched my heart and convicted me, and I
could not go on building without Him. Why would I
want to? I was tired, and the building I was working on

had a crack in it.

How about you? What house are you building, what project are you managing apart from the promises and assurances of God? Your physical house, your spiritual house, your marriage, your job?

God Keeps His Promises

Years ago I was in my daughter's room making her bed after she had gone to school. As I was apt to do on occasion, I knelt down by her bed and prayed for her. She was going through a difficult stage and I needed to consult with God about it. I sensed Him telling me that it was going to be tough to raise her but that one day she would be a powerful woman of God. Now she was only eight years old at the time, and I admit to you that this word about the difficulty of raising her was not something I really wanted to hear. Imagine the thoughts and questions I had at that moment. I didn't want to know that I would be facing years and years – how many, O Lord? – of difficult child-rearing. Would you?

But God was true to His word. Raising my daughter was like what I imagine riding a bucking bronco would be like. I fell off more than I stayed on. And when the hard times hit, you can be sure that I clung to the promise God made to me that day in her room.

Today she is extraordinary. With seven children to raise and a business to run, she does it all by the grace of God.

How To Walk in God's Promises
In order to walk in His promises we must do two things:
- Know His promises by knowing His Word
- Be filled with the Holy Spirit

It is the Holy Spirit who enables us to understand and appropriate His Word for ourselves.

Paul made it clear that without the Spirit God's Word would be like a language we can't understand:

> The man without the Spirit does not accept the things that come from the Spirit of God, for they are foolishness to him and he cannot understand them because they are spiritually discerned. [3]

The Holy Spirit helps us to spiritually discern – to see and know – God's promises in His Word. The Holy Spirit shows us how to grab hold of them and apply them to our lives, here and now.

His Word Is Alive Now
God's Word is alive. It is for you and me right now. It may have been written down thousands of years ago, but it is living and true and applicable for you and me here and now. The Holy Spirit wrote it in the present for the present.

Jesus in the Wilderness
> Then Jesus was led by the Spirit into the desert to be tempted by the devil. After fasting forty days and

forty nights, he was hungry. The tempter came to him and said, "If you are the Son of God, tell these stones to become bread. " Jesus answered, "It is written: Man does not live on bread alone, but on every word that comes from the mouth of God. "[4]

Jesus knew God's Word. He knew His Father's promises. So when the enemy tried to bring Jesus down He used His Father's promises like a sword. When the enemy tried to twist the truth for his own purposes, Jesus spoke the Word as it was written on His heart; He faced the enemy and told the whole truth. He claimed His Father's promises and stood on them in faith.

The Promise Keeper Movement

Have you ever heard of Promise Keepers? It is an organization of men founded in 1990, and it has (at the time of this writing) positively impacted over 5. 5 million men worldwide. A Promise Keeper is committed to:

1. Honor Jesus Christ through worship, prayer, and obedience to God's Word in the power of the Holy Spirit.
2. Pursue vital relationships with a few other men, understanding that he needs brothers to help him keep his promises.
3. Practice spiritual, moral, ethical, and sexual purity.
4. Build strong marriages and families through love, protection, and biblical values.

5. Support the mission of his church by honoring and praying for his pastor and by actively giving his time and resources.
6. Reach beyond any racial and denominational barriers to demonstrate the power of biblical unity.
7. Influence his world, being obedient to the Great Commandment (Mark 12:30-31) and the Great Commission (Matthew 28:19-20).

Promise Keepers is a wonderful organization that has made a significant difference in the lives of many men (and women!). And the true leader and inspiration of this fine organization is the One who never, ever, broke one of His promises.

The Original Promise Keeper

Jesus Christ is the greatest Promise Keeper of them all. As far as I know, He is the only One who kept every promise He ever made. Jesus kept His promise:

*   To His Father to go to the cross and reconcile us to God
*   To His followers (and all of us) to rise from the dead and conquer the grave once and for all
*   To His followers (and all of us) to send His Holy Spirit to live in us and comfort us and teach us and remind us of everything Jesus said, every promise He made
*   To His followers (and all of us) that He would never leave or forsake us

When we open God's Word we receive an amazing gift. The original Promise Keeper allows us to see into another world, into His kingdom, a world filled with hope and joy and His unbroken guarantees.

Great and Precious Promises
Peter spent three years with The Promise Keeper. He heard Jesus and saw Him in action. He saw and talked to his Lord after Jesus rose from the grave, which He had clearly told Peter and the other disciples He would do.

Talking about The Promise Keeper he had come to know so well, Peter said:

> His divine power has given us everything we need for life and godliness through our knowledge of him who called us by his own glory and goodness. Through these he has given us his very great and precious promises, so that through them you may participate in the divine nature and escape the corruption in the world caused by evil desires.[5]

We have a new birth and a living hope when we receive Jesus Christ as our Savior. When we say Yes to Jesus' invitation, we have an inheritance that can never perish, spoil, or fade. That is a promise from the One the disciple John calls Love. That is one of Love's unbroken guarantees.

Our Inheritance
Sometimes when a person dies he or she leaves an

inheritance. Unfortunately, the people to
whom the inheritance is left may sometimes not receive it
because unfaithful stewards have been left in charge. But
there is one inheritance that has been guaranteed to us,
one inheritance that is promised by the One who never
breaks His promises. That is the eternal inheritance we
have in Jesus Christ. The Holy Spirit is the Executor of
the will and He ensures that we will receive the priceless
treasures of Christ.

All inheritance, blessings, power and victory are ours in
Him. All the promises are ours because He has risen, as
He promised to do. They are the great and precious
promises that Peter describes.

Precious is defined in Webster's dictionary as *of great value or
high price; highly esteemed or cherished.* Something (or
someone) is precious because it is rare, priceless. What or
who in your life is precious? I know my list includes my
children and grandchildren, my spouse, my friends and
my health. You too?

Now consider the promises God has made to us through
Jesus, the will our King wrote with His Son's precious
blood, the inheritance He has left us. Isn't it far more
precious, more valuable, than anything we can think of ?
In His Word, through His Son, with the Holy Spirit as
Executor, God promises:
- Life abundant here and now when we choose to
  say Yes and surrender to Him

- Eternal life – abundant life without end – spent with Him when we say Yes and choose Him
- Power and anointing to defeat the enemies in our lives
- Purpose and a call to live a life for Him that fulfills us and brings us joy
- Power to overcome

Precious Treasure and A People of Hope

Paul describes believers as carriers of the treasure of the living gospel, carriers of the good news. He says that although life in this world is often tough, we have the opportunity to demonstrate the power of God as we cling to His promises:

> But we have this treasure in jars of clay to show that this all-surpassing power is from God and not from us. We are hard pressed on every side, but not crushed; perplexed, but not in despair; persecuted, but not abandoned; struck down, but not destroyed.[6]

What makes Christianity unique among all the religions of the world? It is the hope that we have in the resurrection of Jesus Christ. Religions all over the world offer many things – principles to live by, ways to better our lives, even the recommendation of self-denial that will lead to a renewed sense of spirituality. And Christianity offers these things too; but as Christians we present a unique hope grounded in our faith beyond a doubt – our certainty – that Jesus rose from the grave and conquered death once and for all.

Unlike any other group of religious believers, we
Christians know that the founder of our faith is alive and
will never die; He was not just a man who lived on earth
for thirty-three years and taught us how to live life to the
full and then died and was buried; He is God, and we
know that His Holy Spirit leads us now and promises us
eternal life.

Though we live at the crossroads with life's problems,
sorrows, and pain, we have the hope of His precious
promises bought for us on the cross. Peter tells us there
is a new and living hope that depends on God's grace and
promises us that no matter what we face in our lives, no
matter how difficult our circumstances may be, we live in
this powerful hope.

A Living Hope

A few weeks ago, I was feeling discouraged. I began to
read the Bible and came across the story of King
Jehoshaphat. Before he went to battle Jehoshaphat sent
his praise team ahead of him, and the battle was won.
Reading this reminded me that God's Word says He
inhabits the praises of His people. [7] So then and there I
praised God.   Well, the circumstances of my
discouragement did not change, but my attitude toward it
certainly did. Once I began to praise and thank God, I
stopped feeling discouraged. God took the dis away and
left me with courage: courage to face the present
circumstances by claiming Love's unbroken guarantees
and standing on my belief that He is The Promise

Keeper.

The next time you're feeling discouraged, try praising that same God who gave His One and Only Son so that anyone who believes in Him can live forever. [8]

Our living hope is based on His promises, not on things going smoothly.

or ?

The other day I took my car in for a tune-up. I was given a loaner car, and as I was driving home in the loaner I noticed that the gas gauge was nearly on empty. I put seven dollars in the gas tank, but the gauge needle still pointed to E. When I returned the loaner, I told the attendant at the dealership what had happened and said the gauge must be broken. She checked it out and told me, "The gauge says its full. "

I know I had looked at the fuel gauge more than once, and each time the arrow was pointing to E, not F. Crazy? I don't think so. I think the Lord was trying to get my attention. No kidding. I think He was showing me how I – we – can sometimes be deceived. Sometimes we think God's promises are empty; we read His Word and we don't see or hear the life behind the words; we see and read *empty*.

Is that where you are right now? Is all you've hoped for coming up empty?

God's Promises Are Never Empty

Joshua had to depend on God's promises. After Moses died the gargantuan task of leading the Israelites into the Promised Land fell to Joshua. It is true that he had been Moses' understudy and had learned a great deal in preparation for the leadership role. But now the guidance and protection of an entire nation was not just theoretical – it was for real. Do you think Joshua was scared? Would you have been? I know I would have. I bet he was wondering how he was going to do it.

Then God spoke to him:

> After the death of Moses the servant of the Lord, the Lord said to Joshua son of Nun, Moses' aid: "Moses my servant is dead. Now then, you and all these people get ready to cross the Jordan River into the land I am about to give them – to the Israelites. I will give you every place where you set your foot as I promised Moses.... Be strong and courageous because you will lead these people to inherit the land I swore to their forefathers to give them. "[9]

All Joshua had to hold on to were the promises God made – to Moses and to him. God had promised Moses and the Israelites that they would inherit the Promised Land, and now Joshua just had to go in and possess it. *Just!*

The assignment required crossing the Jordan River at spring flood tides; and God parted the river. It required taking Jericho, a well-fortified city; and God gave Joshua a successful strategy. It required fighting his way into the land; and God gave him victory.

Before Joshua crossed the river God promised him that everywhere he put his foot would be his; and He said that He would be with Joshua every step of the way. Joshua had Love's unbroken guarantee, and he carried it with him into the Promised Land.

God's promises are never empty. [10] If you step out in faith and believe His Word, He will do everything He promises.

Broken Promises

The problem we all have is that people (we) break promises. Some of us have experienced broken marriages; we said *until death do us part* – we repeated a vow, made a promise – but the promise was broken. We thought we were promised a long, healthy life, but sickness and disease have disrupted what we thought was a promise made to us. Loved ones have died, lives have been cut short, relationships have soured. When promises are broken, hearts are broken. And the truth is people break promises.

We live in a fallen world with fallen people trying to live as children of God. The best of us break hearts and fail miserably.

What do you do when you lose trust because promises are broken? What do you do when a husband promises to love you as Christ loves the church and you are united as one flesh and he has an affair? Or he doesn't have a physical affair, but he has an affair on the internet through pornography?

What do you do when your husband or wife or friend breaks a promise he or she has made to you?

Rebuilding Trust

If someone close to you has broken a promise, it is easy to hold the hurt and lost trust against God. But your faith in God and your continued intimate, trusting relationship with Him are really what will make all the difference in rebuilding trust with those who have broken promises. Here are some positive action we can take to help rebuild trust with people:

- Go to God with the problem
- Choose to trust God with the problem even though you have lost trust in the person
- Pray about the lost trust; cry out to God about it; hold nothing back; ask for His help and saving grace
- Set boundaries; apply appropriate discipline or consequences where and when necessary
- Get Christian counseling in critical cases of broken trust

Naomi and Ruth

The Old Testament story of Naomi and Ruth illustrates

how God works in our lives in the midst of broken promises. There was a famine in Bethlehem that forced Naomi and her husband (Elimelech) to leave and go to live in the pagan city of Moab. Naomi's two sons (Mahlon and Kilion) married Moabite women, Ruth and Orpah, and then her husband and both of her sons died. Before all this happened, Naomi probably believed that God would allow her husband and two sons to live long lives, but that did not happen. She followed Yahweh, the God of Israel, and she felt that once she got to Moab God let her down.

Naomi could have chosen to turn from God, but the Scripture doesn't indicate that she did that. We know that she was broken hearted. And we know that when she heard the famine in Bethlehem was over she decided to return to her native town. But Naomi wanted the best for her daughters-in-law and she told them to stay in their homeland of Moab. She had nothing left to offer them:

> But Naomi said, "Return home, my daughters. Why would you come with me? Am I going to have any more sons, who could become your husbands? Return home, my daughters; I am too old to have another husband. Even if I thought there was still hope for me – even if I had a husband tonight and then gave birth to sons – would you wait until they grew up? Would you remain unmarried for them? No, my daughters. It is more bitter for me than for you, because the Lord's hand has gone out against me!"

At this they wept again. Then Orpah kissed her mother-in-law good-bye, but Ruth clung to her.

"Look," said Naomi, "your sister-in-law is going back to her people and her gods. Go back with her. "

But Ruth replied, "Don't urge me to leave you or to turn back from you. Where you go I will go, and where you stay I will stay. Your people will be my people and your God my God. Where you die I will die, and there I will be buried. May the Lord deal with me, be it ever so severely, if anything but death separates you and me. "[11]

The Enemy's Plan, God's Plan, Your Choice

Satan's dream – if we can call it that – is to make sure that God's purposes are not fulfilled. But in the story of Naomi and Ruth, what the enemy intended for evil, God used for good. He had a greater plan for Naomi, and Ruth was to play a crucial role. God never broke His promises to Naomi.

God's plan and purposes are tied to His promises, so if the enemy can use the broken promises of our lives to cause us to turn from God, he will thwart God's plans.

Ruth's response to what seemed like a broken promise (the death of her husband, Naomi's son) opened the door to God's greater promise. She could have been bitter, left Naomi and turned away from Naomi's God, but instead

Ruth said Yes to God. And though the enemy intended to rob, steal, and destroy a family line – Ruth's future family – God's promise to Naomi, even though she couldn't see it, was that the Messiah would come from Ruth's genealogy.

Our response to God determines the fulfillment of His promises. Do you believe that?

Every time you say Yes to God you make room for His promises to be fulfilled. Your willing partnership with The Promise Keeper ensures the fulfillment of His promises.

Yes to God is *No* to God's enemy.

God's Word is His promise to you, His roadmap for your life. He has a purpose for your life and a plan to fulfill that purpose. If you trust in Him and hold on to the promises in His Word, He will fulfill your destiny in Him.

Your response, like Ruth's, will determine whether or not the broken promises of your life turn you from God or toward Him.

The choice is yours.

Notes

1. Psalm 127:1-2
2. Phillipians 4:13
3. 1 Corinthians 2:14
4. Matthew 4:1-4
5. 2 Peter 1:3-8
6. 2 Corinthians 4:7-9
7. Psalm 22:3
8. John 3:16
9. Joshua 1
10. Isaiah 55:11
11. Ruth 1:11-17

14 I AM A KING'S KID

I have a secret to tell you. Listen closely because it is a well kept secret. So well kept that most people have not heard it or if they have they do not believe it: *You are the King's kid.* It may be hard to believe that when you receive Jesus Christ into your life, you become His kid entitled to the inheritance of a King. Mary sat at the feet of the King. Scripture says *she sat at the Lord's feet listening to what He said.* I feel certain that He made her feel very special. Because she made space in her busy life to listen He made her feel secure and content. Sitting and listening, she got in touch with who she was and came to realize that her identity was wrapped in Him—that she was royalty. The world will try to give you a false identity dependent on how much money you have, who your friends are, where you live. Our false selves are so used to pretending to be happy we slowly fall in to a pattern of living a sub life never feeling true contentment--- never being content with ourselves. True contentment can only be found in our relationship with Jesus. Listen…. He is whispering in your ear: *You are fearfully and wonderfully made—you are mine and your life is hidden in me.* Oh precious friends if only you could grab hold of this truth. If only you could be like Mary and make space to listen…

In his letter to the believers in Philippi, the apostle Paul describes the secret to being content:

... I have learned to be content whatever the circumstances. I know what it is to be in need, and I know what it is to have plenty. I have learned the secret of being content in any and every situation, whether well fed or hungry, whether living in plenty or in want. I can do all things through Him who gives me strength. [1]

According to Webster's dictionary *content* means *satisfied*. Paul knew that the only way to contentment was to find satisfaction in one thing: his relationship with Jesus, his continuing connection and rapport with The Source of satisfaction.

Contentment. What is it about the thought of being content that makes us sigh, take a deep yearning breath, and fervently hope to capture somehow the elusive essence of it? What is it in us that compels us to ache for contentment, and yet – when we are honest with ourselves – recognizes our powerless- ness to find true, deep, lasting satisfaction?

The Recipe for Contentment

In another letter to the people in Corinth Paul described his difficult circumstances: *Three times I was beaten with rods, once I was stoned, three times I was shipwrecked....* [2] Ah, finally we have the recipe for contentment: to be truly satisfied, one must be beaten, stoned and shipwrecked. How could this be possible – how could Paul say to the Philippians that he was always content when his circumstances and

262

the situations he faced in his ministry were so often difficult, dire, life-and-death? Content? Come on, Paul – really?

He had a secret that he was delighted to share with us. Paul knew that he was the King's kid and that everything belonging to the king also belonged to him. His inheritance was all the intangible riches of eternity: security, peace, joy and righteousness. Contentment. Deep satisfaction. Now-here and always. Paul's enemies could destroy his body, but they could not take away his inheritance as the King's kid.

Do you believe that you are royalty?

I wake up every morning and remind myself in my conversation with God: "Here I am, God, the one You love, your kid ready for the day. " Listen, I know it sounds silly. But I need a reminder because I know that as soon as I get out of bed and my feet touch the floor I will be faced with the darts of the day; and the only way I can fend them off is to remember who I am, *whose* I am. Kings have all sorts of people watching their back, caring for their needs, protecting them from danger. And kings' kids get the same treatment, the same 24X7 security.

As the King's kid, I need to stay close to Him. I need to remember constantly that I am to be in the world but not *of* the world. This was part of Jesus' prayer to the Father for us. When I'm under His loving care – when I ask for it, accept it and acknowledge it – I am content, like a child in her father's or mother's arms.

The Enemy's *Poverty Mentality* vs. The King's *Spirit of Poverty*

The problem is we often choose to live as paupers. So frequently we do not accept our inheritance as a child of the king; we do not remember who we are, whose we are. We give up the life of royalty in the king's palace that Jesus died to give us.

My daughter Hope had a conversation with her two children recently that poignantly describes our distinction as the King's kids. Hope's daughter Ellison kept taking the bow out of her hair so Hope told her, "Ellison, stop taking the bow out of your hair. Princesses wear bows. " Chase, her three-year- old son, said, "Mommy, then why don't you wear bows in your hair? Aren't you a princess?" I could have answered that for Chase. My daughter Hope, Chase's mother, is a princess. Everyone in our family laughs about Hope's princess-status because she has an incredible knack for having everyone wait on her. Truth is, Chase was right. He saw his mother as a princess; he saw her as someone who is special. Special enough to be the daughter of a king. Maybe some of us should put bows in our hair as a reminder of who we are. (Only some of us; maybe the princes among us should wear breastplates with lions on them.)

We sometimes live with a poverty mentality, a pauper

mindset. We live day-to-day as poor orphans who do not take their King's promises seriously. We do not accept our inheritance as a child of the king. Or we give it away like Esau. Remember him? Esau was Isaac's firstborn, Jacob's twin. Once Esau came in from hunting when Jacob was cooking some stew. Esau was famished after days in the wild, and the only thing on his mind at that moment was his empty stomach. So he asked Jacob for some of the stew and Jacob offered it to him on the condition that Esau sell his birthright to him. In ancient times the birthright of the firstborn entitled him to a double share of the father's property when the father died. Esau sold his birthright for a bowl of stew.

You know, it really does not matter how excellent a stew Jacob had cooked up – that was Esau's worst choice as a King's kid.

When we forget the King's promise of eternal life as His child – when we lose track of what Christ has already done for us, ensuring that we can be King's kids – we settle for second-best – sometimes even third- or fourth- or fifth-best. We live as paupers. We give up our rightful inheritance. We give away what is ours, just as Esau did.

God's blessings, our inheritance, entitle us to His justice, mercy, and love. If we don't accept Jesus' sacrifice and offer, if we do not access these blessings, we live with and in a spirit of poverty – giving away what is rightfully ours. We settle for much less than is available. Without realizing it, we slowly starve to death.

We give our inheritance away by believing lies about ourselves and others. We discount what the King has said and done. We believe our title deed is empty or bogus – a title with no benefits. We believe what the world preaches. We think some nice stew today is going to satisfy our hunger tomorrow.

Living with a poverty mentality means we feel as if our resources are limited. Let's be very clear on this: our resources are limited, but God's are not. God's resources are unlimited. Sometimes we think a poverty mentality comes from experiencing financial poverty, but this mindset can also grow out of any feeling of lack: need for love, for affirmation, for positive, life-giving relationship, community. Our feeling impoverished might come from a sense (or messages from the world) that we are not smart enough or are too introverted or shy or unaccomplished at sports or unattractive or … fill in the blank. There are countless reasons you and I can have a mindset that causes us to live like a pauper and not know beyond the shadow of a doubt that we are the King's kid.

There is a crucial distinction between a spirit of poverty and what I have described as a poverty mentality or mindset. Play on words? Absolutely not. There are two kingdoms out there: the kingdom of God and the kingdom of the evil one; the real and the counterfeit; the abundant life and the empty lie. The enemy takes God's created order of things and counterfeits it. He is not able to create anything, but he sure can copy anything and pervert it. In His Sermon on the Mount, Jesus describes in kingdom language what it means to have a spirit of poverty: *Blessed are the poor in spirit for theirs is the kingdom of God.*[3]

To be poor in spirit means that all the possessions of the King belong to those who recognize their need for God. It means that those who seek God and His kingdom and the abundant life He promises are His children, now-here and forever. It means we inherit the kingdom of truth and justice, love and mercy. Poor-in-spirit kids are gladly dependent on their parents. King's kids are joyfully dependent on their King.

The counterfeit poverty mentality operates in the mind. The common syndrome of this twisted spirit is the belief that there is never going to be enough – living in fear, believing the lie that the well is going to dry up. For example, those who suffer from this mindset believe that if someone receives something (pay raise, position of importance, etc) it will diminish some of the provision that could otherwise be theirs. They believe that someone else's blessing will cost them something. [4] This poverty mindset causes jealousy and unhealthy competition, and the enemy loves to use this to divide and isolate people.

Once delivered from this mindset we are free to

encourage and desire the best for others.

One of the enemy's many strategies is to prey on those who feel inferior and who operate from a sense of lack. Deliverance and freedom come when we recognize the lie and identify it in operation in our own lives and begin to agree with God that we are His kid and our inheritance supplies all our needs. We come to understand that the King's well is never dry. Never was, never will be. It is a promise – never broken, never will be.

Paul described his contentment as the King's kid this way: *And my God will meet all your needs according to His glorious riches in Christ Jesus.*[5]   Not a few of our needs or just some – all our needs. Evidence of our deliverance from a pauper mentality is clear when we are able to call out the greatness in others. If we truly believe we are royalty we find ourselves wanting our ceiling to be someone else's floor. We can call out the greatness in others and not feel threatened. [6]

The King's kids need to cultivate an environment that helps others dream huge dreams and believes beyond a doubt that one of the King's greatest joys is to make the impossible possible for those who seek Him and His kingdom.

Jesus characterized those who are *poor in spirit* as people who are humble and recognize their need for God, knowing with a certainty that the entire kingdom is their inheritance. The enemy's counterfeit is based on pride, dependent on self and not on God. It is based on what we can do on our own and it compels people to strive to stay on top.

So ... what do you do if some of this resonates with you, if you recognize that you have a pauper mentality? Do you race through life without really living it, without noticing what is happening right in front of you in the now-here, discovering again and again that you are nowhere, or at least nowhere near where you thought you were headed? Do you see yourself in any of the examples I have offered? Do you feel like royalty or are you driven to prove yourself, your personal value, at all costs?

If life is not fun and adventure-filled; if it is filled instead with unmet expectations and feelings of inadequacy, here is what you do first: recognize that you do not feel or act like royalty and are always fearful of lack. Sit with that recognition a while, let it sink in. Do not let it dishearten you – let it illuminate the path to the palace you are poised to set out on.

Then identify what the source of conflict is:
1. Do you believe God is who He says He is? (see Matthew 16:15-16)
2. Do you believe you are who God says you are? (see 2 Corinthians 5:17 and Galatians 4:6,7)
3. Do you believe that His resources are unlimited? (see Psalm 24:1 and Psalm 50:10)
4. If you do not believe these things that God has

told His kids, are you willing to get to the root of why you do not consider yourself royalty?

5. Take a look at some common signs of living with a pauper mindset:

- Do you struggle to feel valued or significant?
- Do you work yourself to death to keep on "top" for fear that someone will replace you?
- Do you find yourself jealous or competitive with others rather than embracing who you are and the gifts God has given you and releasing others to be who they are called to be?
- Do you relate more to material things than to the King and His kids?

God never intended for us to live in poverty in any area of our lives. The infinite resources of heaven are available to us and we need to recognize that one of the enemy's favorite strategies is to intercept our access to God's resources in Christ through our thought life.

Unforgiveness and False Pride

In addition to the pauper mentality, unforgiveness and false pride are the other two principal reasons we do not receive our inheritance as King's kids and live as the royalty He intended us to be.

Unforgiveness keeps us in prison and outside the palace. If we do not forgive others, there is no way we can be King's kids. No way. God insists that His people forgive one another. We have to take others off the hook so that the King can redeem them. We cannot live in freedom and receive God's abundant provision and resources if we tie them up in heaven with the steel cords of unforgiveness. We need to understand that the debt of sin was paid once and for all by Jesus. He made it possible for all of us to be forgiven – and to forgive one another – by dying for us on the cross. He declared the death of sin and denounced unforgiveness in His final words: *It is finished.*[7]

False pride also blocks or intercepts our receiving God's blessings as His kid. There is a lie that we believe that tells us that any recognition of our abilities or strengths is pride and the only way to deal with it is to demean or devalue ourselves. The truth is, we are sons and daughters of *The King*. Think of that; take however long you need to get it deep inside you: we are princes and princesses – the Prince of Life made sure of that – and we cannot fully realize what it means to be a King's kid until we recognize the gifts He has given us and use them for His glory.

Nelson Mandela put it this way:

> Our deepest fear is not that we are inadequate. Our deepest fear is that we are powerful beyond measure. It is our light, not our darkness, that most frightens us. We ask ourselves, who am I to be brilliant, gorgeous, talented and fabulous? Actually, who are you not to be? You are a child of God. Your playing small doesn't serve the world. There is nothing

enlightened about shrinking so that other people won't feel insecure around you. We are born to make manifest the glory of God that is within us. [8]

Rise up, brothers and sisters in Christ, and recognize what it means to be a King's kid endowed with gifts from your Father to be used for His glory. The revelation of your true identity in Christ will destroy all false pride and enable you to walk in the fullness of your calling.

Sometimes our feeling of low self worth masquerades as false humility. We may try and deflect praise for a job well done, or devalue the gifts that God has given us. True humility acknowledges that the King resides in us and the gifts and talents He gives us are to be freely used to bring Him glory.

> …let your light shine before men, that they may see your good deeds and praise your Father in heaven. [9]

Nehemiah understood what it means to be used by God. He walked in a prince mentality. He knew that he was royalty. By trade he was the cupbearer to the Persian king. Nehemiah had risen to that coveted position, and he was trustworthy and talented. The cupbearer tested the wine to be sure it was not poisoned, and the king held him in high esteem. Nehemiah knew he was a man with a destiny and purpose to serve God, and when the opportunity of his lifetime arrived he did not hesitate to step up and seize the moment.

He was making a good living as the cupbearer to a very influential pagan king, but when God called him to go to Jerusalem to help rebuild the city wall, Nehemiah did not hesitate. He knew he had what it took to accomplish the task and he knew that his God would strengthen him and give him favor to do it. He approached the king and told him that he needed to go back to Jerusalem where his beloved city was in ruins. The broken-down walls left the people vulnerable to attack by their enemies. Nehemiah fasted and prayed and the king gave him permission to go on his mission and more: he gave Nehemiah the supplies he needed and safe passage with letters of access. Nehemiah knew his God would supply his needs and he knew that he had been given the ability by God to be successful.

It was not Nehemiah's power or charisma or strategic thinking or pride that opened the path back to Jerusalem. It was his certain knowledge that he was the King's kid. He knew heaven's resources were at his disposal because he knew that the King would not ask him to do something without giving him all he needed to do it. Everything flowed out of Nehemiah's relationship with the King.

Plan A

In their book *The Supernatural Ways of Royalty*, Kris Vallotton and Bill Johnson describe the call on the church: "God has given the church a great call and therefore it takes great people to accomplish it. If we fail to see our greatness we will fall short of our call. "

False humility has hindered the church and it is time that we recognize we are the King's kids. We have a destiny and the resources to fulfill that destiny.

Eddie Sears writes:
> When Jesus ascended to Heaven to return to His Father, the eleven disciples stood and watched Him rise through the clouds.
> An angel in the clouds nearby saw Jesus pass by and called out, "Jesus, where are you going?"
> "Back to be with my Father in Heaven," he said.
>
> "I thought you were going to bring salvation to the whole world!" the angel protested.
> Jesus said, "I have. The atonement is complete. My work on earth is finished."
> "But who is going to be your witness and go out into the world and spread the Good News and tell people you love them?"
> "They are," Jesus said motioning toward his disciples. The angel looked down on the rag-tag group of disciples.
> "Do you have a plan B?"

My life's life-giving models will never draw crowds to their speeches, or convince world leaders to make peace. They live filled with uncertainty and mundane responsibilities Their lives' worldly aspects keep them "from being so heavenly minded they are of no earthly good " But, because their paths have crossed mine, I am blessed Like them, I want to be a worthy rag-tag member of God's life givers. As it happens, there is no plan B [10]

We the church are the King's Plan A, and there is no Plan B. God's Word is filled with promises of God's provision for His kids…Jesus told us not to worry about our provision, that He would take care of all that if we would simply seek Him:

> *So do not worry saying What shall we eat? Or What shall we drink? Or What shall we wear? For the pagans run after all these things, and your heavenly Father knows that you need them. But seek first his kingdom and his righteousness, and all these things will be given to you as well.*[11]

Go On and Ask

My daughter recently came to my husband and me to ask if we could help her financially. She wanted to go back to school but didn't have sufficient funds. Something she said really struck me. She told us that she had struggled for quite some time with the thought of asking us for the money. She said she had worried whether as an adult with her own family she should come to us with this request. Of course, her Dad and I were delighted to help She is our daughter, and we'll give her anything she asks for if we can…And we know that we don't have to beg our Father in heaven to help us – we don't have to worry about His reaction. He is delighted to meet our needs…We may not always be able to help financially, but we hope that our daughter knows now that she can always ask.

The King waits for His kids to ask. He delights in giving us good gifts: *Ask and it will be given to you; seek and you will find; knock and the door will be opened to you. For everyone who asks receives; he who seeks find; and to him who knocks the door will be opened to you.*[12]

Go on and ask. Your Daddy is waiting.

Do you believe you are royalty? Do you believe you are a child of the almighty King of the Universe? Do you know that He will give you whatever you need to accomplish the things He asks of you? Do you understand that you are an integral part of the King's Plan A and there is no Plan B?

How you answer these questions will determine your destiny and the fulfillment of God's call on your life.

The King is waiting for your answer.

Notes

1. Philippians 4:11-13
2. 2 Corinthians 11:25
3. Matthew 5:3
4. Kris Vallotton and Bill Johnson, The Supernatural Ways of Royalty, 35. Though not always quoted directly, this excellent book was a source for many of the guiding principles in this chapter.
5. Philippians 4:19
6. Ibid. The Supernatural Ways of Royalty, 77.
7. John 19:30
8. Nelson Mandela, 1994 presidential inaugural speech, South Africa.
9. Matthew 5:16
10. Eddie Sears, No Plan B, Christianitytoday. com
11. Matthew 6:31-33
12. Matthew 7:7

15 DO I HAVE TO?

If we can just get a glimpse of the holiness of God – of His amazing Presence – our desire to serve Him will be ignited. I believe that happened to Mary. As she sat at his feet, she was probably concerned about not helping her sister Martha in the kitchen. She was going to help her, but first she had a need--- no a sense of urgency that she must not miss the opportunity to spend a few quiet moments with Jesus. Her: "Do I have to"? waned in comparison to her need to spend time with Jesus. She may not have understood completely, but deep within her she could not do her work until she met with her Master. As she sat at His feet I believe her: " Do I have to?" turned into: " How can I serve you"? When we spend intimate, personal, sit-at-the-feet-of-Jesus time we are filled with His love and desire to serve. There are many things that I don't feel like doing like making up my bed in the mornings, or cooking meals or even more importantly I may not feel like being obedient to God. I don't have time or the motivation to obey. And yet without exception when I spend time worshipping Jesus, when I take time to read His Word and listen to His words to me, I will look for ways to obey. Let's face it. We all say at times: " Do I have to?" Only at His feet will that change to " Send me Lord"?

What is it about being told we have to do something we

don't want to do that causes us to rebel? Is it fear of failure (or success)? Laziness? Good old contrariness? I think the words most often spoken by children – and sometimes adults, although usually not out loud – are: "Do I have to?"

Well, maybe the number one question from kids is "Why?" But "Do I have to?" has got to be a very close second. Right? Were you that kind of kid?

Is *Do I have to* still a favorite response of yours?

Today I asked my five-year-old granddaughter what she thought obedience meant. She said, "It means listening to my mommy and daddy. " Pretty smarts kid, huh? Then she added that it was important to listen to her parents because God uses them to show her what's right and what's wrong. Good Lord – now we're talking brilliant!

Father Knows Best
My granddaughter is so right. God wants us to obey Him because He knows what's best for us. Always. Our view of things is often narrow and shallow, but our heavenly Father's view is comprehensive, to say the least. His view is wide and deep. He sees everything all at once forever. He doesn't miss anything. And He sees our hearts. As the old saying goes, He knows our hearts like the back of His hand.

God knows who we are, how we are and where we are, even when we don't.

Do you remember the TV series *Father Knows Best*? (Dead give away for my age, right?) In that show from long ago, the dad, Jim Anderson, always knew what was best for his family. Always. He was wise, gentle, understanding and compassionate; he had a knowing smile that could light up a living room; and he was always thinking of his wife's and kids' best interests. Jim Anderson was the best dad on Earth.

Much like Jim Anderson – except even better – our heavenly Father (the best dad in the universe) knows what is best for His children; and when He asks us to do something He does it with our best interests in mind. Always.

Obedience Can Be Inconvenient

Though we may often find it inconvenient – sometimes extremely so – we have to make space in our lives to obey God. We have to make it a priority. We have to do things we don't always want to do. My daughter told me recently that she is really cracking down on her four-year-old son. The problem with her crackdown strategy is that her little boy is not only very cute and very smart – he's also always at least two steps ahead of his mother. When she was packing his lunch box the other day, he cautioned her to pack only chocolate. He explained that his teacher allows only chocolate in the kids' lunch boxes. How do you discipline such a clever child?

Have you seen the messages from God on signs along the highway? They have been all over the Internet and those mass distributed emails too. I like them because they give the answer to the *Do-I-have-to?* question in a number of ways. For example:

- My way *is* the highway.
- What part of *No* do you not understand?
- We need to talk.
- They are not called The 10 *Suggestions*.
- Keep using my name in vain, I'll make rush hour longer.
- What part of thou shalt didn't you understand?
- You know that Love Thy Neighbor thing? I meant it.

All of these messages are signed, *God*. And all of them are telling us the same thing: Stop wasting precious time – stop asking, "Do I have to?"

God is telling us, "It's not about *have to* or *want to*. You were *created to.*"

Send Me

In the year King Uzziah died, the prophet Isaiah had a vision of God seated on a throne in the temple. [1] What an incredible gift this vision was. It was a genuine representation of God's glory and hugeness and holiness.

Isaiah saw the seraphs – six-winged celestial beings – and
he heard them 'calling to one another', praising God:
"Holy, holy, holy is the Lord Almighty; the whole earth is
full of his glory. "[2] In this astonishing larger-than-life
moment, standing in God's holy Presence, Isaiah
recognized his own sin and was absolutely undone. He
tells us:

> Woe to me! I cried. I am ruined! And I live among a
> people of unclean lips and my eyes have seen the
> King, the Lord Almighty. [3]

Upon hearing Isaiah's confession, the seraphs took a
burning coal from the fire and touched the prophet's lips
with it – taking his sin and guilt away – and Isaiah reports:

> Then I heard a voice of the Lord saying, "Whom
> shall I send? And who will go for us?" And I said,
> "Here am I. Send me!"[4]

In that profound instant Isaiah was commissioned, sent
out by the King of the Universe to fulfill the destiny for
which he was created.

Once Isaiah saw God's hugeness and holiness and perfect
righteousness, he was never the same. His sin glinted
and burned in the blazing light of God's sanctity and
sovereignty. And once he was cleansed, Isaiah's response
could only be: *Send me.*

The Essence of Obedience
If we can just get a glimpse of the holiness of God – of

His amazing Presence – our desire to serve Him will be
ignited. The reverential fear of the Lord – the genuine
recognition of God's hugeness and absolute authority –
leads to obedience. It has to, doesn't it? It seems to me
that gladly following the instruction of the perfect leader
without asking *Do I have to*? is the essence of obedience.
Think about it: would the perfect leader, the Father who
knows best, ever ask you to do something that was
unnecessary or superfluous? Would that make any sense?

Oswald Chambers reminds us that God did not address
the call to Isaiah; Isaiah was in the Presence of God and
overheard Him asking, "Who will go for us?" Chambers
says that the call is not for the special few but for
everyone. [5]

Others heard it too, but Isaiah responded. He might just
as well have said, "Send me, God. You created me to go."

If We Seek, He Will Speak
Responding to the call of God depends on our hearing
Him call; hearing Him depends on our willingness to seek
His Presence. If we seek, He will speak. It is in His
Presence that we recognize our sinfulness, and it is in His
Presence that we seek holiness – because He is holy and
we respond with reverence when we hear His voice, hear
His question.

Obedience comes from a place of intimacy with God. It
comes when we surrender.

The Cost of Discipleship

Dietrich Bonheoffer, a German pastor martyred at 39, wrote eloquently about single-minded obedience in light of costly grace:

> Costly grace is the gospel which must be sought again and again, the gift which must be asked for, the door at which a man must knock. Such grace is costly because it calls us to follow, and it is grace because it calls us to follow Jesus Christ. It is costly because it costs a man his life, and it is grace because it gives a man the only true life. [6]

Obedience always costs us something. It costs us our lives in exchange for Christ's own. Nevertheless, the question haunts us: *Do I have to?*

Why?

Isn't there another way?

We each have to face that question, no matter how it's phrased. And it all comes back to grace; it all comes back to seeing the Lord high and lifted up, huge and overpowering and holy. And like Isaiah's response, ours must also be: *Send me. I was created to.*

Counting the Cost

Abraham was told by God to leave his comfortable life and all the things he was familiar with and to go to an unknown place ... to do only God knew what. Abraham had seen God; maybe not the ethereal vision that Isaiah had, but he had seen Him and understood God's hugeness and perfection and holiness. And Abraham obeyed. He was tested on Mount Moriah – asked to sacrifice his only son – and he was willing. [7]

Abraham sought God, and God spoke. God instructed and tested. God said, Go and do as I say, and Abraham went and did.

Obedience costs us everything … and it is the key to everything. If we are to be obedient, we must be willing to trust God with our very lives and the lives of the ones we love.

Are We Willing?

Tonight I received e-mail from a beautiful Christian woman whose husband has just been diagnosed with cancer. Her response was to quote a few famous lines from an anonymous source:

> This is the beginning of a new day. God has given me this day to use as I will. I can waste it or use it for good. What I do today is very important because I am exchanging a day of my life for it. When tomorrow comes, this day will be gone forever, having something in its place I traded for it. I want it to be a gain, not a loss; Good not evil; success not failure, in order that I shall not forget the price I paid for it.

Each day can be used for good, or wasted. We are to follow God's plan in obedience, and we are to remember that when tomorrow comes this day will be gone forever.

What is God calling you to do today? What has He been asking you to sacrifice?

Are you willing to say, "Send me"?

But I Want It My Way

Why did God give us free will? It's an age-old question that often trips us up, especially when we're considering how inconvenient obedience can sometimes be. But we have to remember that our Creator wants us to be in deep relationship with Him, and this requires that we freely receive His love and freely – that is, by our own free will – give Him our love in return.

Few people live with their free will focused entirely on God. So many things get in the way. For one thing – maybe the *main* thing – our fallenness gets in the way. I was watching my grandchildren playing the other day. The four-year-old brother had a toy that the two-year-old brother wanted ... so the two-year-old grabbed his brother by the hair, the toy flew out of the unclenched four-year-old fist, and – voila: victory! Well, victory for a second or two. Then the four-year-old brother exercised – maybe I should say *unleashed* – his free will, and there followed a spirited battle involving fists and feet – all four fists and feet seeking the coveted toy.

Sometimes people have trouble believing that the human will can be sinful or selfish, but it is true – it can be, and it often is. Go to your dictionary and look up *willful* and you will be reminded of how we have most often exercised the free will our heavenly Father gave us. *Willful* means *headstrong, stubborn, obstinate, wayward, unruly* ... and ever since we were told to leave the Garden of Eden – as a result of the first misuse of our God-given free will – our sinful and selfish will has been a defining bottom-line characteristic of the human condition.

A Key to Obedience: Surrendering Our Will

Let's face it: our wills often cross God's will. Paul understood this very well:

> We know that the law is spiritual; but I am unspiritual, sold as a slave to sin. I do not understand what I do. For what I want to do I do not do, but what I hate I do. And if I do what I do not want to do, I agree that the law is good. As it is, it is no longer I myself who do it, but it is sin living in me. I know that nothing good lives in me, that is, in my sinful nature. For I have the desire to do what is good, but I cannot carry it out. [8]

Paul continues by thanking and praising God for sending His Son Jesus Christ to rescue him from this body of death.

One of the keys to obedience is the surrender of our will to Christ. Dallas Willard reminds us that in our fallen world few people live with a focused will, a determination to follow God in obedience. [9]   We all want things done our way, and it is only when we have a heart yielded to God's purposes that we are able to fully and fearlessly obey.

Until we surrender our will to Jesus, obedience is not *natural*; once we surrender, it is. Once we surrender – that is, *give in* – obedience becomes *second nature*.

Another Key: Getting Unentangled

In his second letter to Timothy, Paul described single-minded focus:

> No one serving as a soldier gets involved in civilian affairs – he wants to please his commanding officer. Similarly, if anyone competes as an athlete, he does not receive the victor's crown unless he competes according to the rules. [10]

Obedience flows from focusing on the commanding officer – the Father who knows best – and not getting entangled in other things. Our default *Do-I-have-to?* attitiude changes to an enthusiastic *Send-me!* commitment.

The writer of the book of Hebrews puts it this way:

> … let us throw off everything that hinders and the sin that so easily entangles, and let us run with perseverance the race marked out for us. Let us fix our eyes on Jesus, the author and perfecter of our faith….[11]

Another key to obedience is getting unentangled – single-mindedly fixing our eyes on Jesus so that we can run freely and fulfill our call. So that our will is His will.

Freely Receive, Freely Give

When Jesus commissioned his disciples to go out and heal the sick, He gave them clear instructions to go to the lost sheep of Israel and preach the message of the kingdom of heaven – that it is near and it is offered to everyone. He reminded His followers that they had freely received from Him and now they were to freely give back to others. [12]

Maintaining An Attitude of Gratitude

Obedience comes when we recognize and are thankful for all that Christ has done for us; when we are so full of gratitude we can't help but want to serve obediently wherever He sends us. My New Year's resolution for 2010 is to have an attitude of gratitude so that I will not grumble or complain about the things God asks me to do. Every day is filled with surprises when I maintain that attitude in all the places He sends me and with all the people He calls me to care for.

My children now have children of their own, and they don't have much money; they find themselves in a season of their lives when they need me again. I have had to examine my schedule, confront my own inflexibility and make myself more available to help. Sometimes I feel as though I am being pulled in a million directions, but maintaining an attitude of gratitude helps me stay balanced in the midst of the craziness of life.

The Throne of *I Can Do All Things*

The other day I began with my usual list of meetings and activities – places to go and people to see – and by 9am I felt like I had been shipwrecked and washed up on a deserted island. All my best-laid plans were suddenly swept overboard. Around 9:02am my Heavenly Father spoke to me through my earthly father, reminding me of the advice Dad had given me this past summer. He had told me to use the gifts God had given me and to delegate the things that I wasn't called or gifted to do. But here I was right back in the same situation: trying to do all things and forgetting the last part of Paul's confident can-do message: "*I can do all things through Christ who strengthens me* (emphasis mine). "[13]

So around 9:03am that morning I transferred my day back to the Lord, remembering that He has

called me to do one simple thing every day: follow His will. That's it. That's all.

I am not the master of the Universe – He is. Thank God!

Do you ever find yourself on the throne of *I can do all things?* If so, when the throne is about to crumble under the weight of all those things you think you can do on your own, and whenever the Father who knows best reminds you who's in charge and who you are to follow, just get off that rickety gold-plated throne, re-adopt your attitude of gratitude, and remember: *freely you have received, freely give.*

Give What You're Given
You can only give what God has first given you. Otherwise, you will end up like I did that morning – washed up on the island of despair, crushed under the weight of *all things.* He straightened me out and pulled me to my feet, and the rest of the day was amazing.

God's perspective is a beautiful thing. We all have days like that, and it is so very good to know we are not alone.

He is incredibly generous. So should we be.

Willing or Willful
When we ask the *Do I have to* question, what we really mean is: Do I have to *in my own strength, through my own will?* This is the core issue, the question we are really asking; this is the fear and discomfort and impossibility we are really feeling. We have discussed our human will and willfulness. Now, how do we surrender our will to God's so that our joyful obedience comes from free willingness and not willfulness?

Plain and simple: our will must be surrendered to God's love. It is only in this surrender to

God's love that we can willingly obey. Anything else is striving, performing, coaxing our will, and begrudgingly obeying God. David Brenner describes this beautifully:

> If the core of Christian obedience is listening to God's will, the core of surrender is voluntarily giving up our will. Only love can induce us to do this. But even more remarkable, not only can love make it possible, it can make it almost easy. Surrender to anything other than love would be idiocy…. Ultimately, of course, this means that absolute surrender can only be offered to Perfect Love. Only God deserves absolute surrender because only God can offer absolutely dependable love. [14]

Genuine love calls us to a deeper place of trust and connection with God, which in turn enables us to respond with bold anticipation and a genuine desire to serve Him.

A Surrendered Heart

Over 2,000 years ago, the angel Gabriel approached a teenaged girl named Mary and told her that she was highly favored by God and had been chosen to be the mother of His Son. Gabriel told her not to be afraid. Are you kidding – who wouldn't have been afraid? Seeing an angel, hearing the news about her pregnancy, being told that she was going to be the mother of the Son of God? This was the epitome of Information Overload; this was way too much to process – for anyone, much less a teenaged girl who had never been sexually intimate with a man.

Or was it? After only a moment's reflection, Mary said to
Gabriel:

> "I am the Lord's servant.... May it be to me as you
> have said. "[15]

Does this sound like a woman who was panicked and
ready to run as far from the angel as she could get? To
me, Mary sounds like a girl who became a woman in an
instant – a woman who surrendered her heart and risked
her very life. This is the epitome of obedience and trust.

Mary surrendered because she understood that her Father
knew best. She trusted Him. And we are called to do the
same. You and I are called to surrender to Jesus,
choosing His will *for us*, His life *in us*.

Surrender and Obedience

David Brenner draws a distinction between surrender and
obedience:

> But we can and frequently do offer a substitute for
> surrender – something that looks superficially
> enough like it that we easily confuse it with
> surrender. We can offer obedience. [16]

A heart surrendered to the love of God offers us the
ability to *choose* to obey. A heart surrendered to God's
unconditional love leads us to obey. We gratefully receive
God's love and then pour it back out in obedience.

Just Love Me

I have to be truthful: this is where I am right now, the place where the Lord is testing me. I am asking my Father, "Do I have to?" And guess what He says back to me. "Have to what, Joanne?"

"Do I have to pour out my life in ministry and help with 10 grandchildren and be a good wife –   which, by the way, in my family means cooking, among many other things, and I don't like to cook – and be a devoted daughter and a devoted sister and a devoted friend? Do I have to do all *that*? Not that I don't want to be all those things, but, Lord, come on – there are not enough hours in the day. There aren't enough hours, period!"

And my patient Father who knows best listens to all my desperate hopeless-sounding ranting about what's possible and what's impossible, and how many hours there are, and He says gently, "Did I say you had to? All I said – all I've ever said – is *receive my love and love me back by passing it along.* The rest will take care of itself. If you try to do it on your own you will be frustrated, always striving to be perfect, almost always falling short. I didn't create you to do *anything* on your own. Just love me and live out of that love, Joanne. Then you will see how easy it all becomes. "

Father does know best. Always. No matter what things look like.

Floating On Your Back

Brenner describes the cease-striving thing as floating on your back. He took some people out to learn how to swim. Having earned their trust in therapy sessions, he wanted to demonstrate how to let go. He describes the exercise and one woman's response:

> They trusted me when I told them that they would have to float, and lo and behold, when they took off their life vests and lay back in the water, they did just that. And they trusted me when I told them that they could breathe through the snorkel without having to lift their heads out of the water; and lo and behold, this also proved true. They had learned to surrender to God, so learning to trust in this situation was relatively easy. With delight one woman exclaimed: "Nobody told me that you don't have to do anything to float!"[17]

That's what Father is saying to you and me: All you have to do is float, and to float you don't have to do anything.

In my quiet time, I imagined myself floating in the sea of God's love – effortless, held up by the water, arms stretched out and relaxed. Try it: take a moment, close your eyes. .. imagine floating on the water. Don't bother to take all your burdens, worries and schedule with you. They are not needed. Just float in Perfect Love. Sounds like some weird exercise, huh? But sometimes we need a visual to get us to take the leap – the leap from striving to obeying to surrendering to love.

Others May Pay for Your Obedience

What happens when God asks you to do something and you are unwilling because "duty" calls – your family needs you, your job is demanding? How can you follow the call of obedience when there are so many things that demand your attention? Jesus addressed this issue:

> He said to another man, "Follow me". But the man replied, "Lord, first let me go and bury my father. Jesus said to him, "Let the dead bury their own dead, but you go and proclaim the kingdom of God. Still another said, "I will follow you, Lord; but first let me go back and say goodbye to my family. " Jesus replied, "No one who puts his hand to the plow and looks back is fit for service in the kingdom of God."[18]

If you have ever seen the movie *My Big Fat Greek Wedding* you have a pretty good picture of what my family is like. We are Greek and we are all animated; when we get together no one can hear anyone else talking because we all talk at once. We are happy, loud, fun, and there are lots of us! I love being with my family. But as God has called me deeper into ministry, the people I love so much have paid a cost. My obedience to the call means there are times I can't do things with them because *there aren't enough hours in the day.*

A few years ago a friend of mine said, "Your family has had to count the cost of your involvement in ministry, haven't they?" It's true. And when my friend made that observation I was feeling especially concerned about my children. So I went to them and thanked each of them for supporting me in what I am doing. I told them I recognized that even though they are adults now and need me less, they have had to count the cost too.

I tell you all this because it is sometimes difficult to be obedient if you think that others will have to count the cost too. Jesus understood it, but He clearly told His disciples that they needed to be single-minded in their devotion to following Him. Of course, this does not give anyone license to neglect his or her family.

The point is to seek the Lord first, last and always. He promises to take care of all your concerns for your family.[19]

Obedience Marked by Grace: Moses and Gideon, You and I

Oswald Chambers writes that every time we obey our obedience is met by supernatural grace. [20]   Think about that: obedience and grace intersect. Where obedience is, grace is also. Grace is often referred to as *God's riches at Christ's expense.* Our obedience is an indication of God's grace at work in us – our thankfulness and love in response to God's great love and sacrifice for us.

Recently God and I had a talk. Well, I did the talking and He listened. My husband is right: it is difficult to get a word in when I am in my process-out-loud mode. I was talking to God about some things I sensed He was asking me to do. I was sort of like Moses when he questioned God about the exodus assignment. Don't get me wrong – God was not asking me to do something on that grand scale; this had nothing to do with leading the Israelites out of Egypt. In fact He was asking me to do a few simple things. But it didn't feel that way to me at the time.

Moses told God that he didn't think he was the best candidate for the job; after all, he wasn't particularly articulate, he was 80 years old, he'd never led an exodus before – and who knows what other excuses Moses made. God wasn't thrilled with his response. In fact He was angry. But He told Moses he would provide Aaron to be the spokesperson. [21] When God asks us to do something, He knows we can do it. He doesn't set us up for failure. What would be the sense in that? Father knows best, but we still fear failure; we doubt the call. *You can't mean me, can you? Me? I don't know anything about exoduses!*

We doubt our abilities to obey the call. God knew that Moses could do it, but Moses didn't believe it. How about Gideon? An angel appears with the message that God is calling him to deliver the Israelites from the Midianites. The Midianites destroyed the Israelites' crops and killed their cattle, and when the Israelites cried out to God for help, the Father who knows best chose Gideon to be their deliverer. But Gideon, like

Moses, was ready to bolt:

> The angel of the Lord came and sat down
> under the oak in Ophrah that belonged to Joash
> the Abiezrite, where his son Gideon was
> threshing wheat in a winepress to keep it from
> the Midianites. When the angel of the Lord
> appeared to Gideon, he said: "The Lord is with
> you Mighty Warrior. " "But sir, Gideon replied,
> "if the Lord is with us, why has all this
> happened to us? Where are all his wonders that
> our fathers told us about when they said: 'Did
> not the Lord bring us up out of Egypt?' But
> now the Lord has abandoned us and put us into
> the hand of Midian. " The Lord turned to him
> and said, "Go in the strength you have and save
> Israel out of Midian's hand. Am I not sending
> you?" "But Lord," Gideon asked, "how can I
> save Israel? My clan is the weakest in Manasseh,
> and I am the least in my family. " The Lord
> answered, "I will be with you, and you will strike
> down all the Midianites together. "[22]

Gideon was a wreck. Why would the angel call him a
mighty warrior? Why would the Lord ask him to fight the
Midianites when his clan was considered weak and he
considered himself the weakest of them all, the least able
to deliver God's people?

Like Moses (and I, and maybe you too), Gideon was full
of doubt and questions. Maybe God was mistaken;
maybe he didn't hear God correctly; maybe God didn't

see his shortcomings. But the Lord's response was: "*Go in the strength that you have.*" Gideon saw himself as a weakling, unable to obey God's call, but God saw a mighty warrior.

Well, after my pep talk with God and his reminder about Moses and Gideon, I felt better about what He was asking me to do. After all, He was just asking me to do a few simple things, not lead a nation out of Egypt or lead an invasion against the Midianites. The truth is, no matter how small or large the act of obedience, God is with us.

He sees in us what we do not see: a mighty warrior.

Harbor Pilots

Here is a problem we all face: how do we know if God is speaking? How do we discern the call? Over the years, I have struggled with discerning God's voice among all the others that vie for my attention. To put it another way: how do we tune out the world and our own fears and tune in the Holy Spirit who will gladly lead and direct us if only we'll allow?

In my experience, the voice of God is quietly persistent. God doesn't scream. He is never pressed for time, never panicked. He doesn't try to out-shout anyone.

I most often hear His voice when I'm reading Scripture. Sometimes as I read I sense a nudge from Him to do something. At other times I hear His voice through a friend or family member, even a stranger. When I am considering whether or not God is speaking, I often refer to what I call the *harbor pilots*. Are you familiar with real-life harbor pilots and what they do? I am because I live on the ocean. Harbor pilots are men and women who guide big ships into port, lining up the harbor lights, giving expert counsel, leading the way safely to shore. Three of the harbor pilots I rely on when I'm trying to confirm God's voice and direction are:

- The Word of God
- Circumstances lining up
- The peace of the Lord

The Next time you sense God is calling you to do something, see if the harbor pilots illuminate the way for you. And as you step out in faith, remember that if you are obedient, He will be with you. That's a promise.

Must You Go?

Peter was not happy with Jesus' decision to go to Jerusalem. The Lord told His disciples that He would suffer many things at the hands of the elders, chief priests, and teachers of the law; He told his friends He would be killed. And Peter wanted to change His mind. Remember Jesus' reaction?

> Peter took him aside and began to rebuke him. "Never, Lord!" he said. "This shall never happen to you!" Jesus turned and said to Peter, "Get behind me Satan! You are a stumbling block to me; you do not

301

have in mind the things of God, but the things of men. "[23]

Have you ever had someone try to convince you that you haven't heard from God, particularly if the call is a difficult one – a call to be a missionary in another country, to change jobs, to distance yourself from a relationship that you sense is not from God? Jesus loved Peter, but Peter had his mind and heart set on things remaining the same. He didn't want Jesus to die. He didn't want Jesus to obey the call.

That happens, doesn't it? Well-meaning friends or family members try to convince you to keep the status quo. They love you, but fear of things changing and never again being the same drives them to stand in the way.

Jesus knew His Father had sent Him. He knew there was an exorbitant cost. And He kept His eye on the call:

> Let us fix our eyes on Jesus, the author and perfecter of our faith, who for the joy set before him endured the cross, scorning the shame, and sat down at the right hand of the throne of God. [24]

We must fix our eyes on Jesus. He is the harbor pilot, He is the light. He is the way. And it is through our single-minded obedience to Him that true joy will fill our hearts.

When God Says Go and We Say No

You know what happens when we ask God, "Do I have

to"? We find reasons not to do what He asks. Chocolate hurts my stomach when I eat it, but I eat it anyway. I can find so many reasons to eat chocolate: I need the caffeine boost; I need the comfort; I need the sweetness; I hear there are benefits to eating dark chocolate. I love those e-mails that say: "You only have one life to live. Eat ice cream. " Have you ever seen those? They help a lot. Same thing with God's requests. I can think of so many reasons why it might not be God asking or why He wouldn't ask me to do *that*. I am pretty good at it. I've had lots of practice.

But here's the problem: if we disobey God, our spiritual growth is stunted; our spiritual ears become dull, and our ability to hear His voice is inhibited. Why? Because our reasoning crowds out the space for God; our excuses fill our thinking space with reasons that keep us from obeying.

One of my grandsons is so funny. His mother was working with him to teach him that it is not okay to hit the other children in school. The other day on the way to school he said, "Mommy, would it be okay if I hit someone today?" Can you imagine my daughter saying, "Well, all right, honey – but just today." Her little boy had figured out that generally it was not okay to hit the other kids, but then he began to reason that maybe there were some days that it would be okay. Sort of like in a card game when there is a wild card and it can be anything you want it to be. *Hitting is allowed on Tuesdays and every other*

303

Saturday. If Tuesday or Saturday is a national holiday, hitting may occur on the weekday immediately following. When in doubt, ask your mother.

We are like that sometimes. We hear God speaking and we try to wiggle our way out of it, or at least we search for an opt-out clause, or we reinterpret what we're hearing to match what we would have preferred to hear. Right? We try to find an obedience loophole. The problem is that when we do this, we lose a God-given opportunity to grow in Christ-likeness; we give up an opportunity to see God's faithfulness and to experience His nearness.

Fully Persuaded

There are some keys to obeying God's call that we should consider, and Abraham shows us what it takes. Abraham:

- knew His God to be faithful;
- was fully persuaded that God could and would do what He said He would do; and
- knew that God could raise from the dead anything that He took away

The result of Abraham's surrender and obedience is that from this one man came a nation, descendants as numerous as the stars in the sky:

> By faith Abraham, when called to go to a place he would later receive as his inheritance, obeyed and went even though he did not know where he was going....

By faith Abraham, even though he was past age –
and Sarah herself was Barren – was enabled to
become a father because he considered him faithful
who had made the promise....

By faith Abraham, when God tested him, offered
Isaac as a sacrifice. He who had received the
promises was about to sacrifice his one and only son,
even though God had said to him: "It is through
Isaac that your offspring will be reckoned. "
Abraham reasoned that God could raise the dead,
and figuratively speaking, he did receive Isaac back
from death.[25]

Tucked in the pages of the great faith chapter in the book
of Hebrews is one of the essential keys to obeying God.
The writer of this book begins by defining faith as the
assurance of what we hope for and the certainty of what
is unseen. [26]

It takes faith to obey God. We must believe that He
rewards those who seek Him and that He pours out His
love upon us to motivate us to respond in obedience:

And without faith it is impossible to please God,
because anyone who comes to him must believe that
he exists and that he rewards those who earnestly
seek him. [27]

Abraham and the many other biblical men and women of
faith were certain of the things that they didn't see

because they trusted God. They believed Him for the impossible.

Are we fully persuaded that God is who He says He is? *Are we fully persuaded that we are who He says we are?*

Are we fully persuaded that God will do what He says He will do?

These are questions that we must all wrestle with as we seek to grow in our faith. But as we relentless- ly, single-mindedly pursue Him, as we make space for faith in our lives and for His perfect love to fill us and light our way, we will be able to do more than we ever imagined. Exceedingly more. He says so. He has said so again and again. And He knows best. Always.

Once we are fully persuaded, when we next hear His call and instruction, we will remember His promises to us, and we will see a mighty warrior in the mirror, and we will say with absolute assurance: "Here I am, Lord. Send me."

Notes

1. Isaiah 6:1
2. Isaiah 6:3
3. Isaiah 6:5
4. Isaiah 6:8
5. Oswald Chambers, My Utmost for His Highest, 14
6. Dietrich Bonheoffer, The Cost of Discipleship, 47
7. Genesis 22:1-19
8. Romans 7:14-18
9. Dallas Willard, Renovation of the Heart, 153
10. 2 Timothy 2:4-7
11. Hebrews 12:1-2
12. Matthew 10:8
13. Philippians 4:13
14. David Brenner, Surrender to Love, 59
15. Luke 1:38
16. Ibid. , Brenner, 55
17. Ibid. , Brenner, 61
18. Luke 9:59-62
19. Matthew 6:33
20. Oswald Chambers, My Utmost for His Highest, 283
21. Exodus 4:10-16
22. Judges 6:11-16
23. Matthew 16:22-23
24. Hebrews 12:2
25. excerpts from Hebrews 11:8; 11-12; 17
26. Hebrews 11:1
27. Hebrews 11:6

16 EXTRA GRACE REQUIRED

I wonder if Mary had people in her life that drove her crazy? I wonder if her sister Mary was bossy or just tired the day that she rebuked Mary in front of Jesus for not helping her? Poor Martha. I think she was tired. I think she wanted to do what Mary was doing but her sense of duty called and she needed to cook and prepare the meal. Who knows if Martha was an extra-grace-required person. Perhaps Mary's brother Lazarus was difficult to get along with but I don't think so. He was a friend of Jesus, but then I guess Jesus walked in such love that irritating people didn't bother Him. We don't know about Mary's siblings, but we do know that she must have had some people in her life that were difficult to get along with. She probably carried each of them in her heart. I say that because she obviously was a sanguine personality type, who often have a gift of mercy. She brought them with her to the feet of Jesus; those people who may have burdened her with their needs and who were self absorbed. In the Presence of Christ, she felt this shift…. those people she carried with her felt lighter. Could it be that Jesus took her burden? Could it be that Jesus gave her a heart to love them deeply (even though they drove her crazy) and that he taught her how to be yoked to Him and not to them? *Close your eyes for a moment. Listen to the words of Jesus: Come to me all who are weary and burdened, and I will give you rest. Take my yoke upon you and learn from me, for I am gentle and humble in heart, and you will find rest for your souls.* Now take every person you are carrying and hand them over to Jesus. He can do far more for them than you can.

Are there people in your life who drive you crazy? These people can fall into many categories; it really depends on *what makes us crazy*, doesn't it? For example: people who ask you the same rhetorical question over and over again, as if there might be some point to the question (or some answer that would satisfy them); or people who apparently talk with the sole purpose of hearing what their voice(s) and opinions sound like; or people who are just flat-out rude or insensitive or oblivious to the feelings and experiences of those around them. Or ... fill in the blank. You know who they are and you know what makes you crazy.

People who drive us crazy are, frankly, a fact of life.

And every now and then – like it or not – they are divine appointments, chosen for us by God, as surely as were our parents and sisters and brothers.

So, okay – the question is not *do we have people in our lives who require extra grace*; the question is: when those people appear and the making-crazy begins, what do we do about it – what do we do about *them*?

Making Space, Extending Grace

At the heart of this book is the imperative of making space for the living God in our everyday 24X7 lives, allowing His Holy Spirit to lead us and teach us how to be like our Lord Jesus, how to follow after Him, and how to eradicate our own stinkin' thinkin', our critical attitudes and judgments as though they were stained and mismatched clothes we've put on, outer garments that clash with our authentic God-given inner desires.

When we are able to deal with these wrong-hearted thoughts of ours, the judgments and attitudes, we make room for love, mercy, and justice. Making space for God involves moving out the things in our lives that run contrary to Him and His heart's desire for us and moving in the Godly counterparts. As we depose ourselves from the throne of our lives – as each of us takes me out of the center and puts Jesus there – our King will have the room required for us to follow Paul's advice; we will be able to allow Him to live and move and have His being in us.

How to Allow

You know how I do this – how I allow God to live and move and have His being in me? Like repentance, it is an everyday thing, an everyday commitment: every morning I begin my day by saying, "Self, get off the throne; Lord God, please take your rightful place on the throne of my life. " I know it may sound overly simple, even foolish, but it works for me.

I declare something that God has given me the invitation and authority to declare. In my own voice and my own words, I accept His invitation and in the same breath offer an invitation to Him.

I need practical ways to get myself out of His way, and this works for me.

Room For Whom?

Is there room for God in your life or are your spiritual spaces cluttered with people who are so difficult they end up sucking the life out of you? At the end of the day, do you often find yourself angry, frustrated, or crazy? You haven't accomplished what you intended to accomplish –

all you've done is react to the crazy-makers. Do you end up bitter and resentful toward the people you have invited into those spiritual spaces inside you, the people you have given the most time and energy and attention to?

This is not the way relationships are supposed to be, is it? How do we end up there? Maybe you don't, but if I am going to be honest I must admit that I sometimes find myself drained by a needy person rather than figuring out how to deal with him in a loving and truthful way – in a way that honors him, me and God.

Remember: God may have brought these people directly to us; if not, He has at least allowed them to be in our lives, and though we are often not able to discern His purposes in the moment, we can be absolutely certain our King never does or allows anything without a perfect purpose.

As we said earlier in this book, God calls us to *bloom where we are planted*, and often we are planted by people who demand our attention and slowly (or not so slowly!) suck out our patience, draining us of any desire to be like Jesus.

The Trap The Enemy Wants Us In
In his letter to the Colossian church, Paul tells them/us to clothe ourselves with compassion, humility, gentleness, and patience, and he makes it very clear that this requires *grace*. [1]   But sometimes we aren't able to take off the spirit-smothering apparel of anger, stress, impatience, or judgment; sometimes just the thought of doing so seems draining – let alone putting on the spiritual apparel of love, mercy and justice. This is a trap. And it is just where the enemy wants us: on the hamster wheel dealing with

each exhausting encounter, and with each encounter becoming less willing to forge through to God's intent for us, which is to be in deep relationship with Him and more like His Son.

So how do we address the reactionary Spirit-less hamster mentality in ourselves? How do we climb out of the enemy's trap of dealing with the people who are so needy that they drain us?

EGR People

One of my favorite books is *Balcony People* by Joyce Heatherley. The book is about the *lethal poison of rejection and the healing antidote of affirmation.* [2] Heatherley distinguishes between worldly affirmation (people pleasing) and Godly affirmation (God pleasing). Extra-Grace-Required people, whom we'll refer to as *EGR people*, need an extra measure of love and affirmation. They are often wounded, broken, disillusioned, deeply dissatisfied people who wind up being rejected because of their (wounded, broken, disillusioned, deeply dissatisfying) behavior.

Do you know anyone like that? You can see it in them, and if you pay any attention at all, you can see them setting themselves up again and again to fail in relationships. Their brokenness leads the way and their deeply dissatisfying relationships flow out of their hurts, hang-ups and habits.

More times than I can count, I have wanted to say to these EGR people, "Look at what you're doing! You are driving people crazy – talking incessantly, trying to get attention, always engaging in obnoxious behavior that pushes people away. "

Are you like me in this? Do you just want to be honest enough to tell the EGR people in your life what they are doing? Do you sometimes want to hold a mirror and a tape recorder up to them and show them what you see and what you hear when you're around them?

The thing is, the EGRs' brokenness and repeated life-draining behavior, and our inability to deal with their needs in ways that will actually honor and change them, keep us on the hamster wheel– just where the enemy of abundant life and grace and justice wants us – and keeps us dancing the same jagged graceless dance, draining our ability to put on the spiritual apparel of mercy, love and truthfulness.

What People Need

Here's a shocker: people need love and affirmation and grace. I mean *all* people – EGR people, of course – and you and me too. We all need love and affirmation and grace. We are lost without them. And here's the shocker-shocker: the same exact love and affirmation and grace (*unmerited favor*) that God extends to you and me is what we have to extend to the EGR
people in our lives.

How do we get to the place where we not only do not reject EGR people, but where we also begin to bless, affirm and speak truth-with-love to them?

Who are these people? As we said, they are often the ones who have experienced rejection; and they are often the people who are closest to us – family and friends. (Could that be God's design?) And the ones in our lives who seem to be the most difficult to love are the ones who need it the most.

You Cannot Give What You Don't Have

Before we can become affirmers, truth tellers, mercy givers, we must accept God's mercy ourselves; we must be merciful to ourselves and deal with our own stuff – the stuff that keeps us on our own hamster wheel – the stuff that makes us crazy when another EGR person does it, says it, brings it to us.

Jesus made it very clear that we are to love our neighbors as *ourselves*. That's right. We cannot love others like Christ loves us until we love ourselves like Christ loves us. Give it any thought at all and it makes perfect sense, doesn't it?

Oxygen and Grace

We all know the drill when a commercial airplane takes off: the stewardess goes through the motions of explaining safety measures to all the passengers. Toward the end of her presentation, she tells us that in case of emergency – if the cabin loses pressure – the oxygen masks will drop from overhead (a fitting metaphor); she holds up an oxygen mask and reminds us that adults traveling with children should put their masks on first before assisting their kids.

Same with us and the provision of love, truth, affirmation and grace. We must first accept and put on God's love for us; we must love ourselves the way God loves us. We must first allow Him to heal our broken wings before we can fly – certainly before we can help others fly.

314

Before we can give the oxygen of extra grace to the unlovable, grace-starved people in our lives, we must first accept it from the source of grace.

We cannot extend to others what we do not have ourselves. Doesn't this make perfect sense?

Judge Not
The hardest thing to do when we have difficult people in our lives is not to judge them. Or to put it another way: the easiest thing to do with EGR people is to judge them. They deserve it, and we're right. Right? They are difficult and unlovable, and the truth about them (and how difficult and unlovable they are) is obvious. Their deplorable condition is as plain as the noses on their faces. Right?

And who are the best ones to recognize the nose on someone's face? Why, those who have noses on their faces too! In his letter to the Christians in Rome, Paul said:

> You therefore have no excuse, you who pass
> judgment on someone else, for at whatever point you
> judge the other, you are condemning yourself;
> because you who pass judgment do the same things.[3]

Jesus was definitive and uncompromising on the subject too:

> Do not judge, or you too will be judged. For in the same
> way you judge others, you will be judged, and with
> the measure you use, it will be measured to you.
> Why do you look at the speck of sawdust in your
> brother's eye and pay no attention to the plank in

315

your own eye?[4]

Judge is the source for the English word *critic*. Another form of the same root is translated *hypocrite*, implying a critical, judgmental or self-righteous spirit.

The hard part about dealing in a Godly way with the EGR people in our lives is that it is so very easy to be judgmental, critical, or hypocritical in our relationship with them.

Got Planks?

Jesus is saying that before we look at the speck in someone else's eye we ought to extract the large piece of lumber from our own eye. *Speck* was used in classical Greek to describe material used to make a bird's nest – bits of small plant materials. The plank, or log, was an obvious overstatement, hyperbole – a form Jesus used often to convey a truth. He exaggerated His point to make sure we got it. Sometimes it's difficult to see the point when you have a plank in your eye.

Our Mask

Hypocrite was used to describe a person who performs behind a mask; it came from two Greek words meaning *to judge* and *under*. In Greece a hypocrite acted one way on the surface and another way under the surface; one way in the light, seen by others, and another way in the dark, unseen.

Sometimes it is easier to deal with EGR people by putting on a hypocrite's mask: judging them harshly in our hearts and minds (underneath), but saying something completely different to them (on the surface).

But the easy way is not the way God would have us go with the EGR people in our life. What we must do – what Jesus tells us unequivocally – is remember to deal with the plank in our own eye (the nose on our own face) before attempting to speak truth into the lives of EGR people.

We are called to extend to EGR people the grace God has already offered to us.

Judas: An EGR Person For The Ages
Jesus was friends with His disciples. It was true that He had a close-knit group of three (John, Peter and James), but He was friends with *all* His disciples. We know this because He
told them that He no longer called them servants, but friends. [5] Remember, Judas Iscariot was one of the disciples, and therefore one of Jesus' friends. And yet Judas betrayed Jesus for a handful of silver coins. Jesus knew that Judas was going to betray Him and He mentioned it during their last meal together:

> The one who has dipped his hand into the bowl with me will betray me. [6]

Judas had the audacity to ask: "Surely not I, Rabbi?" Talk about extra grace required. The one who was going to betray Him played dumb in front of the other disciples, and Jesus knew it. [7]

I don't know about you, but at that point I would have exposed Judas. I would have at least kicked him out of our last meal together. I would have called him a

317

hypocrite. Not Jesus though. He just said: "It is you. "

Have you ever been betrayed? How did you handle it?
Were you able to extend grace?

God's Way: Grace Extended
My twelve-year-old granddaughter, Mary Catherine, told
me that there is someone at her school who continually
lies to her friends. When it happened again last week, it
was the last straw as far as Mary Catherine was
concerned. The girl was spreading lies about Mary
Catherine, and my granddaughter's other friends turned
on the liar. They decided they did not want to be her
friend any more. They shunned her.

But not Mary Catherine. My granddaughter decided to
extend grace. She confronted the girl who had lied about
her and asked her what was going on in her life. Mary
Catherine did not excuse the girl's behavior but tried to
find out what was behind the lying.

The girl told Mary Catherine that her parents were in the
middle of a bitter divorce. She was sad and angry and she
had lied about Mary Catherine because of the way she
was feeling. Mary Catherine listened and understood and
offered to help the girl. They agreed that if she would
quit lying, Mary Catherine would help her walk through
this hard time.

Talk about making a grandmother proud. I wanted to tell
everyone the story – even random people I saw that
week.

Now, thinking about my granddaughter and how she

extended grace, I wonder if I would have done the same. I wonder if I would have taken the much easier path and joined the other girls and turned my back on the liar. Would I have allowed my initial indignation and hurt and self-righteousness to rule me? Would I have withheld the grace that the sad and frightened girl so desperately needed?

A Little Help From Our Friends

Sometimes we need the help of others to deal rightly and compassionately with the high-stress people in our lives. Depending on the situation, that helper might be our boss or closest friend or spouse. Sometimes we cannot see clearly enough to understand how to best deal with the EGR people in our lives, and God speaks through others to show us the way.

David and Jonathan

How about our old friend King David? He keeps showing up in this book, doesn't he? When you read David's incredible story, it doesn't seem like he had too many friends. King Saul was the number one EGR person in David's life, at least at the beginning of David's journey, and it was Saul's son, Jonathan, who most helped David deal with Saul. Jonathan was a friend at a time when David didn't have many but surely needed them. And it was Jonathan who helped David deal with his EGR person.

David had the opportunity to kill Saul but refused to do so. He said that he would not touch God's anointed. Saul was pursuing David to kill him but David, with Jonathan's help and counsel, refused to harm him.

Peter: A Model EGR Person

And then there was Peter. He's made an appearance or two in this book as well. Peter was a beloved disciple of Jesus, and he was certainly one of Jesus' EGR people from the beginning. He was in Jesus' circle of closest friends, but don't you think he must have required more grace than the others? Now right here we have to admit that pretty much every person Jesus ever ran across was an EGR person. Right? Didn't Jesus need to extend extra grace to every human being on the planet? Wasn't Jesus' agony and death on the cross the ultimate extension of forgiveness and grace to *all* of us?

Imagine Peter jumping out of the boat onto the water without even thinking. Imagine Jesus watching this EGR person walking toward him, then losing focus, his now frightened eyes noticing the wind- whipped waves surrounding him.

I picture Jesus seeing it all and saying, "Wait a minute, Peter. Listen to me, keep your eyes on me…. Peter, you're sinking. No wonder I nicknamed you 'The Rock' – you're sinking like a rock right now! Oh, Peter – so little faith. Here, take my hand. I've got you. "

Or impetuous Peter in the garden of Gethsemane seeing the temple guard coming for Jesus, running up to the guard, pulling out a sword and cutting off his ear. In that tense, life-defining moment, Jesus gently said to Peter: "Put your sword back in its place, for all who draw the sword will die by the sword. Do you think I cannot call on my Father, and he will at once put at my disposal more than twelve legions of angels?"[8]

It is as if Jesus is saying to this EGR Hall of Famer: "Peter, I don't have time for this now. Haven't you heard *anything* I have said?" And He reaches over to heal the guard's ear.

Or what about Peter saying he would never deny Jesus – that everyone else would, but not he. Can't you just hear Jesus telling him: "Peter, don't go there, my precious little blow-hard EGR disciple. You'll regret it. " But Peter went there; in the EGR World Series, Peter batted 1000; and then he denied his Lord and Savior, his best friend, three times. Jesus had predicted it, knew it would happen. But He let Peter be Peter; and then He forgave him and died for him and conquered the grave and poured His love and mercy and grace on Peter and instructed him to go to the ends of the earth and tell everyone what he knew to be true.

Your EGR People: Hard Questions, Harder Answers
Some EGR people are like Peter: impulsive, hasty, hot-headed; not thinking before they act; speaking too soon, saying the wrong things when they speak. Some EGR people seem to feel that their very lives depend on their being the center of attention.

We all know the type: you have just opened your heart and shared with him or her that your marriage is falling apart or that you have a terrible illness, and he or she interrupts (often saying something like, "I don't mean to interrupt, but...") to tell you in great detail how hard his or her life is right now. Nobody's life is as hard as theirs.

We all know people who suck the life out of us. When we think about the EGR people in our lives, and we consider our relationship with them, we need to ask:

- Why does God allow those people in my life?
- Is there something in me that attracts annoying people?
- What am I called to do about them?
- God allows these people into our lives because they are broken and need attention … and the King of the Universe has chosen us to be the ones to extend grace. We are called by the Source of Grace

— the same One Who has extended grace to us more times than we can count – to extend grace to those who need it.

In the chapter called *When He Says No* we discovered that God allows stressful people in our lives to transform us and help us be more like Him. Did you not want to hear that? Me either.

Wouldn't it be easier if we could read a book about how to deal with these people and follow a few clear and simple steps? This is one of those cases when a formula would be very nice.

Diamonds In The Rough

Apparently Jesus sees us as His 'diamonds in the rough' and wants to do some refining and sanding in us to make us smooth and beautiful.

I would rather be a diamond or opal or some other rare and precious gem that does not need to be polished. What about you?

Broken People Attract (and Seek) Broken People

Let's look into the second question about our attracting these annoying people. Could it be that people who have experienced rejection or brokenness attract difficult needy people? Could it be that those of us who have experienced deep hurts are more understanding and tolerant of those in need? Sometimes people with deep rejection issues become people pleasers and attract the needy because they are unable to set boundaries, driven by an irresistible desire to please and be accepted.

It's really not complicated. Broken people are like broken pieces of pottery looking to see where they fit in the vase of life; where does their piece fit to make a beautiful piece of pottery?

And there are also people who are so broken that they do not see any way they will ever fit in the vase of life; they are convinced they will never be mended, never whole, never a well-designed part of anything of value. People like that need people like us; people like that need broken people who've had grace extended, again and again; people like that need former members (or recovering members) of the EGR Club who now know beyond the shadow of a doubt that they do fit, they fit beautifully. God says so:

> He has showed you, O man, what is good. And what does the Lord require of you? To act justly and to love mercy and to walk humbly with your God. [9]

The prophet Micah spoke these words after God had presented His case against His people, the Israelites. They had forgotten (once again – sound familiar?) that God had delivered them from Egypt. They offered sacrifices to appease God, but all God required of His EGR people was to act justly and to be filled with love and mercy.

Bearing Burdens, Not Carrying Them

What sacrifices are you offering God to appease the situation with the EGR people in your life? Are you trying to deal with this person your way or God's way? God's word tells us that His love (*agape*) is supernatural – *above the natural*. We are called to bear one another's burdens, but we are not called to carry them. We are called to take the burden of the EGR relationship and give it to God. Let His character grow in you; let Him shoulder the burden and help you set good boundaries; let Him show mercy. God's mercy isn't always what we think.

Once again, we are faced with making space for doing things God's way – with His mercy, His justice, His love.

We need to walk in God's grace, humility and mercy for sure but not fall off the other side of the horse. It doesn't mean we let EGR people walk all over us. It doesn't mean we do not set boundaries; and it doesn't mean we affirm EGRs when they need correction instead.

My granddaughter, Mary Catherine, did it God's way. She offered unconditional love by saying the friendship with the lying girl meant a lot to her; she was fair-minded, not judging the girl but confronting her with justice; she was merciful and honest, neither running away from the friend nor painfully enduring the barbs. Mary Catherine dealt fairly and compassionately – God's way.

My granddaughter taught me a lesson and illustrated God's Word in the way she extended grace to the EGR person in her life.

Abigail's EGR Challenge

I Samuel 25 tells the story about Abigail and her EGR person, her husband Nabal. He was a man filled with pride and a bad attitude; he was someone who required extra grace to live with. In describing Abigail and Nabal, Samuel says:

> She was an intelligent and beautiful woman, but her husband, a Calebite, was surly and mean in his dealings. [10]

David had been very kind to Nabal, watching over his property for many months. Yet when David asked for supplies for his troops, Nabal responded:

> Who is this David? Who is this son of Jesse? Many servants are breaking away from their masters these days. Why should I take my bread and water and the meat I have slaughtered for my shearers and give it to men coming from who knows where? [11]

David in his anger set out with his men with swords drawn. One of the servants told Abigail what had transpired, that Nabal had insulted David, and Abigail lost no time:

> She took two hundred loaves of bread, two skins of wine, five dressed sheep, five seahs of roasted grain, a hundred cakes of raisins and two hundred cakes of pressed figs, and loaded them on donkeys. Then she told her servants, "Go on ahead; I'll follow you. " But she did not tell her husband Nabal. [12]

Abigail set off to find David and set things right. David had extended grace to Abigail's graceless husband (whose name meant fool), and Abigail knew exactly what she must do:

> When Abigail saw David, she quickly got off her donkey and bowed down before David with her face to the ground. She fell at his feet and said: "My Lord, let the blame be on me alone. Please let your servant speak to you; hear what your servant has to say. May my Lord pay no attention to that wicked man Nabal. He is just like his name.... [13]

Abigail walked in grace. She overlooked her husband's arrogance and humbly went to David to give him what he needed. She dealt with her EGR person with humility and with a willingness to cover his mistake.

Proverbs 17 tells us that love covers an offense. That is what Abigail did. Sometimes it is the only way we can deal with the EGR people in our lives.

John The Baptist: EGR With A Divine Purpose
John the Baptist didn't look the way an evangelist should look. He dressed in camel's hair and tied a leather belt around his waist. He ate wild honey and locusts. John was not someone you would want to invite to dinner, let alone allow him to baptize you.

My guess is that he was the type of person who did not take *no* for an answer. (Well, he could take the Father's *No*, but not anyone else's.) John talked straight; he got right to the point. Small talk was not his forte; he was downright blunt.

He was the type who would tell you to "turn or burn" – get your life right, repent, or you would end up in hell. If the people John spoke to had written him off as a loon, a fanatic – an EGR person with no sense of propriety – if they had not been willing to hear his message, they never would have met Jesus. John was called by God to prepare the way for the Savior. And that is exactly what he did.

Sometimes the people who require an extra portion of grace are the ones God sends our way to speak the truth into our lives. Often we are unwilling to listen to these specially appointed EGRs because of the package they come in and the way they deliver the message.

But they are sent our way to prepare us to grow in love, mercy, and justice. We have to learn to recognize them and pay attention.

Practical Ways to Deal with EGR People
- Deal with your own brokenness, hurt and rejection first: accept God's unconditional love and recognize the countless times He has offered grace to you.
- Look for ways to authentically affirm and not tear down the EGR person.
- Ask God to give you a heart for this person.
- Pray for them.
- Evaluate the situation but do not judge.
- Be gently honest with them: do not pull punches BUT do not hammer them with the truth either; telling the truth without love is of no value (or is of negative value).
- Cover their offences with love, justice and mercy.

Putting On The New Life

We have to take off the spiritless apparel that causes us to be bitter, angry or frustrated with the EGR people in our lives. God calls us to put on the spiritual apparel of patience, kindness and mercy, which He designed for us, and which He designed us to wear.

> You were taught with regard to your former way of life, to put off your old self, which is being corrupted by evil desires; to be made new in the attitude of your minds; and to put on the new self, created to be like God in true righteousness and holiness. [14]

Where The Rubber Meets the Road

So this is where the rubber of reality meets the road of self. This is where *Kum Bay Ya* (literally *Come By Here*) changes to I would rather not have to deal with you. This is where you feel like you are the road and God's commands are the tire that is crushing you.

Yet God's Word is clear: we do not get a free ride; we do not get to choose which EGR people we will respond to, extend grace to. It is costly to lay down our lives and show grace, love, and mercy. No one likes to die to self – there must be another way. You can run from your EGR person – if I avoid them they'll go away – but they or someone like them will knock at your door soon enough. We can run and we can try to hide, but sometime, somewhere, through some EGR person or another, God will get a hold of us and we will have to die to self in order to deal with the EGR in a Godly, graceful way.

Isn't it interesting how so often the most difficult people – the ones who require extra grace – are often in our own family? Coincidence? Well, let's call it a *Godincidence*. He

328

planned it that way. He had a perfect purpose in allowing it.

Jesus did not run from Judas. He walked toward him.

Jesus did not run from the cross. He carried it through the streets of Jerusalem and up the hill and allowed His persecutors to nail Him to it.

Neither did He run from us. Instead ... *while we were still sinners Christ died for us.* [15]

We are His disciples, and He promises to give us the grace we need to stop running. He will pour out His love upon us and through us and show us how to love the unlovable, just as He has loved us.

And in the process we will be utterly changed. We will begin to look more and more like our Father in heaven.

Notes

1. Colossians 3:12
2. Joyce Heatherley, Balcony People, 9
3. Romans 2:1
4. Matthew 7:1-5
5. John 15:15
6. Matthew 26:23
7. Matthew 26:17-25
8. Matthew 26:52
9. Micah 6:8
10. I Samuel 25:3
11. I Samuel 25:10
12. I Samuel 25:18-19
13. I Samuel 25:23-25
14. Ephesians 4:22-24
15. Romans 5:8

17 WHEN HE SAYS NO

We know very little about Mary. We know that she valued worshipping Jesus above all else. Two of the times we see her in Scripture she is either sitting at the feet of Jesus or pouring oil over his feet preparing Him for burial. She had tapped into the secret of knowing that in His Presence there is fullness of joy; that in His Presence every need is met and even the "nos" of life take on a new meaning. She must have been told no many times. All of us grew up hearing 'no'. When my children young I used to tell them: "What part of no do you not understand?" We all understand the word no but that doesn't mean we have to like it. Mary, sitting at the feet of Jesus, came with her own disappointments in life. She came with her bucket full of the times she had wanted to do something but could not. She came with her desires, her needs, and she hoped that she would hear yes. We do not know if she asked Him for anything at all, but what we can be sure of is that what she thought she wanted changed in the Presence of Jesus. All of her disappointments, all of her desires for someone to say 'yes' to her were lost in the pool of His refreshing Presence. As she gazed into His eyes she didn't have a care in the world.

Sometimes we want something so badly and it doesn't work out the way we wanted. You may have prayed for a loved one to be healed and they died. You may have wanted a broken relationship to be restored and it wasn't.

We have all suffered through tragedies, heartbreak and sorrow, and I think we have all gone through those times when we've wondered: *Where is God – what is He thinking? What is He doing (or not doing)?* I know I have, more than once. How about you?

Where are you, God? How can you allow these things to happen to me and the people I love? Why won't you give me what I need? Why don't you answer me?

What Do We Do When …
There are some things we will never understand on this side of eternity. We may get glimpses –

God-given clarity on certain issues, partial revelations, prophesy regarding specific time-bound events, situations or people. But we do not have the full revelation. I don't think the Lord wants us to know yet – I'm not sure why. Maybe it is just too much to know – maybe we can't handle it.

Two of my husband's three sisters died in the same year. It was so hard. They were in their thirties, and that is just too young to die. But they did die – one very suddenly, completely unexpected – and my husband and I, and our entire family, were faced with the question: *What do we do when God says No?*

What do we do when God does not give us the long life we expected (maybe even took for granted)? What do we do when disease and sickness strike and even our best friends' words of compassion and support and hope suddenly don't have meaning.

At these times we just want to hear from God. We want to know why He refused to fix things, or to give us what we think we need (or deserve). We want to know why the One for whom nothing is impossible said No. Sometimes doors closed that we had hoped would open wide for us; other times doors open that we did not want to open. And always the lingering question: *God, where are you? Are you really for me?*

Sometimes we stop dreaming – or we lose hope, or maybe we just get tired and give up. Is that where you are right now?

Broken-Winged Birds
Langston Hughes said: "Hold fast to your dreams for if your dreams die, life is a broken winged bird that cannot fly."[1]

Have you let go of your dreams? Have you stopped dreaming? Have you allowed your dreams to die because you no longer believe you will realize them? Have you become a broken-winged bird, unable to fly – unable (or unwilling) to soar and meet (or exceed) the expectations you once had?

The Enemy Loves It When We Are Wounded
The enemy is in the business of destroying human hopes and dreams, and when God says *No* to us the enemy always tries to capitalize on our woundedness; our vulnerability immediately following a *No* from God – an apparent defeat, a set-back that momentarily crushes our hope – becomes fertile ground for Satan's lies and recriminations and misdirections. Dreams flow out of our desire to bring God glory, so if the enemy can steal our

hope or crush our dreams by twisting and perverting the *No's* of life, then he will have robbed us of the opportunity to give God glory.

When we get a *No* from God, when we suffer defeat or dire situations, tragedy or pain, some of the questions we simply cannot avoid are:
Is God Sovereign?
If He is sovereign, why did God design a world in which there is suffering and evil? Does God cause the suffering or trials in our lives?
If He doesn't cause them, why does He allow them in our lives? Why does God say No and close doors that seem so right, so good, so meant-to-be?

Job (Speaking of Hard Questions)

Do you remember the discussion about Job in the chapter called *In The Eye of The Storm*? We looked at Job's story and experience from the angle of how he handled himself when the storms of life hit him. We focused on his trust in God and how that unfailing faith and belief led him into the eye of the storm, the true and deep peace of God. We heard Job say that although God had slain him, he would nevertheless trust Him.

Let's take a look at Job again and use his story to provide a Godly perspective on the subject of theodicy – how to justify or defend God in the face of evil, especially human suffering. How do we view a sovereign God in the face of the *No's* of life and specifically the suffering of the innocent?

Job responds to the question of human suffering by explaining that God uses the suffering to trans- form us, to refine us, to make us more like Him:

> My ears had heard you; but now my eyes have seen you. [2]

God strengthened Job during his trials. Job had heard about God before He allowed Satan to test Job and take him through horrific ordeals; and Job had trusted God to a degree. After his trials, though, Job saw God in a very different way. The depth of his trust in the sovereign God grew, and he saw the goodness of God with his own eyes.

Is God pressing on you now to move to a deeper place of knowing Him – or not just knowing but truly seeing Him? Do you understand – and believe – that you are no less precious to God than Job was?

Knowing God's Character

In the midst of writing this I received an e-mail from a good friend of mine. He told me that a mutual friend's son has a brain tumor and that the prognosis was not good. As I read the e-mail I wondered how I could best respond. What to say? How do I reply in a way that is authentic, Godly, encouraging? I struggled with whether to give the well-intended responses to the trials in life that we all give; you are likely familiar with these; you may well have said them yourself: "God is in control. " "God will turn this for good. " "God will see you through. "

In the middle of the storm sometimes the best help we can give is to hold the person's hand and say nothing. The ones who share this difficult storm-news with us are often not looking for the shore at that moment, maybe not even looking for a life preserver. They simply need the ministry of our presence beside them. Though well intended and based in truth, words at times like these seem frivolous.

The key to withstanding the toughest ordeals of life – what we need to move though the inevitable pain and suffering – is the certain knowledge of who God really is, now and always, and who He is not. The key is knowing God's character.

Job was strengthened in, by and through the Lord because of the trials God allowed. He grew in his knowledge of, and trust in, the character of God as a direct result of the ordeals he withstood.

The way to grow when the answer is *No* is to know the character of the King.

David: Character Through Chaos
What about David? As a young man anointed to be King of Israel, he watched his quiet life as a shepherd turn into a chaotic and extremely dangerous journey to the throne. David got a promotion and his world was turned upside-down as King Saul relentlessly chased him and tried to kill him.

Has that ever happened to you – get a promotion and things get tougher? Much tougher? Have a breakthrough with one of your children and the other child falls apart? Get caught up financially, then your house needs major repairs? That's what happened to David.

At first, it must have seemed to the young giant killer as though the world was his to take. But that fantasy was

short-lived. Once anointed King over Israel, David had
to run and hide in the caves. Then, when he thought that
things could not possibly get worse – while the town he
was planning on hiding in was set on fire and women and
children were carried off – his rag-tag army blamed him
for all their troubles and were ready to stone him. It is at
this point in David's incredible story that we really see his
understanding of God's true character. When God said
No the young shepherd-turned-king ran *to* God as his
only place of shelter and hope:

> When David and his men came to Ziklag, they found
> it destroyed by fire and their wives and sons and
> daughters taken captive. So David and his men wept
> aloud until they had no strength left to weep.
> David's two wives had been captured – Ahinoam of
> Jezreel and Abigail, the widow of Nabal of Carmel.
> David was greatly distressed because the men were
> talking of stoning him; each one was bitter in spirit
> because of his sons and daughters. But
> David found strength in the Lord. [3]

Everyone was distraught. Notice they *all* wept, and that
included David. His emotions were just as raw as the
other men. The men were bitter and distressed and
seriously considering stoning David. Yet David's
response was not to become bitter but to *find strength* in
the Lord.

Your Choice: Pity Pot or God's Heart?

Can you say that you would respond in the same way
David did? If you lost your family and your home was in
flames and your companions and colleagues turned
against you, would you turn to God for strength or would
you sit on your pity pot?

I have done both. The pity pot approach did not turn out all that well. Maybe yours was a bitter pot or a victim pot or a life-stinks pot. There are almost as many pot choices as there are human beings to choose them.

Turning to God in the midst of your current trial requires knowing Him and the depth of His character. We fall into more pits (and pots) when we assume that we know God and then can't find Him in the midst of our ordeal because we're looking in that pathetic little box of assumptions we've relegated Him to.

David did not fold when God kept saying *No*. He knew he could depend on God because he had a deepening knowledge of God's character; he had already begun learning about it, hadn't he? So far in his life, David had already seen his heavenly Father's character up close and personal – on the battlefield against Goliath, and in the caves when he was on the run for his life, and even when he was a twelve-year-old shepherd defending his father's sheep against wild predators. David was able to draw strength from God because God had provided that strength before. David was able because of His understanding of the eternal King's character. David was able because he trusted what he knew to be true.

The principle at work with Job and David is this: when bad things happen; when doors seem to slam shut everywhere we turn; when life appears to be senseless or out of control or desperately disappointing, we get our strength from knowing God's eternal, unchangeable character. Job and David knew and re-learned again and again that God is good all the time; we matter to Him more than we are capable of imagining; He knows what we need, and He wants the best for us, now and always. Now and always, the King of the Universe is:

Our Shepherd

David writes:

> The Lord is my shepherd, I shall not be in want. He makes me to lie down in green pastures, he leads me beside quiet waters, he restores my soul. [4]

In want here does not mean a lack of things. On this side of eternity you and I may lack things; we may lack finances or 'creature comforts'; we will almost certainly be disappointed; we will undoubtedly experience sorrow and pain. When David says he (and we) will not be *in want*, he means we will never lack contentment or satisfaction as long as we are in the Shepherd's care.

Did you know that it is nearly impossible for sheep to lie down if a few basic requirements are not met? It's true. Sheep cannot lie down peacefully – rest, be content – if they are not free from:

- fear
- parasites or flies
- hunger

The shepherd will even break a sheep's leg if it keeps wandering away from the flock because he knows that the sheep will die if it strays near predators. And if he is forced to break a sheep's leg in order to protect it, the shepherd will carry the sheep wherever it needs to go from then on.

David knew all this very well. And in the twenty-third psalm he spoke from his practical working knowledge of sheep and his personal knowledge of God's character to confirm for us that our Shepherd, the Lord of Lords, provides these freedoms and protections for us just as the natural shepherd does for his flock.

How like the sheep we are! Sometimes our Shepherd allows our broken wings or legs so that He can carry us. Sometimes we need to know the side of God that is so deeply merciful and caring that only His allowance of a tragedy or disappointment will enable us to see the truth and find our way.

God does not look down at us and think up ways to break or punish us. He finds ways to save us. He is the way.

Sovereign

God is the Creator and King of the Universe. He is the Supreme Ruler. There is no one and nothing above Him. He is sovereign. Knowing that He has things under control is not only comforting for me – it gives me confidence to know that I do not have to trust in myself. More often than not, I can be fickle, confused, misled, and have my own agenda. So why would I ever want to be in control of my crazy life?

The prophet Jeremiah tells us that God has a plan for our lives – and it is a better one than any of us could come up with:

> I know the plans I have for you, declares the Lord, plans to prosper you and not to harm you; plans to give you a hope and a future. [5]

Our Lord declares it. The solid foundation of our hope and our future is the fact that we are not in control – He is.

340

Passionately Compassionate and Merciful

Years ago, as I was driving my son to a tennis lesson, he became disrespectful with me. Can anyone relate? I got so mad that I turned the car around and sped back toward home. I told my son there would be no tennis lesson that day. I may have suggested that there would never be another tennis lesson again, ever, until the end of time. As I pulled into my neighborhood a flashing blue light appeared in my rearview mirror. Of course I immediately said to my son: "See, you made me speed and now I'm going to get a ticket because of your smart mouth. "

As you might expect, my son's response was: "No, Mom – you did that on your own. "

So the policeman pulled me over and asked why I was speeding. Why do they always ask that? They must enjoy hearing all the crazy stories we tell them. I told him the truth – that my son had been disrespectful and I was taking him back home at the speed of light because I most certainly was not going to allow him to enjoy the privilege of his tennis lesson.

The policeman walked around to my son's door and asked him to roll down his window. "Son," he said, "have you ever read the Ten Commandments?"

"Yes, Sir," my son replied very respectfully.
"Do you remember the one about honoring your mother and father?" "Yes, Sir. "
"Well, you did not honor your mother today. I'm not going to give her a ticket, but you must honor her. You got it?"

341

"Yes, Sir. "

I wanted to high-five the policeman. A mother's dream-come-true. I imagined the headline: *Policeman tickets disrespectful boy for back-talking mother, cites fifth commandment.*

I loved it. My son didn't have quite the same reaction.

Our God is passionately compassionate and merciful. He does not miss any opportunity to teach and raise up and redeem. Sometimes He uses policemen; sometimes mothers or dads; sometimes shepherds; sometimes kings. God notices the one lost sheep and goes after him; He looks for the one disobedient or disrespectful son and disciplines him in a way he will remember. He loves us so much, He will not leave us to ourselves. He knows we might easily wander away from His safe pastures. And our loving Shepherd does not want a single one of us to be lost.

Sometimes when God seems to be saying *No*, He is allowing the courses of our own actions to play out. He is allowing the consequences, but He is never banishing us from the flock.

The Promise Keeper's Greater Yes
Could there be a higher purpose in pain and suffering, in God's closed doors? I believe there are some things we can all agree on:
- We cannot escape the laws that govern our universe. Forces of nature like gravity and fire and other natural disasters can lead to tragedy. Fire is excellent for warmth and helpful in your stove, but if it is allowed to get out of control,

fire can destroy.
* Sin brought a curse on the earth and the curse includes disease and death.
* We are a social race; our lives are intertwined, so we sometimes suffer when the sins of others affect us.

But God looks beyond the natural laws of the universe and sees the supernatural truths of eternity. As Alpha and Omega – beginning and end – He sees what we cannot see, and He takes the hopeless situations and turns them into opportunities for Him to reveal His glory. Paul said:

> ... it seems to me that God has put us apostles on display at the end of the procession, like men condemned to die in the arena. We have been made a spectacle to the whole universe, to angels as well as to men. [6]

In the world's eyes Paul and the apostles were condemned, always forced to the margins of society, always made a spectacle. But they were God's people, they were His obedient servants, and they were victorious. Because of this small band of men and women, who fearlessly proclaimed the gospel of Jesus of Nazareth, the world was turned upside-down. They spread the good news throughout the world, and what at first may have seemed like a big *No* became God's greater *Yes*.

Sometimes we don't understand why our fruitfulness, our dreams, our desires are cut off by the *No*'s of life, but God will allow spiritual barrenness in order to produce the kind of desperation that will make us totally available for His purposes, His greater *Yes*.

God never goes back on His promises. When He makes a promise He fulfills it. He is the great Promise Keeper. Confusion enters when we think that God has promised us something (longer life, better job, ever-obedient and respectful sons and daughters, etc.) and then whatever it is does not happen and we blame God for not coming through with the goods.

Abraham had enough faith to trust the promises of God. He left the safe and familiar surroundings of his home country to go where God said to go and do what God told him to do:

> By faith Abraham, when called to go to a place he would later receive as his inheritance, obeyed and went, even though he did not know where he was going. [7]

Somehow, Abraham got a hold of the greater *Yes*.

Jesus suffered a horrible *No*, and three days later had a profoundly greater *Yes*. His Daddy had looked down through the ages and knew that humanity needed a Savior; He knew that He had to send His one and only Son to save us because there was not one among us who could accomplish the task. God the Father looked beyond the devastating pain and suffering of the cross to the greater *Yes*, and the world was changed forever.

God's No Transforms Us

One year I bought a beautiful white blooming cactus at Christmas. After the cactus finished blooming I continued to water it, but after a while I forgot about it and left it outside where temperatures dropped below freezing. The cactus made it through the winter but I rarely watered it and it appeared to be near death. By the spring, though, it perked up; I began to water it again (feeling so guilty that the plant was hanging onto life in spite of me and my neglect), and the following year it bloomed profusely.

I read about cacti after that because I was so surprised that this little plant had hung in there. Cacti are distinctive and unusual plants that adapt to extreme arid environments and learn to conserve water. Their stems have an expanded succulent structure that contains the chlorophyll necessary for life and growth.

How like the cacti we can be! The difficult tests of God's *No*'s give us the opportunity to send our roots down to the Living Water:

> He is like a tree planted by the water which yields its fruit in season and whose leaf does not wither. Whatever he does prospers. [8]

God transforms us when He says *No*.

Faith Built, Refined and Perfected

In her study of Daniel, Beth Moore, well-known speaker and author, notes that our faith is always affected by how we are delivered from our fiery trials; and she points out the crucial role that the trial itself plays in our deliverance. Moore says that when we are delivered *from* the fire, our faith is built; when we are delivered *through* the fire, our faith is refined; and when we are delivered *by* the fire, our faith is perfected. [9]

If we turn our ordeals, the *No*'s, into a relentless pursuit of God and His desire for us, we will be transformed, delivered and set free. And we will become available to God in ways we never imagined.

Yes-But-*No*: A Link in the Dream-Chain

Have you ever started a project that you knew was divinely inspired and others took over? Perhaps your part was to plough the ground and someone else spread the seeds and brought the dream to fruition. You had the vision and someone else saw it through.

Once again, King David's experience provides a great example for us. Remember the wonderful dream he had, the fantastic vision he wanted to see through to completion? We mentioned it briefly in Chapter 5 (*Increasing The Feast*). David looked at his cedar-paneled walls and lamented that he had a magnificent dwelling but the Ark of the Covenant – the symbol of God Himself, His glory and presence – was located in a tent outside the city. David was concerned that he lived in luxury while God's house was in a tent. He wanted to build a splendid temple to house the ark and be a fitting home for God.

But God said *No*. Well, maybe it was a *Yes*-but-*No*. The King of Kings told David that his son would build the temple; He instructed David to hand over the fulfillment of his dream to Solomon. Solomon tells us:

> My Father had it in his heart to build a temple for the Name of the Lord the God of Israel. But the Lord said to my father David, 'Because it was in your heart to build a temple for my Name, you did well to have it in your heart. Nevertheless you are not the one to build the temple, but your son, who is your own

flesh and blood – he is the one who will build the
temple for my Name. '[10]

God said *Yes* to David's dream; He said that David's
dream was great; David was just the wrong person to see
it through. So what did David do in response to God's
Yes-but-*No*? He had a clear choice: he could take a seat on
the pity pot (or the bitter pot or the it-was-*my*-dream pot),
claim exclusive rights to the temple-construction idea, and
bury it forever; or he could become a link in the dream-
chain and hand it over to his son with excitement and joy
and give it to Solomon to complete with his help.

David said *Yes* to being a link in the dream-chain. And
what a link! With God's instructions and approval, David
turned the dream into a project; then he put up the funds
and gathered all the materials and supplies necessary to
build an extraordinary temple; and then he gave it all to
Solomon with his blessing.

Waiting On The Dream Planter
It is God who gives us the dream in the first place. He is
the Dream Planter. And it is up to
Him to tell us the part we are to play in the fulfillment of
the dream. Maybe we are to see the dream through to
fruition, start to finish. Maybe we are to be an important
link in the dream-chain but not the finisher. Maybe our
part is to dream the dream and pass it on, and not see it
fulfilled. Whatever our part is to be, just remember: God
will fulfill the dreams He plants in our hearts.

He is so faithful. He can't help it. It is a part of His
character, and He does not change. Just as He is Love
and Relationship and Truth and Joy, He *is* Faithfulness.

347

Remember this about Him. Remember that He knows your heart, He knows exactly what you need, and when He says *No* He is preparing you for blessing beyond belief.

We will be blessed beyond our wildest dreams when we surrender ourselves into His loving hands. The Dream Planter will carry us as we wait; the Promise Keeper will transform us as we despair; the One for whom nothing is impossible will encourage us to send our spiritual roots down deep into Him, and He will faithfully call us to look up expectantly and see His greater *Yes*.

Notes

1.   Langston Hughes, The Lincoln University Bulletin 67. 2, 1964, 1-8
2. Job 42:5
3. I Samuel 30:3-6
4. Psalm 23: 1-2
5. Jeremiah 29:11
6. 1 Corinthians 4:9
7. Hebrews 11:8
8. Psalm 1:3
9. Beth Moore, Daniel: Lives of Integrity, Words of Prophecy, Week 3 of 12 (referring to Daniel 3:3-18)
10. 2 Chronicles 6:7-9

18 CONNECTING

Connecting with God and then connecting with others is the only thing that brings true joy—I am not talking about happiness which is dependent on so many external factors, but true joy which springs up from connection with God and with others. When Mary connected with Jesus, He became her center; the place from which she could connect with others. What she learned in her relationship with Jesus she was able to take into her relationship with other people. Jesus is the true friend---the one who sticks closer than a brother. Jesus is the One who loves us completely without reservation and without strings attached. When Mary made room for Jesus in her life and put Him first, she in turn made room for other healthy relationships. Jesus brings into each relationship the perfect model of a perfect friend. I think that Mary learned a lot from Jesus about the value of being connected to others. She may have heard through the grapevine (no pun intended) that He spoke with his disciples about the vine and the branches. Jesus indicated that He was the vine and that they were the branches. This intimate connection enabled the branch to be nourished by the vine and produce fruit. When we are connected to Jesus, our relationship fruit is healthy, fresh, truthful, and loving. When we make room for God, when we connect with and bless one another, our King looks for ways to bless us. And one of God's favorite ways of blessing us is through relationships.

Today I was thinking about a behavioral pattern I have noticed in Old Testament people. It is a pattern that is repeated, story after story, even as the Bible's narrative moves from the Old to the New Testament. What I've noticed about some of these Biblical characters – okay, *most* of them – is that they would first choose to follow the One True God (Who by the way made covenants with them and parted the sea for them and fed them when there was no food naturally available and led them in victorious battles against all odds) and then – often seemingly in the same week or immediately subsequent to some awesome supernatural saving act by the One True God Himself – these same people would choose to follow some other god.

They repeatedly rejected the Living God Who had actually spoken to some of them and proven His love and righteousness to them again and again and again, and they decided that some other god – an idol made by the locals out of stone or gold or some well-regarded building material – might be a good substitute for the real thing.

So, considering these people and their recurring flip-flops between believing in the Living Almighty God and Dead Building Material, my assessment of them was: *Fickle*! That's what I was thinking: *Look at them! Good grief! How fickle – how God-forgetting stupid – can you be?*

Fickle Updated
Right about then the Living God gave me a heads-up and I noticed I was knee-deep in *judgment* mode. The Only One qualified to judge led me into a deeper and more realistic consideration of those people back-then; He invited me to compare and contrast then and now, them and me.

As He so often has to do, God suggested that I look for myself among those people I was judging. He suggested that I consider how closely connected to them I really am.

So, okay – I guess I'm fickle too. One minute I'm running hard after God and the next minute I am off to follow other gods, other idols – the ones the world makes it so much easier (and so much more respectable) to follow: money, success, self-interest, personal agendas. Fill in the blank(s) for yourself if this applies to you.

It's not a very pretty picture, is it? But it's true, isn't it?

Big Surprise: We Are They

This may not be a new revelation for you; it is not really new for me either, yet I am amazed at how regularly I forget this truth and how often I must be reminded. It is the same concept of the repeated-behavioral-pattern thing I noticed about Old Testament people: I'll learn some basic eternal truth from God's Word again and again and again – something He and His Son and His Holy Spirit have shown me in just about every Bible story – and yet I seem to have to re-learn it on a regular basis. I know why, too; I know why I need constant reminders: because I do not like this truth. It says something about me that I would just as soon hide or deny or repress.

I do not enjoy knowing that I am so closely connected to these fickle people, that I am exactly like the Old Testament characters I judge so easily.

Since 'misery loves company', and we all know God's Word is not just about me, I have to report something you probably already suspect: you and I are in the same boat; you are just like all those Biblical characters too. That's why they are there: to hold a mirror up for us. If this is a surprise for you, I'm sorry, but in the interest of full disclosure (and conceding that misery does indeed love company), I had to tell you.

But for the gap of thousands of years and the radical variations in clothing styles, there is not much difference between you and me and the rest of God's fickle people across the ages: today we draw close to God and then tomorrow the world pulls on us and diverts our attention and we chase after other things.

Yep. We are they.

He Never Forsakes
In his extraordinary Holy Spirit-inspired book, the prophet Isaiah describes the Israelites of his day. True to form, they had deserted God, and He had allowed the consequences: barrenness, isolation, desolation and a deep, desperate feeling of having been forsaken. God allowed His Covenant people to feel as though they had received what they actually deserved.

Through Isaiah God tells His covenant people that they will be brought back from captivity, the place of isolation, and that He will restore the tribes of Jacob; and hidden in this magnificent chapter is a reminder to Israel (and to all of us fickle folks) that God will never forsake us:
> But Zion said, "The Lord has forsaken me, the Lord has forgotten me. " Can a mother forget the baby at her
> breast and have no compassion on the child she has borne? Though she may forget, I will not forget you!

See I have engraved you on the palms of my hands;
your walls are ever before me. Your sons hasten
back, and those who laid you waste depart from you.
Lift up your eyes and look around; all your sons
gather and come to you. [1]

In Isaiah we see the once-great city of Jerusalem
abandoned, desolate, in ruins. Here Jerusalem is a
metaphor for God's people (for us), who require constant
reminders, old revelations newly revealed. We too can
find ourselves feeling abandoned, isolated, cut-off and
forsaken, but God tells us He will never forsake us. He
tells us to look up and see that there are others gathered
around us.

He reassures us and tells us clearly that we are not to
believe the lie that we are alone.

He Gives Us Each Other

The Living God goes on to tell the people of Israel that
though they were ruined and desolate and their land made
waste, there will be a time when they will say that they
need more land; what was once deserted and void of
people will be filled with children:

Though you were ruined and made desolate, and
your land laid waste, now you will be too small for
your people, and those who devoured you will be far
away. The children born during your bereavement
will yet say in your hearing, "This place is too small
for us; give us more space to live in. "[2]

The fickle amnesiacs, once deserted and in need of little
space, now need to expand in order to have room for all

the promises of God; room for God to fill their once-empty lives and connect them with family, friends and fellow believers.

Designed To Be 'One-Anothers'

Then and now, God wants us to give Him room to live and move and have His being in us. He wants us to be connected to Him and to one another. After His One and Only Son Jesus, it is the *one-anothers* in our lives who are His greatest gift to us. And we are the one-anothers with whom and through whom God wants to move.

The Creator calls us to befriend, comfort, protect and deeply connect with one another. We are each designed to be a one-of-a-kind 'one-another'.

Connection: Making Room for God's Blessings

As we think about God's desire for us to make deep connections with Him and with one another, we each need to answer two questions:

- What keeps me from connecting with God and with those He has put around me?
- Am I willing to make space for God to connect me with others?

Do you know the story in 2 Kings 4:8-17 about the Shunammite woman? The prophet Elisha passed by her house on a regular basis and from time to time would stop in for a meal. One day, the woman asked her husband if he would be willing to build a room for the man of God so that Elisha could stay overnight and rest on his journeys. In ancient Israel roofs were flat and served two primary purposes: as a gathering place for the family, and as a temporary accommodation for guests.

The Shunammite woman recognized the importance of building a more permanent structure for their guest.

Re-reading this story makes me think how I sometimes just want God to come by for a visit. I give Him a temporary place to stay, but when He wants a more permanent space I get edgy. The truth is my God and King does not want to be a sometime visitor – here today, gone tomorrow. He wants to be a welcomed and honored part of my life, a central thought and not an after-thought. He wants to be housed in a permanent dwelling, a place of habitation, not just visitation.

Elisha was touched by the Shunammite woman's generosity and asked her what he could do for her in return. She replied, "I have a home among my own people. "[3] The Shunammite woman had a family and was wealthy, and she was telling Elisha that she had all she needed. But she had connected with him in a deep way, and Elisha persisted in his desire to bless her. He asked her servant, Gehazi, what he could do for the woman, and Gehazi told Elisha that the Shunammite woman had always wanted a child but her husband was too old.

Elisha happened to be connected to the Living God and knew that nothing was impossible for Him. The prophet was able to go to the woman and tell her that this time next year she would have a child. I wonder what she thought when she heard that! Maybe she was filled with hope; maybe she doubted. It didn't matter. She had connected with Elisha and, through him and his deep connection to God, her heart's desire was fulfilled.

When we make room for God, when we connect with

and bless one another, our King looks for ways to bless us. And one of God's favorite ways of blessing us is through relationships.

Isolation: The Enemy's Scheme

There is an enemy out there who does not want to see you blessed with meaningful relationships. His assignment is to keep you isolated, feeling abandoned, hopeless and alone. If he can keep us isolated from one another, he can keep us from fulfilling our purpose on earth. Our destiny in Christ can be fulfilled only in relationship with one another; we were created for relationship. It's in our DNA. So the enemy sends out his cohorts to whisper in our ear, to twist us into self-centered knots with stinkin' thinkin', to divert us from relationships and talk us into withdrawing from connection with God and His people. The enemy's assignments include:

- Using our trials to convince us to withdraw from one another and doubt God's promises
- Introducing depression, anxiety and rejection in our minds and hearts: when we need people the most, we often pull away; we remove ourselves from people for fear of failure; we build walls
- Instilling pride, resentment and bitterness
- Telling us we are just too busy to connect with others; suggesting that our schedules are more important than our relationships

Walls and Native Stones

All walls are not bad; some are necessary; some should be constructed and maintained. Back to the passage in Isaiah: when God told His people that their "walls" were before Him,[4] He was referring to the walls of Jerusalem, which had been broken down by Israel's enemies, who were then able to freely come in. God saw the destruction of walls that were built originally to keep enemies out. Israel should have maintained those protecting walls, and the people of God paid a steep price for having allowed their destruction.

But there is another kind of wall that our God sees too. He sees the walls we build around our hearts and minds to limit or destroy the connections He wants for us – the walls we erect to keep God and our one-anothers out.

In her book, *The Wall*, Gloria Jay Evans describes this second kind of wall: I don't know when I first began to build the wall.

> I suppose it was when it occurred to me that I could keep people out of my life by building a simple wall. The wall would be a kind of boundary – a kind of protection. At first the little wall was only knee high. It was really quite attractive, made of native stone I had found in my life. [5]

Let's face it: we have all built walls with our own 'native stones' – fear of rejection, pride, busyness. What stones have you used to build your walls?

We were created for relationship with God and with our God-given one-anothers, and the enemy works overtime to keep us from forging those deep, lasting, life-changing connections. The enemy knows very well that God's grand design has relationship as its foundation. And the enemy knows that when we connect – really connect – we impact our world for good; we walk and talk and live our King's good news. We prove in very practical ways that

Love is the most powerful force in the universe. Why would our enemy want that?

From a Child's Perspective

Another story about my wise granddaughter. I asked Mary Catherine what she thought are the two most important things that enable us to connect with others. She said, "Trust and vulnerability. " She said that we need to know that our friends, the ones we are connecting with, can keep confidences. She knows that vulnerability is a delicate willingness to let others in, and friends need to know that when you expose yourself it is a precious thing. It is a gift that is not given to everyone.

Mary Catherine told me that no one should have to worry that his or her vulnerability, the raw expo- sure of self, will ever be used against them.

As our friend Isaiah also said: ...*a little child will lead them* [6] This granddaughter of mine is brilliant. Thank you, God, that You have given me the gift of connection with Mary Catherine. I am so grateful that she is a one-another of mine.

What Connecting Depends On

It seems to me that connecting with our one-anothers depends on four things:
- Loving God with our whole being
- Staying connected to Jesus, the Vine
- Loving ourself as God loves us
- Loving others through serving and self-sacrifice

Love the Lord your God with all your heart and with all your soul and with all your mind. This is the first

and Great Commandment. And the second is like it:
Love your neighbor as yourself. [7]

The first commandment in Deuteronomy 6:5 was
repeated twice daily by faithful Jews. The idea was that if
you were devoted to God you would obey Him, which
meant obeying the laws He had given to Moses. And the
Jews had a boat-load of laws to obey. Each of the
synoptic gospels (Matthew, Mark and Luke) includes the
words *heart* (emotions, will, and deepest convictions), soul
(the immaterial part of a person's being) and *mind*
(reason). Matthew alone lacks the term *strength* (how a
person uses the abilities he has).

How does God want us to be fully devoted to Him? With
all our heart, soul, mind and strength.

How We Know
How do we know if we love the Lord with all of our
being? In his book *Abide In Christ,* Andrew Murray gives
us a hint:

> Who would after seeking the King's palace be
> content to stand in the door when he is invited in to
> dwell in the King's presence and share with Him in
> all of the glory of His royal life?[8]

If you are content to stand at the door and not enter fully
in, then the question you must ask is: *Do you love something
or someone more than God?*

Jesus posed the same question to Peter: "Simon, son of
John, do you truly love me more than these?"[9]

To stand in the door of the palace – one foot in, one foot

out – means that we are not fully devoted to God. But God persists; He even commands that we love Him with our heart, soul, strength and mind. He wants us to enter the palace, His Presence, and live there. He offers the invitation to everyone. *Everyone.* There are no exceptions, no fine print on the invitation.

Our King knows that our connection to Him is vital to our relationship with others. And He knows that when we love Him with our whole being there is no room for anything else to take center stage. He knows that if we cannot love Him completely, we cannot love others with His complete unconditional love.

The True Vine: The Ultimate Connector
Staying connected to others is dependent on staying connected to Jesus the Vine:

> I am the true vine, and my Father is the gardener. He cuts off every branch in me that bears no fruit while every branch that does bear fruit he prunes so that it will be even more fruitful. You are already clean because of the word I have spoken to you.
>
> Remain in me and I will remain in you. No branch can bear fruit by itself; it must remain in the vine. [10]

And then:

> My command is this: Love each other as I have loved you. [11]

Jesus reconnected us to the Father by dying on the cross. His love for us made Him the great Reconciler, the ultimate Connector.

For God was pleased to have all His fullness dwell in

Him and through Him to reconcile to himself all
things whether things on earth or things in heaven by
making peace through His blood shed on the cross.[12]

Jesus told us that He is the vine and we are the branches;
all the vine possesses belongs to the branches; and all the
branches possess belongs to the vine. We do not have to
accomplish anything, do anything. We must simply abide.
Our weakness becomes His strength. We come empty
and helpless each day to receive His love.

Remain and Rest: Velcro

This is for all you overachievers and perfectionists,
including yours truly. Jesus wants us to rest. He calls us
to come to Him and remain there, fixed, and rest in Him.
Jesus wants us velcroed to Him. He says, *Fasten yourself to
me, and then relax. I am Love and Relationship. I am what you
need. I have things under control. Everything. Do nothing but* be in
me.

If we take more time to relax in Him than doing things
for Him, we will find ourselves connected to His power,
His love, and His nourishment. Just like the branches are
connected to the vine. We will find that relationships will
flow out of a place of rest rather than a place of striving.
We will see that we can have authentic, deep and fulfilling
relationships with our spouses, our children and our
friends – all our one-anothers. His life in exchange for
ours: that's a good deal, isn't it?

Loving Ourselves

If we are to connect with others, we have to love
ourselves. That is a must. That is a command from the
King.

Take a moment and look in the mirror. What do you see?
Do you see someone wonderfully and fearfully made?[13]
Do you see someone made in God's image?

Or do you see failure, rejection, hurt, hopelessness?
David wrote in his Psalm that his frame was not hidden
from God when he was being made, being knit in his
mother's womb. David saw that he was a masterpiece
because his Father in Heaven said he was.

You know what our number one enemy is? Self-hatred.
Not liking who God created. There's that four-letter
word again – S-E-L-F – back on the throne, vying for
center stage, threatening to keep us isolated from God
and our God-given one-anothers.

We must love ourselves as God's beautiful creation, as
His own children, before we can truly love others. It is
not a nice-to-have; it's a must-have.

Loving Others Through Self-Sacrifice

Service is a natural byproduct of loving others. We serve
when we carry the burden of others, when we lay our
lives down, when we put others' needs above ourselves'.
There's *self* yet again. We have to sacrifice self and self
does not lie down easily. Self puts up a fight. Jesus was
the only one willing to wash the dirty feet of the
disciples.[14] No one else picked up the towel that evening.
Who knows where those feet had been? But Jesus loved
those fickle disciples from head to toe. And the love He
demonstrated when He washed the disciples' feet was the
same self-sacrificial love He would demonstrate the next
day as He hung on the cross and gave Himself for all of

us.

David Benner paints a beautiful picture of what love is:
> Christian conversion is not merely encountering love.
> Nor is it developing new ideas or values about love.
> Nor is it committing myself to be loving. Christian
> conversion involves becoming love. But like all
> becoming that occurs on the spiritual journey,
> becoming love involves death.... Love always
> involves saying yes to someone and saying no to
> self.[15]

I don't like to cook. It is a known fact among my family
and friends. It is a real sacrifice, but during the week I
make sure there is a meal for my husband on the table.
What would it be for you? What self-sacrificial act would
demonstrate your love for your one-anothers? Washing
the dishes after the evening meal? Running errands?
Giving a back-rub? Holding a hand? Helping put the
children to bed?

Where and how do you need to love others through
sacrifice?

In his letter to the church in Galatia, Paul writes:
> Do not be deceived: God cannot be mocked. A man
> reaps what he sows. The one who sows to please his
> sinful nature, from that nature will reap destruction;
> the one who sows to please the Spirit, from the Spirit
> will reap eternal life. Let us not become weary in
> doing good, for at the proper time we will reap a
> harvest if we do not give up. [16]

If we want to be connected to one another we must

sacrifice. We must kick self off the throne and wash some feet, do some dishes, prepare some meals.

One Body, Many Parts

You and I need each other. God designed it that way. We who believe in God and His Word and follow after our Lord Jesus are not only His foot-washers on Earth – we are His feet too. We are His body, His hands and eyes and ears and feet. God's blueprint calls for us – the members of His body – to be connected to one another. Check out part of Paul's meditation on connection:

> The body is a unit, though it is made up of many parts; and though all its parts are many, they form one body.... The eye cannot say to the hand, "I don't need you!" And the head cannot say to the feet, "I don't need you!"[17]

God says, *Abide in me and connect with one another. Love and serve. Extend my grace. Your life depends on it.*

Relationships *do* require trust and vulnerability – a willingness to both ask for help and be the help. Wayne Jacobsen describes relationships that thrive:

> Relationships are not built on illusions; they are built on the real struggles of life.... What endears people to one another is the reality of their struggles, doubts and weaknesses. Without that honesty our relationships will remain shallow. [18]

We need each other, and we need honest, open, vulnerable relationships. Our dependency on one another, and our self-sacrificial serving, will impact our world for good.

Busyness: Satan's Yoke

The worst trap of all in terms of keeping us disconnected from God and others is being busy: BeingUnderSatan'sYoke. Who would want to confess that? The truth is we wear our busyness like a banner:

"What are you up to?" "Just real busy. "

"How are you doing?" "Busy. Really busy. "

You know it's true. Right? Most replies to those queries are the same. We are infected with the "busy" virus. Even if we are not busy we say we are because it is some kind of badge of honor.

I recently took my laptop in to be fixed. It was running so slowly that I could drink a glass of water, watch a program on TV and have a phone conversation in the time it took my computer to boot up. Turns out there were 400 viruses on my laptop. The technician told me that when you go to some websites, there are viruses attached. I had no idea what he meant. Anyway, 400 viruses sounded scary, so I asked, "What do you give the computer to get rid of them?"

Poor man. I think I scared him more than the viruses scared me.

Caution: Technology and Garage Doors May Cause Isolation

My husband and I do a technology relationship sometimes. Now don't think I'm weird – well, not too weird anyway. We live in the same house, right? His office is on the first floor, mine is on the second. We text each other, we e-mail, we voice mail … and we are in the same house! Talk about substitution for relationship. It's quick and easy, but it takes away the personal interaction. We have now set aside time each day to catch up face-to-face.

You know what else blocks interaction between people? Garage doors. There was a time in my life when I did not have a garage door, so when I parked my car outside the house I spoke to my neighbors, caught up on their lives and then went inside. (I can be one of those obnoxious neighbors who likes to get personal.) But now my new house has a garage door. I drive down my driveway, punch my garage opener and then close myself into my own little world. I'm not kidding – the garage door has impacted my relationship with my neighbors.

I told my husband that I'm going to park my car outside so that I can talk to the neighbors. He thought I was as crazy as the computer technician did.

The Manifold Wisdom of God
Paul wrote an amazing letter to the church in Ephesus. He told the Ephesians that the manifold (many-faceted) wisdom of God would be made known through the church. Hey, that's us. We are the church; we are the body of Christ in the now-here. We together, connected to God and one another, will make God's wisdom known to a world that isn't always so wise. Paul encouraged his friends in Ephesus by telling them that he was praying for them:

> For this reason I kneel before the Father from whom his whole family in heaven and on earth derives His name. I pray that out of his glorious riches he may strengthen you with power through his Spirit in your

inner being so that Christ may dwell in your hearts through faith. And I pray that you, being rooted and established in love, may have power, together with all the saints, to grasp how wide and long and high and deep is the love of Christ, and to know this love that surpasses knowledge – that you may be filled to the measure of all the fullness of God. [19]

Do you get it? Paul is praying that his friends in Ephesus have deep roots in the love of God so together (connected) they might be filled with the fullness of God. He recognized that our connection to God and one another through God's love was the power that we needed to impact our world with the wisdom of God. And wouldn't you agree that the world needs wisdom?

The people in Jerusalem looked at their broken walls. They looked at their deserted city and then God spoke: *your walls are ever before me.*

He speaks down through the ages to us: *You are not forsaken; you are not isolated. Look up and see all those who stand ready to help. Get connected. Your life and the lives of your one-anothers depend on it.*

And we will reply: *give us more space to live in.*

And God will fill that space with His love and the love of others.

Notes

1. Isaiah 49: 14-18
2. Isaiah 49: 19-20
3. 2 Kings 4:13
4. Isaiah 49:16
5. Gloria Jay Evans, The Wall
6. Isaiah 11:6
7. Matthew 22:37-39
8. Andrew Murray, Abide in Christ, 13
9. John 21:15
10. John 15:1-4
11. John 15:12
12. Colossians 1:19
13. Psalm 139
14. John 13:4-11
15. David Benner, Surrender to Love, 86-87
16. Galatians 6:7-9
17. 1 Corinthians 12:12, 21
18. Wayne Jacobsen and Clay Jacobsen, Authentic Relationships, page 124
19. Ephesians 3:14-19

19 BRINGING HEAVEN TO EARTH

Jesus taught His disciples to pray: *My Kingdom come, my will be done on earth as it is in heaven.* For years, I prayed this by rote never thinking about what I was saying. One day it occurred to me that I was asking, no, I was seeking to have God's kingdom invade earth. To say that truth totally changed my view of the Lord's prayer is an understatement. From that time on, when I pray for God's will for my family, ministry, relationships, or whatever is a concern to me, I simply pray: " God, bring your kingdom into that area of my life. " It may sound peculiar, but think about it. Jesus told us to pray that way. As Mary sat at the feet of Jesus, she could not see heaven with her earthly eyes invading their space together, but she knew that the space on earth where she sat had been transformed. She was sitting at the feet of the *King* of the Kingdom and wherever He was, His kingdom was. That space of earth was invaded by heaven. Mary was able to see things and hear things from a kingdom perspective and the sound of heaven sounded quite different from the sound of earth. In that moment, Mary knew what heaven would be like someday. Do you pray the Lord's prayer by rote? Try praying it now and ask Jesus to bring heaven wherever you have a need: *My kingdom come, my will be done....*

My husband and I just returned from a trip to Idaho where we fished and hiked. I use the term 'fished' loosely regarding my participation; what actually happened was that we went on a float trip on the Salmon River, and I read a book while he fished. (The book I was reading had nothing whatsoever to do with fishing.)

We did do a lot of hiking, and it was on the hikes that I sensed the Presence of God. God is perhaps most poignantly seen in the beauty of the earth He created, and in my humble opinion, Idaho – the Saw Tooth Wilderness to be precise – is among His most precious works of art in the United States.

Two of our hikes were profound spiritual experiences for me, and each one was straight up a mountain. God spoke to me as I climbed and revealed Himself to me in ways He never had before.

The View From the Top

The objective of our first hike was to see hollyhock flowers in such profusion that it was considered a local phenomenon. We had been told that hollyhock seeds can lie dormant for as long as a hundred years and blossom only under the 'right conditions'. About halfway up the mountain we found the flowers in full bloom, and they were exquisite. After my husband snapped what seemed like hundreds of photos, we started to head back down. Suddenly a woman approached us and suggested we keep climbing. "The most magnificent flowers are at the top," she told us. "Believe me, you don't want to miss them. "

Truthfully, I was tempted to just take her word for it and not go higher. The flowers we had seen were wonderful, we got the idea – we had about a thousand pictures to prove it. But we didn't want to miss the best, right? So we huffed and puffed our way to the top. Okay, I was the one huffing and puffing. I think my husband may have been whistling.

Well, when we reached the top of the mountain the scene was absolutely breathtaking. The fact is, *breathtaking* is a cliché that falls far short as an adequate description. The hollyhocks were extraordinary – abundant and ablaze. And as I looked at them and marveled at God's dazzling creativity, He spoke to me: "If you press on with me, if you climb the tough mountains and don't settle for less, I will show you magnificent things."

Over the years my Heavenly Father has taught me that when He says this kind of thing, it is a promise. It is not a tease, it is a guarantee. And when He says *magnificent*, He means exactly that: superb, splendid, glorious.

The next day we hiked up another mountain to see Washington Lake. We had been told that it was not a difficult hike, which is not exactly true for someone like me who lives most of the year at sea level and can hardly breathe in the mountain altitudes of Idaho. Anyway, we took the hike and climbed to the lake … and were disappointed. It wasn't spectacular. But at least we had made it. My husband took a picture or two to prove we had seen Washington Lake, and we started back down the mountain.

Once again – you've probably already guessed it – someone stopped us and told us to go higher. "The view at the top is worth the climb," he said.

I was beginning to think that this was some kind of conspiracy among the crafty citizens of Idaho to get two South Carolinians to crawl on their bellies up the mountain – straight up, as it turned out. I wanted to stop.

I wanted to quit. I'm a mountain climbing wimp, I admit it. But the truth is I knew it was not our two fellow hikers calling my husband and me higher. It was God, reiterating His invitation and promise of the day before. Reiterating a promise He has made from the beginning of time. God was clearly saying, "The view at the top is worth the climb. "

Mountain climbing wimp though I am, I did not want to miss the best view of all. So we said Yes to the invitation, and on we went. Not surprisingly, I huffed and puffed all the way.

Wintley Phipps says an old Southern lady once told him: "Son, if the mountain was smooth, you couldn't climb it."[1] I was not thinking about that as I struggled straight up the mountain, but as I reflect on it now, I know that the Creator designed the mountains so that we could climb them.

When we reached the summit we were at 10,000 feet; we had climbed 1,000 feet above the lake; and I saw the most beautiful, vast, breathtaking view I have ever seen. The two sea-level South Carolinians were surrounded by majestic mountains that dropped down into a canyon called Ants Basin. As my eyes and heart filled with this magnificent jewel of God's creation, I sensed the Lord saying to me: "Tell my people to climb the mountains – the difficult testing mountains – and take in the view from the top. Then take the view from the mountaintop into the valleys of life. "

Like the mountains in Idaho, the mountains in our lives are made perfectly for God's purposes. If He had made them smooth, we couldn't climb them.

Something Better

Reflecting on the Lord's clear instruction to me, I was reminded of Caleb in the Old Testament. Remember him? Caleb was one of the 12 spies who cased out the Promised Land to see what the Israelites would have to face when they entered. Twelve spies were chosen but only two – Caleb and Joshua – were willing to press on. Ten of the spies feared the giants in the land; two feared only God.

That same courageous Caleb pressed into the Promised Land. He knew there was something better. And there came a day when the land had to be divided among the 12 tribes of Israel; each tribe would receive its inheritance in the homeland God had promised. Most of the tribes asked for the lush valleys, but Caleb asked for the mountains. He knew his inheritance was on the mountain and he refused to allow the difficulties of the land – the climb, the terrain, the rough places – to get in the way. Caleb accepted and allowed the difficulties to *be* the way.

God doesn't take us around. He leads us through.

God spoke to me on those two mountains in Idaho. He showed me how easy, how natural, it is to settle for less – in this case smaller, fewer, less impressive hollyhocks and the rather mundane sight of Lake Washington. He told me to go higher and, like Caleb, I knew the King of Creation – the One Who made the mountains climbable – had something better for me. It occurred to me that the *Something Better* that God promises always requires hard work, accepting His direction, giving in to His way and letting ours go, huffing and puffing, resisting the temptation for easy and smooth and 'isn't there another way?'

God invites us to climb the mountains and promises that when we reach the top He will show us things that will profoundly affect our lives in the valley. Our lives and the lives of those we touch.

The valley-to-mountaintop-and-back-down journey is a great illustration of what it takes and what it means to bring heavenly resources to earth. God has unlimited storehouses in heaven and He wants to open our spiritual eyes so that we can see our inheritance and then bring the Kingdom's wealth to earth.

We are not to wait to 'get to heaven'; we are to participate in bringing heaven to earth. Now.

Consider again, the Lord's Prayer – probably the most well known prayer in Christian history – the one Jesus used to teach us how to pray. [2] He taught us to pray simply and boldly for His Father's kingdom to come and His will to be done on earth as it is in heaven. [3] It is a present-tense prayer, not a future-tense prayer. Jesus gives us this unadorned and powerful request as a key to unlock heaven's inexhaustible and eternal resources and bring them to earth, here and now.

The Eternal Perspective: On Earth and In Heaven
The word *economy* comes from the Greek *oikonomia*, which combines *oikos*, meaning 'house', and *nemein*, meaning 'to manage'. *Oikonomia* means 'steward' or 'manager'. The

archaic definition of economy is 'management of household or private affairs'. Today the dictionary definition is 'careful management of available resources. '

Followers of Christ must never forget: the King's resources are unlimited and eternal. And our destiny is inextricably linked to our willingness to cooperate with God, climb to the top and see the things of Earth with and through an eternal perspective.

Recently, reading through Ecclesiastes, I noticed one line that stuck with me all week: *God has set eternity in the hearts of men.* [4] Think of that: God has put in our hearts the knowledge of, and yearning for, eternity. We are born with it. From the beginning, He created us for more than earth. He created us

for heaven and for eternal relationship with Him. He designed us to have heavenly resources as our inheritance. That is the desire of the Designer's heart.

Paul put it this way: *We fix our eyes not on what is seen but on what is unseen. For what is seen is temporary but what is unseen is eternal.* [5]

God's kingdom economy is as different from the world's economy as the view from the mountaintop is from the valley. And if God has set eternity in our hearts, then as managers of His resources we must have an eternal perspective – not a temporal one. Our Creator is not time-bound, and He does not want us to be either.

We have been given dominion over the earth [6] and it is our God-given duty to manage earth's resources –

finances, government, families, businesses, entertainment, science and medicine – with and from a faith-filled mountaintop-to-valley perspective.

We Are Called

We are called to invade our culture by being counter intuitive, counter cultural – kingdom cultural – and to influence our world with the principles of the kingdom economy, with God's eternal rule and reign. We are called to perceive with our spiritual eyes, not our physical eyes.

Take a look at this diagram, which my 11-year-old friend Olivia McGuirk drew for me, and ask yourself: *do I live by what I can see with my physical eyes or do I see with spiritual eyes?*

Mr. Eternal or Mr. Temporal?

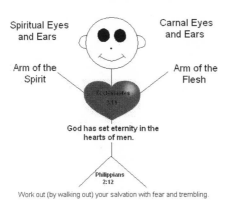

Spiritual Eyes and Ears

Carnal Eyes and Ears

Arm of the Spirit

Arm of the Flesh

Ecclesiastes 3:11

God has set eternity in the hearts of men.

Philippians 2:12

Work out (by walking out) your salvation with fear and trembling.

It is such a daunting challenge for us to answer this because we live in a culture that has fully embraced a materialistic, physical (carnal) worldview, which rules out spiritual reality as 'pie in the sky' and makes the material realm the definition of reality.

So in order to catch sight of the jewels God has for us – the unlimited wealth of His kingdom – and manage heaven's resources as He has designed us to, we must learn and practice walking in the spirit, using our spiritual eyes to see what is promised.

Exiled To Babylon

Babylon is an apt metaphor for describing the culture and world system – the valley – we live in today. Ancient Babylon was a city filled with luxury, wickedness, idolatry, excess, opulence, and greed. Sound like any culture you're familiar with? When God's people turned to idols and forgot their one true King, He used Babylon as an instrument of His judgment. He exiled the Israelites to the valley of Babylon and gave them over to the lifeless pursuits and hollow idols they had chosen.

The Spirit of God is exhorting us today to invade the culture of Babylon and help bring His kingdom and perfect will and promises to earth. Especially here and now when crises are the new reality in the valley, plaguing every earthly economy and virtually any area of society we are willing to honestly examine.

Jesus taught us to pray for this invasion of heaven over 2,000 years ago, as if it were yesterday and there was no tomorrow.

The Authority to Serve

In his book *Dreaming with God*, Bill Johnson tells us:

> Any Gospel that doesn't work in the marketplace

doesn't work. We have been given authority over this planet. It was first given to us in the commission God gave in Genesis 1 and then restored to us by Jesus after His resurrection in Matthew 28. But Kingdom authority is different than is typically understood by many believers. It is the authority to bring heaven to earth. It is the authority to serve. [7]

The authority to serve. The authority to participate in bringing our Lord's kingdom to earth. We are God's Plan A – there is no Plan B. And as a called people with a destiny we must press into God and influence our communities with His resources. We must be Calebs who insist that our inheritance is on the mountaintop, nothing less than the unlimited abundance of God's kingdom. And then take what we see from the summit – what He has promised all along – into the valley where we live.

Can you imagine the impact on our world when we as Christ followers decide to get involved in the entertainment industry, business, government? Can you imagine? Can you see it with your spiritual eyes?

Do you remember the story about the talents in Matthew 25:14-28? In Jesus' time a talent was a measure of money; today it represents our gifts and callings. *All* the servants are given gifts and a call. The servant with five talents doubled his investment; the servant with two did the same. The servant with one buried it. He did not use his God-given gifts, did not climb to the top and catch the view, did not fulfill his calling.

Remember the hollyhocks in Idaho? They bloom

prolifically given the right conditions – if the forest has been burned and just the right amount of rain falls. The mountaintop my husband and I climbed to was filled with hollyhocks because all the competition had been burned around it. The truth is if we do not use the gifts God has given us to advance His kingdom on earth – money, time, talents, imagination, fire, rainfall, powerful prayers – He will allow the circumstances of our lives to burn out any competition.

As stewards of the earth, we must seek eternal seeds to be buried in our lives and used for Kingdom purposes. We are Plan A: God wants spirit-led followers of His one and only Son to bring His kingdom's influence to bear on our governments, families, businesses, and financial institutions.

And we are called not just to catch a glimpse of heaven's resources and promises, but to bring them back to the valley. We are called to be expert witnesses about the view from the top of the mountain. We are called to boldly, authentically, and lovingly participate in the manifestation of heaven on earth. So that His kingdom comes and His will is done, here and now.

We are called to 'bring up there down here'.

But the truth is we cannot give what we do not possess ourselves. We can't help bring heaven to earth if we haven't climbed the mountain and claimed the promises.

Practical Applications of Kingdom Economy Principles

So … nice ideas – yes, by all means let's bring heaven to

earth, count us in. But how? How do we do this? How
in God's name do we practically sharpen our spiritual
eyes and see the view from the mountaintop, the view of
heaven's resources and the King's promises? How do we
get our instructions from God?

Consider these few practical ways we can draw near to
God and allow Him to invade our lives in the Now Here;
a few steps we can take to allow God to show us the
unseen:

- Study God's Word: pay attention to what "pings"
  at your heart. I take a notepad and write down
  what I am hearing as instructions from God
- Pray that the Lord will use the time, treasure, and
  talents He has given you
- Discern the talents God has given to the people
  you know, those in the community around you,
  and exhort them to join you in bold, authentic
  and loving participation in God's plan
- Ask God to show you what is in heaven by
  praying His will to earth as it is in heaven; keep
  these basics in mind:
  - o The world belongs to God: *the earth is the
    Lord's and everything in it* [8]
  - o We have been given dominion over the
    world: Genesis 1:26-28 and Psalm 8:6
  - o Our resources are eternal, stored in heavenly
    storehouses

Jesus tells us that His sheep hear His voice. [9]   To the
degree that we stay close to our shepherd and follow Him
and are obedient when He gives us His gentle
instructions, we will not only find our way up the

381

mountain, we will have the strength required to return confidently to the valley. He will never leave us. If we stray from the path, He will bring us back.

Our Heavenly Father is looking for spirit-filled Christians who will follow the Shepherd up to the mountaintop and take news of the view back down into the valley. He wants us to be people who are willing to follow and obey the Shepherd so that we can make a difference in the world in the most practical ways: boldly and authentically sharing the love of God and the promises and principles of His eternal Kingdom economy.

The King's promises are here today and gone never. He promises to show us how to use our talents, treasures, and time, and He will teach us how to access His resources in heaven through prayer, faith and obedience to His Word.

Step by step we climb closer to Him and open ourselves to Him and make ourselves available for His Spirit to work through us.

Notes

1.   Wintley Phipps is president of the U. S. Dream Academy, a ministry for children of prisoners. Mr. Phipps is a wonderful singer who offers an excellent history of Amazing Grace and
some revelatory insights on the composition of negro spirituals; see http://www. youtube. com/watch?v=DMF_24cQqT0
2.   Matthew 6: 5-13
3.   ...your kingdom come, your will be done on earth as it is in heaven: Matthew 6:10
4 Ecclesiastes 3:11
5. 2 Cor. 4:18
6. Genesis 1:26-28
7. Bill Johnson, Dreaming With God, 87
8. Psalm 24:1
9. John 10:4

20 STAYING CONTENT

Sometimes God places us in circumstances that are less than satisfactory. That is putting it mildly. Sometimes we feel stuck in places that are simply miserable. We hardly know anything about Mary and the circumstance of her life. We have discussed the various scenarios that might have been going on in her life but we don't really know. I feel sure however that she was a normal young girl discontented with certain things in life. Depending on her age, she could have been obsessed with her looks, her figure, or her friendships. Most women are so hard on themselves. Perhaps Mary was rejected by her friends when she started hanging out with Jesus. They probably thought she was peculiar or even worse, if they were strict Jews, they could have been shocked that she would bring a would-be-Messiah into her home. So she, like us, came to Jesus with her basket of woes---the places where she was discontent and wondered why she had put herself in this position. She could have chosen to be like the other girls, not offended anyone and been content. Or would she have been? I don't think so and here is why. When we are confronted with the One who can bring us true contentment and yet chose to go in the other direction, we will always be restless. Why? Because our hearts are bound to be restless until we find our rest in Him. We were created for Him and in Him only are we able to find true contentment.

Do you ever find yourself asking these questions: "Why doesn't God deliver me out of these miserable circumstances? Why do I have to stay in this depressing job?

Why does God put us in these impossible places, with difficult people?"

Or Does He?
Do you find yourself going round and round with questions when you are faced with difficult circumstances? Do you sometimes wonder if the familiar "fight or flight" mechanism describes your only choices? Do you sometimes think everything would be better if you were *anywhere but here*, if you were in any situation but the one you're in?

Our lives can be very tough when we are faced with the grave difficulty of blooming where we are planted. Let's face it: sometimes we cannot fight or fly away because neither strategy will work. Sometimes we need to just get a grip and bear it. Right?

Is it possible to bloom in the desert?

As we make space for God, He will enable us to do things we never dreamed of. The King of all things will show us how to not just endure tough times, but – hallelujah! – how to bloom in the most difficult of times. No kidding: if we persevere and do things *God's* way, God will show up and amaze us. Astound us. Bloom us!

You Be Jesus
I well remember as a child being told to do to others what I would want done to me. But as a typical child I just wanted to get even with my siblings for what they did to me, which was rarely what I wanted done to me, and rarely pleasant. I wasn't content to adhere to Jesus' so-

called Golden Rule.

Sometimes as children – and even (and especially) as adults – we simply do not want to bloom where God has planted us. We want a different family, a different job, a different home. We want a different set of circumstances altogether. Most of the time we can't believe that any God with half a brain could have planted us here in the first place! Right? Ever felt like that?

A little boy put it very succinctly: *Dear God: Did you really mean "do unto others as they do unto you"?* Because if you did, then I'm going to get my brother good! Well, that's not exactly what Jesus told us, but….

Or there's the familiar tale of the mother who was preparing pancakes for her sons – Kevin, 5, and Ryan, 3. When the boys began to argue over who should get the first pancake, their mom saw the opportunity for a moral lesson. She told her sons, "If Jesus were here, He would say, 'Let my brother have the first pancake, I can wait'." Kevin turned to his younger brother and said, "Ryan, you be Jesus. "

What about you? Are you discontent with yourself, your situation*, your life as you know it?* How about with the people who are in your life – your family, friends, co-workers? Are you dissatisfied with your job?

The last thing we want to be is a flower in the midst of what we consider a desert! But remember: God sent His Son to save us; the heavenly Father sent Jesus to do for us what we could never do for ourselves – and Jesus of Nazareth had to bloom in a desert. Remember, too, that

He told us to do the same.

Jesus told us to trust Him no matter where we find ourselves – desert or oasis or somewhere in between – because He has a perfect plan and it is for our good.

Do you believe that God has planted you in a certain family, or a particular job, or a specific neighborhood or community so that you can make a difference to those He has brought into your life, and so that they can make a difference in your life? Some of you may not want to consider these possibilities. Some of you might have been thinking the flight option was looking pretty attractive.

Some of us spend way too much time fighting the very people, situations and opportunities God has ordained.

God Set You Apart
God told Jeremiah: *Before I formed you in the womb I knew you; before you were born, I set you apart....*[1] Grab the reality of this: God knew you before you were you. He knew your name and He knew your destiny.

He had, and has, a master plan for your life. The people He puts close to you in your family, job, and community have needs that only you can fill with the leading of the Holy Spirit.

God sets the agenda, and He does not make mistakes. Are you ready to meet the challenges that come with reaching out to the people and into situations He has placed in your life?

So … how do we recognize the needs and bloom where we are planted?

Producing Fruit

In John's gospel, Jesus tells us:

> I am the vine and my Father is the gardener. He cuts off every branch in me that bears no fruit, while every branch that does bear fruit he prunes so that it will be even more fruitful. [2]

Stop right there. I am not interested in cutting off stuff that I need to hold on to. Is Jesus saying that if I am discontent, grumbling, not really interested in being changed – but more interested in changing others – I may be cut off from Him? Is He telling me that if I don't conform to His image (which means bear fruit) His Father will cut me off, disconnect me from Jesus?

And is He saying that just when I think I am blooming like crazy and everyone notices my beautiful garden I need to be pruned? Is this what He's telling us?

I think so. You see, God is interested in our bearing fruit. He wants us to look like His Son. We are the branches, Jesus is the vine, and no branch can bear fruit by itself. It must remain in the vine. [3] So where does that leave us when we are discontent, dissatisfied, grumbling, focused inward instead of on the vine?

> I am the vine and you are the branches. If a man remains in me and I in him, he will bear much fruit; apart from me you can do nothing. [4]

Now it's been said. That is clear, isn't it? No need to fight or fly: the Word is out and cannot be denied.

We are worthless without the vine; you and I cannot expect to bear fruit without Him; and the fruit we do produce needs to be pruned so that even more fruit can be made.

The Gardener ... Everywhere, Including the Desert

God is the gardener: He plants you somewhere and then He removes the dead life and prunes the fruit-bearing life in order that your life will have greater impact in the place He has put you. Throughout our lives, that place is going to be the desert every now and then. Count on it. And count on the Gardener to be there too – pruning, perfecting and producing.

Some Thrive, Others Don't

Why do some flowers thrive and some do not? Soil, light, fertilizer, and constant loving care are all necessary for healthy flowers and fruit. And that constant care must include guarding against pests, foragers and disease. All these factors impact the flower that is planted and the fruit that is produced.

The same is true of us. We started in the perfect Garden, and God has been growing us ever since. In order to thrive, we need to make more space for Him in our hearts; and we need to ask the constant Gardener to till the soil, to fertilize with His Word, and to guard our hearts against pests and disease.

Depending on the Gardener

The Gardener plants you in certain places, with certain people, in certain times, and He always has The Plan in mind. Your destiny is an integral part of His plan, and

He never, ever, forgets the part He has chosen you for.
Never.

We are dependent on the vine that nourishes us. This is
the key: dependence on the vine, dependence on Jesus.
The trouble comes when we are planted somewhere we
decide don't want to be, or when we think we can do
things our way. Then comes the blossom end rot.

Blossom End Rot: Tomatoes, Jobs, and Attitude Adjustments

This past summer my son planted a beautiful garden.
Everything came up quickly and he invested time in
caring for the garden. Only problem was that the
tomatoes would bloom and then the blooms would rot
before they produced fruit. Previous to the planting, his
father had warned him that this same thing had happened
the year before, and that the nursery professionals told us
that it might help to move the garden elsewhere. There
was a strong indication that whatever was in the soil
would remain in the next planting season. Obviously
something in the soil was causing the tomatoes to rot
before they could produce fruit.

God once planted me in a job that at the time I was very
thankful for. That is, until I realized that I was not
equipped to handle the administrative tasks I was
assigned. My gifts most definitely lie elsewhere, and I
learned this lesson the hard way. I needed the paycheck
but what I needed even more was an attitude adjustment.

I complained daily about my job. One day, reading my
Bible and praying, I took my problem to the Lord. I told
Him I wanted another job. I may have gone on about it,

detailing all the issues and my inability to do what was asked of me. Well, God's answer was quick and clear:

My grace is sufficient for you, for my power is made perfect in weakness.[5]

Surely He didn't mean that I needed to stay in the job ... right? I mean really – I'm supposed to continue doing what I'm no good at (and do not enjoy) because His power would be complete in my place of misery?

Uh, yes – that's exactly what God meant.

So ... I stayed. And guess what? No kidding: He perfected. I agreed to be obedient; I became the branch to the Vine, and the Gardener worked in me. I bloomed where I was planted.

Not that I wanted to. That was His idea. But it worked – as it always does when we obediently say Yes – and I was changed for the better. I grew ... and I produced fruit.

Not My Choice

God often calls us to do things that we would never choose to do. Michael Brown says that how we respond reveals how open to God's Presence we really are. He underscores his point with a story from the life of St. Francis:

One of the many legends surrounding the life of St. Francis of Assisi illustrates how persons of faith are asked to do that which we would not ourselves have chosen. Francis, it is told, was terrified of leprosy, and understandably so. Thus he avoided lepers intentionally and consistently. One day while riding his horse through the country, he rounded a curve and came upon a ragged leper standing in the roadway. The man was so shabby and pitiable that somehow Francis' fear gave way to sympathy. His sympathy gave way to epiphany. He saw Jesus in the sufferer. Suddenly he remembered the words of Christ. "In as much as you have done so unto the least of these, my brothers and sisters, you have done so likewise unto me. " We often fear where God plants us, but how we respond to where God calls us determines how open we are to His Presence. [6]

Some Secrets to Blooming

There are many people in the Bible who knew the secret to blooming where God planted them. Abraham is an excellent example. He shows us that one of the keys to blooming involves trust. Abraham had quite a journey, and God continued to test him by pruning him. As is true of all of us – no one is immune – Abraham failed some tests and passed others. God told Abraham to leave his comfortable home, the country of his birth and upbringing, and to go to an unknown place. Then God told him that he would be the Father of many nations. What the heck did that mean? Abraham didn't have any more of a clue about it than you or I would have had in the same situation. But he went where God told him to go.

Going and Doing As We Are Told
Abraham

Finally, in the biggest test of all, God told Abraham to sacrifice his son, Isaac. God said, "Kill your son on an altar as a sacrifice to me." I am not even going to ask you if you can imagine this. Now the crazy thing is that Isaac was the son from whom the nations (that God had promised Abraham) would come – and Abraham knew very well that God had promised this. But he went where God told him to go, and he did what God told him to do: he made a three-day journey to the mountain, took his son up to the top, and prepared to kill Isaac on a stone altar.

Would you call that *trust? Fanaticism? Idiocy?* Call it what we will – it doesn't much matter – the point is that Abraham did exactly as he was told, and his son was spared. And an entire nation – descendants as numerous as the stars in the sky and as the sand on the seashore[7] – came from Isaac.

It is not easy when God asks so much of you. A friend of mine has said more than once *that what God asks of us is almost always simple, almost never easy.* Abraham stayed on course when flight in the opposite direction would have at least seemed to be the easier option. And in the end, the writer of Hebrews tells us that Abraham was faithful because he was fully persuaded that God was faithful and would keep His word.

That's really the first secret to blooming wherever God has planted you: *trust.*

Moses
Moses is another fine example of blooming in the desert. The Gardener first planted Moses in Egypt; then when he was 40 years old, Moses was transplanted to the desert, where he spent 40 years; then one otherwise ordinary day (when Moses was approximately 80 years old), God caught Moses' attention in a very unique way, and the pruning and blooming process began in earnest. Moses

had the shock of his life (so far) when he saw a bush that was on fire but not burning up. Flames engulfed the bush but did not consume it. Hmmm.

If that wasn't enough, God then spoke directly to Moses from the blazing bush and told him to lead His people out of Egypt. Which he finally did … and then wandered with a bunch of complaining Israelites in the desert for another 40 years. When Moses died at 120 years of age, he still had not entered the promised land.

If you found yourself in Moses' situation, would you run? No sense fighting a burning bush, but how about the old flight option? I admit I've never found myself in exactly the same situation as Moses did with the burning bush, but, still, I am pretty sure I would have chosen flight.

And yet Moses did not run. Maybe after you've spent 40 years on the backside of nowhere being a shepherd, you're naturally open to anything that promises some excitement. Maybe when a burning bush gives you some clear instructions, you tend to pay more attention than usual.

But all Moses said was, "Who am I to go to Pharaoh?"

So … I think the second secret to blooming where God plants you is humble obedience, which in this example specifically means not automatically making the natural human assumption that you can do it (whatever *it* is) without God. Who could? When relationships get messy and you want out, better not to look for (or fabricate) an opt-out clause; better to trust and obey and see what the burning bush can do.

More Keys
Paul

Paul gives us another key to blooming in his letter to the Philippians:

> I have learned to be content whatever the circumstances. I know what it is to be in need, and I know what it is to have plenty. I have learned the secret of being content in any and every situation, whether well fed or hungry, whether living in plenty or in want. I can do everything through him who gives me strength. [8]

He knew the secret of being content, but how did Paul learn this one? And how did it enable him to bloom where he was planted?

He knew the secret of dependency on God. He knew that all his resources came from God and not from himself. He came to understand and trust that it was God who had made him take the road to Damascus that day; it was his destiny. And Paul grew in his trust and he followed his destiny from that day forward, acknowledging the road was hard and knowing that Jesus would work all things out for good.

Paul knew that Jesus, the One whom He had met on the road to Damascus, would give him the strength and whatever else he required to bloom where he was planted. Paul planted churches, and they bloomed where they were planted because Paul bloomed where he was planted.

Trust, dependency on God, and strength from God. Have you made space in your life for these? Or are you like so many of us who refuse to trust because they want to be in control?

I am coming to understand that I cannot be in control of the planting or the blooming. Instead, I am seeing again and again that *I can do all things through him who gives me strength.*

Once Paul figured that out, he was content. Then and only then.

Jesus

Paul describes Jesus to give us another key to blooming where we are planted:

> Who being in very nature God, did not consider equality with God something to be grasped, but made himself nothing, taking the very nature of a servant being made in human likeness And being found in appearance as a man, he humbled himself and became obedient to death – even death on the cross![9]

The Vine learned that the key to blooming is willingness to die. Denying self in full obedience to the Gardener. Who wants to do that? But wrapped within that self-denial, coated in humility, we find ourselves again – a new life of contentment no matter what the world and the present situation dish out.

Think about it: difficult marriage, relationship struggles, financial stress, health issues, job struggle, the aging process. Can contentment be found?

More Secrets to Bearing Fruit

Love is the strongest force on earth -- it cannot be quenched or defeated or undone. [10]   Love covers a multitude of sins,[11] and it can break through even the most hardened heart to produce healthy seeds of life.

When Jesus looks out over the vineyard and points to the vine and the branches and explains that He is the vine and we are the branches, He is teaching about love:

> As the Father has loved me, so have I loved you. Now remain in my love. If you obey my commands, you will remain in my love, just as I have obeyed my Father's commands and remain in his love. I have told you this so that your joy may be complete. My command is this: Love each other as I have loved you. Greater love has no one than this, that he lay down his life for his friends. [12]

Love is one of the secrets to blooming in the desert. It's the biggest and best of them all. We are to love big, love deeply, love sacrificially. It is impossible to be content if you refuse to love others. We cannot be content without loving and being loved. Love is a command because it covers sins; and it breaks through discontentment, discouragement and anything else that causes us to have bloom rot.

Love is the most powerful force for change on the earth. Love is the most powerful force in the universe. And Jesus demonstrated that power on the cross. His love held Him there and His love took the force of discontentment and replaced it with a deep joy – a joy that only obedience can bring.

So … Maybe a Little Pruning

So maybe it's time to cut off any dead branches that are causing discontent; branches that are not directly connected to the vine and are not producing fruit. The Gardener knows exactly which branches need to go.

Maybe you have lived so long in a fruitless desert you think this is just your lot in life. But that isn't so. The Gardener wants to cut away anything that keeps you from thriving. He made you to thrive, and He wants to till the soil of your heart and prepare for new growth.

What needs to be cut away? Is there malice, envy, hypocrisy, or unbelief that keeps you from blooming? Lies? The comparison trap?

What about the martyr syndrome? You know that one: the one that says you must endure at all costs, you must just bear up under the stress and strain. Any of that at work in your life right now?

What needs to be cut away and thrown into the fire?
> If anyone does not remain in me, he is like a branch that is thrown away and withers; such branches are picked up, thrown into the fire and burned.[13]

How about dead branches of perfectionism, people-pleasing, hurt, rejection, shame?

Blooming From a Place of Rest

God's Word says that we can do all things through Christ who strengthens us. Jesus does not tell us that we can do all things if we knock ourselves out trying, working, striving. Blooming where you are planted involves working from a place for rest and trust in Him. [14] The only Word I know that says we are to strive is the one that tells us to strive to enter God's rest. The context is that if anyone enters God's rest He must rest from His own works just as God did:

> For if Joshua had given them rest God would not have spoken later about another day There remains, then a Sabbath rest for the people of God; for anyone who enters God's rest also rests from his own work, just as God did from his. Let us, therefore, make every effort to enter that rest so that no one will fall by following their example of disobedience. [15]

Blooming in a desert – being in a place where you do not wish to be and yet flourishing – requires entering the rest of God, a place of deep peace that obedience to God brings. All the energy we spend in fighting our circumstances does not bring rest; only obedience brings it. And when we are content in knowing that God is in control. Rest comes when we stand on Jesus' promise that His *yoke is easy and His burden is light.* [16]

Summing Up: Truths About Blooming

1. Believe that God is who He says He is; that He is a faithful Gardener who places you in just the right place, with just the right people
2. Trust that your heavenly Father knows best, and allow Him to be the Gardener, to remove branches that are not fruitful – works of the flesh, lies we believe, dead works, dead places in our lives
3. Allow Him to prune the fruit-producing branches
4. Surrender in obedience knowing that it is the joy

of obedience which produces fruit
5.   Receive God's love and give His love away,
allowing Christ to live His life in you. That
requires dying to self and praying "Christ, You
must increase, and I must decrease." In a world
filled with the philosophy that it is all about you
(and me), the Gardener requires us to deny
ourselves and pick up the cross.

Lingering Questions

What if you are in an abusive marriage – must you stay?
Should you assume God put you there, so you must stick
it out hoping to bear fruit some day?

What if your job is so stressful, it's harmful to your health
and your family members?

What if a relationship has died and all your efforts to
resurrect it have failed?
Jesus told us:
> … seek first his kingdom and his righteousness and
> all these things will be given to you as well.
> Therefore do not worry about tomorrow, for
> tomorrow will worry about itself. Each day has
> enough trouble of its own. [17]

The Lord of Love, forgiveness and grace wanted to make
sure that we understood that whatever is going on in our
lives – whatever is going on – we must seek Him first. He
will guide us; He will make our paths straight. He will
answer the questions that stop us in our tracks and keep
us from blooming. If we seek His kingdom first, every
single thing we need to live an abundant life will be
added.

Where should I be planted? Am I in the right place? Am I doing the right thing? Do I need to make a change?

He will get you on track. He will deliver you from past mistakes. Seek Him, lean into Him, ask Him. Allow Him to till the soil of your heart. He promises to plant you in soil that is fertile and rich; He will not abandon you in your places of unrest if He wants you to stay.

When you need Him to be your Deliverer, He will be. He is now, and He always has been.

Believe, trust, obey, love … and bloom where you are planted!

Notes

1. Jeremiah 1:5
2. John 15:1-2
3. John 15:4
4. John 15:5
5. 2 Corinthians 12:4
6. Michael Brown, Bottom Line Beliefs, 33
7. Genesis 22:17
8. Philippians 4:10-13
9. Philippians 2:6-8
10. Song of Solomon 8:7
11. I Peter 4:8
12. John 15:9-13
13. John 15:6
14. Philippians 4:13
15. Hebrews 4:8-11
16. Matthew 11:30
17. Matthew 6:33-34

21 A PLACE OF AUTHORITY

We each have a place of influence. Maybe you have not given it much thought. But someone is following you. It is a sobering thought. It may be your children, your spouse or a friend, but you can be sure we are all leaders leading someone. The question we need to be asking ourselves is this: "Am I demonstrating and using the authority that God has given me to be a Godly influence in those who are watching and following me?" Mary was a courageous woman who chose to be a friend of Jesus. What Mary may not have known is that she had people watching her. Her lavish devotion towards Christ and her transformation were evident to many. After she sat at the feet of Jesus, she was no longer the same person; she seemed to walk in such authority. The people of Jesus' day questioned how He walked in power and authority. They did not get it. He was the Messiah. He was *The Authority*. This fact did not fit into their God box (which by the way was very small). They could not think outside the box to consider that the Messiah was in their midst. I suppose there were people who knew something was different about Mary after she had been with Jesus, but they could not get out of their box either. They could not imagine that anyone, let alone a woman could walk in power and authority of God. That is the problem with the church today. We have forgotten or we never believed that we have the authority of Christ. But here is something to think about it. If Jesus lives in us, then His authority does too.

Does the church today have less authority than the church that Peter and Paul and the first Christians began to build in the first century? Does today's church – the living body of Christ here on Earth – have any authority at all?

Are the miracles and astonishing supernatural movements of the Holy Spirit that are routine in Luke's Book of Acts simply interesting phenomena or legends from the distant past?

Do you believe – really believe – that God can and will fight His children's battles today, like He did back-then? If you do, are you willing to make space for God to fight your battles?

The Role of The Redeemed

The role of the redeemed – that is, we sinners bought-and-paid-for by Jesus, we Christians – is to joyfully live and breathe and proclaim the good news of Jesus' gospel to those He brings into our lives and life stories; and to be joyfully proactive in our response to the assaults on the advancement of the kingdom of God in our personal lives and the world in which we find ourselves. We are called by the King of the Universe to devise and implement strategies that penetrate and weaken the influence of evil. We are God's Plan A, and there is no Plan B.

Satan wants to divert people from Christianity. He is bent on the destruction of Christ's Kingdom. It sounds crazy doesn't it? Really, at best, the idea of a war raging between the forces of good and evil sounds made-up –

right? I know it does – I know it seems crazy, and not just a little fantastic. I am also certain that Satan is counting on that. Satan is counting on this whole War-Between-Good- and-Evil-For-Our-Souls thing sounding radical – even loony – to all human beings, all the people God loves and wants deep relationship with, people like you and I.

Who But A Fool?
The enemy will do his very best to make this war-for-the-universe appear silly or stupid or divisive – the lurid creation of a dangerous lunatic fringe.

Who but a fool would believe that we are now – and always have been – in a war between God and the enemy of God? Who but a fool would think that those who believe in God and His One and Only Son must strap on our armor and go to battle?

And yet it is the truth: the war for the minds, bodies, lives and souls of the human race is raging all around us, and we fools for Christ have to recognize it and put on the armor the Captain has fashioned for us and show up on the battlefield. If not us, who? If not now, when? If not Plan A, which plan?

Great News, Straight From the Top
The great news we fools for Christ can rely on is that this war we are in has already been won. God saw the war coming before time began, and He secured the final victory before you and I breathed our first breaths. He made us to play integral parts in this incredible drama; He made us to joyfully and proactively share the great news with anyone and everyone He brings into our lives. We

were created not only to recognize the war raging around us, and to expect the present battles, but also to ensure that His victory is proclaimed, here and now.

We are expected to put on the armor, show up ready for battle, and follow the Captain wherever He leads.

Making History: Winning A War Already Won

Do you remember your World War II history? On June 6, 1944 ("D-Day") the Allied Army landed on the beaches at Normandy, France had launched the largest amphibious invasion in the history of the world. The battles over the next several weeks were incredibly dangerous and bloody – Allied casualties alone were estimated at 10,000 – but the invasion was successful. For all intents and purposes, the war in Europe was won as a result of the D-Day invasion, but the fighting continued until May 8, 1945; VE Day was not declared until almost a year after D-Day.

So it is for us Christians and this war in which we find ourselves, this 'war to end all wars'. Jesus Christ died on the cross over 2,000 years ago, and with His last breath on the cross and His resurrection from the grave three days later, He declared D-Day. He conquered death once and for all, and He conquered the enemy: victory was (and is) His. But still we time-bound believers are at war; still we Christ followers fight the enemy who continues to prowl around seeking whomever he can devour.

The Great News Continues

Now here is more great news: we have authority over the enemy. It is worth repeating: you and I and anyone who believes Jesus is who He says He is and has done all He's said He's done – we who believe God is as good as His Word – we have authority over Satan! We were made to defeat him.

Jesus' victory on the cross ensures believers of the power and authority to put the devil in his place. In his gospel, John states it this way:

He that is in you is greater than he that is in the world. [1]

Our King and Captain is greater than the enemy who prowls around. We may give Satan a foothold for a little while, but when we come back to our senses we have the authority to send him flying. John Eldredge makes it even clearer:

The thief comes only to steal and kill and destroy; I have come that they may have life to the full. [2] Have you ever wondered why Jesus married those two statements? Did you even know he spoke them at the same time? I mean, he says them in one breath. And he had his reasons. By all means, God intends life for you. But right now that life is opposed. It doesn't just roll in on a tray. There is a thief. He comes to steal and destroy. In other words, yes, the offer is life, but you're going to have to fight for it because there is an Enemy in your life with a different agenda. [3]

The enemy wants you to be scared, to cower; he wants you to feel powerless; he doesn't want you to learn about the authority you have in Christ. He would like nothing more than to defeat you anytime he wants. And he will do everything he can to keep you from learning the truth about the authority you have over him.

Making Space for His Authority

Does this frighten you? Don't be scared. Remember, remember, remember: your King loves you and is with you "to the very end of the age"[4]; He will never abandon you; and He is greater than the enemy – so much greater!

Let's make space for God to use the authority He has given us as Christ followers. Let's learn how to take a stand against the enemy's onslaughts, against the spiritual warfare leveled at us as individuals and the church community, the Body of Christ. Some battles we face are battles of the flesh (the unspiritual person); some are battles caused by the influences of the world; and some are sent from the devil and his cohorts.

So what do we make of all of this? Think about the authority a policeman has. If you run a stoplight or rob a store or are in a traffic accident, the policeman has the authority to give you a ticket or arrest you and take you to jail or write up an accident report. We have written laws and granted this authority. The value of this authority rests in the power behind the authority, in this case the elected lawmakers, the government.

In *The Believer's Guide to Spiritual Warfare*, Thomas White quotes Jesus in order to remind us of the heavy responsibility we have as leaders: "As you sent me into the world, I have sent them into the world. "[5] White says:

> Spiritual authority is to be exercised in efforts to personally overcome evil, to walk in truth, and to help set others free from sin and Satan. [6]

We are called to be in the world and not of it, to exercise

the authority Jesus clearly has given us, and to confront everyday battles in our lives from our position in Christ.

Seated in Heavenly Places

In his letter to the church in Ephesus, Paul instructs the believers in their walk with Christ and explains how to confront the battles they face:

> ... God raised us up with Christ and seated us with him in the heavenly realms ... in order that in the coming ages he might show the incomparable riches of his grace expressed in his kindness to us in Jesus Christ. [7]

Earlier in the same letter, Paul prayed that the spiritual eyes of the Ephesians would be open to know the hope to which they were called and to know the power that they have to fulfill their call in Christ. [8] Later he reminds them to live a life worthy of their call, walking in holiness and standing against the schemes of the evil one.

In essence Paul is telling them, and subsequently all of us believers through the ages, that there are four reasons we are able to effectively confront the battles of life with our position and power in Christ:

- We are seated in heavenly places
- The same Holy Spirit power that raised Jesus from the dead is available to us
- Walking in holiness empowers us with the authority Christ gives us
- We can proactively stand against the schemes of the enemy

Have you ever meditated on the fact that you are seated in heavenly places? Although you are physically here, as a believer you are spiritually seated with Christ, and He sits at the right hand of the Father. Stop for a moment and think about that. Let that sink in. Isn't it absolutely amazing? If we can grasp that truth, if we can know it deep-down without a doubt, doesn't it have to radically change the way we face the interruptions and trials and struggles life throws in our paths?

When I find myself in the heat of some battle or other, I try to envision myself seated with Christ – the King of Kings sitting next to me – having His mind, drawing from His knowledge and wisdom.

Resurrected Power

We have the same power available to us that raised Christ from the dead:

> I pray that the eyes of your heart may be enlightened in order that you may know the hope to which he has called you, the riches of his glorious inheritance in the saints and his incomparably great power for us who believe. (emphasis mine) That power is like the working of his mighty strength which he exerted in Christ when he raised him from the dead and seated him in the heavenly realms.... [9]

Stop and take this in. The same power that raised Christ from the dead is available to us who believe. How could anyone not want to believe? We all need power to live our lives, don't we?

Walking in Holiness: Where The Rubber Meets The Road

How do we make room for God's authority and power? How can we expect to call on that power and authority in our daily lives? Paul makes it crystal clear in the fourth chapter of Ephesians. He has just told the new Christians at Ephesus that they have position and power in Christ Jesus, and now comes the hard part. Paul says that the authority we have is dependent on how we live our lives:

> As a prisoner for the Lord, then, I urge you to live a life worthy of the calling you have received. Be completely humble and gentle, be patient, bearing with one another in love. [10]

It is one thing to have power and position, and it is quite another to have to be humble and patient. It is a tall order for some of us, isn't it? Paul doesn't let us off the hook. He tells the Ephesians that it is time to quit acting like infants tossed back and forth by false teachings; it is time to speak the truth in love and to grow up. Now he's done it. He has invaded our personal lives and is pressing on every nerve.

We must live lives worthy of the call. In order to bring God's power and authority to bear, we must live out Jesus' humility and gentleness and patience and love. We must extend to others the same grace that the King of Kings has extended time and again to us. We must walk in holiness in the here-and-now, in the midst of our less-than-perfect lives, in the midst of the war raging all around us. This is where the rubber meets the road.

Walking The Talk

My grown-up married daughter was going through some trials this week. Sage that I am, I instructed her in the strategies of spiritual battle. I told her to remember her position (seated with Christ) and her power (available through the resurrection), but I saw that it was time to

411

speak the truth in love. It was not easy for me to tell this daughter I love so much that her walk did not match her talk. That is what I felt I must do, though. I told her that if she wanted authority over the junk going on in her life she needed to walk in a manner worthy of her calling in Christ.

I did pretty well. My daughter wasn't too pleased. But in the end she took the high road; in the end, she took the highway of holiness.

This is where we often detour or crash in our battles. We want the power and the position that Christ gives us, but we do not want to make the sacrifice; we are not so excited about putting off the old self and putting on the character of Jesus. [11] Easier said than done. But that is exactly what we must do in order to claim the King's promises of power and authority.

Ready To Stand

Paul makes it clear that after we recognize and accept that we are seated with Christ we can draw from His power and walk in holiness. Notice that we are *seated*, which means it is *His* effort that wins the battles, not ours. Now, finally, we are ready to stand – but only in His power, not ours:

> Finally, be strong in the Lord and in his mighty power. Put on the full armor of God so that you can take your stand against the devil's schemes. [12]

Time to strap on our armor and stand. But what exactly does that mean? Do you know about King Jehoshaphat?

Jehoshaphat's Recipe for Victory

The Moabites, Ammonites and Meunites joined to make war on Jehoshaphat, king of Judah. When Jehoshaphat was told that a vast army was coming against him from Edom, the first thing he did was seek God and proclaim a fast. Jehoshaphat's Plan A was to be sure that this was God's battle to fight and to get his strategy from the Captain.

Jehoshaphat stood in the courtyard of the temple, God's house, and spoke to God. He recalled all the faithful acts that the Lord had done for the people of Judah, and he recounted them for God and thanked Him for everything. And as he remembered how wonderful God was, and is, Jehoshaphat's faith grew. He reminded himself and openly admitted to God that he had no power apart from God to face this enemy army. And finally Jehoshaphat declared that his eyes would be on God alone.

This is a powerful example of fighting battles God's way. God wants to fight for us, and Jehoshaphat shows us how you and I can call on the Eternal King to do just that.

After Jehoshaphat's fast and prayer time, acknowledging God's past victories and asking Him to lead as only He could against the enemy army, Zechariah, a Levite, prophesied:

> Listen, King Jehoshaphat and all who live in Judah and Jerusalem! This is what the Lord says to you: "Do not be afraid or discouraged because of this vast army. For the battle is not yours but God's. "[13]

When the King and the people of Judah put their trust in God to do battle for them, their enemies were defeated. That time and every time.

King Jehoshaphat never met Paul but both men understood that power, position, humility (the way we walk) and standing against the enemy (trusting God to do battle) were the only ways that would ensure that their enemies would be defeated.

God has given us three things to ensure victory:
- His name
- His power
- His authority

His Name (Above All Names)
Did you know that the name of God is powerful? There are many descriptions or names of God in the Old Testament. For example, *Jehovah Jireh* means He is our provider; *Jehovah Shalom*, our Peace; *Jehovah Rohi*, our Shepherd; Jehovah Raphe, our Healer. The list goes on. Eskimos have many different words for snow because they see lots of different kinds of snow – nuances of snow. God's people have many different names for Him because through the ages we have seen Him manifest Himself – His characteristics, His attributes, His unbroken promises – in many ways. Every name of God reveals another facet of His character and goodness towards us. Those who know His name(s) will trust Him and be protected:

> The Lord is a refuge for the oppressed, a stronghold in times of trouble. Those who know your name will trust in you, for you, Lord, have never forsaken those who seek you. [14]

414

We hide under the shadow of the Almighty[15] and His
name is a strong tower of refuge. We all have been given
a name. Some of us like our names. I never liked my
name until I discovered that it meant *full of grace*. I liked
that. I actually hid under the shadow of my name
knowing that I was under God's grace: undeserved,
unmerited favor.

We live under the shadow of the name of our Savior
Jesus Christ. Salvation is found in no one else. [16]

I am telling you all this because you and I represent God's
name; it is God's name we proclaim; it is God's name that
invokes the power of God and penetrates the darkness
that threatens to overtake us. His name is powerful.

His Power

We already mentioned the power available to us through
Jesus' resurrection, but we need to under- stand that His
power is available to us through His Holy Spirit:

> I am going to send you what my Father promised;
> but stay in the city until you have been clothed with
> power on high. [17]

Filled with His Spirit, we wear His power like clothes.
We are not left naked or vulnerable; we are clothed with
His anointing and power. Now I don't know about you
but that makes me want to shout. It is a power-promise
that gives me confidence – not just that the battle is
God's, but also that He empowers me to stand against
whatever daily assaults I face.

Here are some of the things my family and I are facing
today or have faced in our past … or may well face in the

days to come:
- Illness
- Depression and anxiety
- Loss of job
- Wayward kids
- Broken relationships

What about you? What are some of the things you are facing right now or may be facing tomorrow?

Do not ever forget: He has clothed you with His power. He has told you to *sit*, not march in and invade; He has called you to *stand in His strength*; not run and be weary. Does it sound foolish to you? Are you willing to be a fool for the One who has never, ever, broken His promises?

What about Jesus? He won the greatest victory of all when He hung on the cross. He was a fool for His Father. Our Lord surrendered completely. He knew that the battle could only be won with His life.

His Authority
> The crowds were amazed at his teaching, because he taught as one who had authority and not as the teachers of the law. [18]

The law and the teachers who taught it were powerless to fight the kingdom of darkness, but the authority of Christ packed a punch against the dark kingdom and advanced the kingdom of God through healing, deliverance, and the forgiveness of sins. Talk about proactive. Even nature bowed down to His authority:
> The men were amazed and asked what kind of man is this?

Even the winds and waves obey Him. [19]

Jesus was a man of authority; He told us so Himself:
All authority in heaven and earth has been given to me. [20]

Authority Given, Then and Now

Jesus gave the 12 disciples authority to drive out evil spirits and to heal. He told them He was sending them out as sheep among wolves;[21] He told them to preach and demonstrate the kingdom of heaven. Having freely received, they were to freely give. Their Lord instructed the disciples to seek a place of peace (be receptive vessels) and use their authority to advance God's kingdom. And He gave them the authority to do these things.

Then there was a man named Stephen:
Now Stephen, a man full of God's grace and power, did great wonders and miraculous signs among the people…. These men began to argue with Stephen, but they could not stand up against his wisdom or the Spirit by whom he spoke. [22]

The anointing and power of God began to spread to those outside of Jesus' original disciples.

On Pentecost, upon being filled with the Holy Spirit himself, Peter spoke to a crowd in Jerusalem. He told them about Jesus and who He really was and what He had accomplished with His death and resurrection. Peter told them that they should be baptized and receive the Holy Spirit. Luke says: *Those who accepted his message were baptized, and about three thousand were added to their number that day.*[23]

Philip went down to Samaria and proclaimed Christ, and when the crowds heard him and saw the obvious authority with which he spoke and witnessed first-hand the miraculous signs he did, they all paid close attention to what he said. [24] Wouldn't you?

The Book of Acts is an incredibly powerful, extraordinary, astonishing account of the Holy Spirit's movement among those first-century Christ followers. The power of God spread like wildfire beyond the disciples and the Holy Spirit was at work filling believers with power and authority.

Jesus made it very clear that we have the same power as the first-century church:
> I tell you the truth, anyone who has faith in me will do what I have been doing. He will do even greater things than these because I am going to the Father. And I will do whatever you ask in my name, so that the Son may bring glory to the Father. You may ask me anything in my name and I will do it. [25]

We will do *greater* things? Maybe before we get to the *greater* things we should start by doing the things that Jesus did.

Battles Close to Home

I may be headed for trouble now. I'm going to get personal. But you know what? Taking authority in the name of Jesus, with His power, begins at *home*. My home and your home. God's instructions for spreading the good news about Jesus and the Kingdom of God began at home, in Jerusalem. The Spirit-filled Christ followers were to start there because that is where they were. Then, from Jerusalem they were to go to Judea and Samaria and ... the ends of the earth.

His strategy for exercising kingdom authority was to begin first at home. The parable of the talents illustrates this principle:

> You have been faithful with a few things; I will put you in charge of many things. [26]

Well ... what has God put you in charge of ? Have you been faithful? Faithfulness starts at home. So we start at home and begin with issues related to our here-and-now, things that personally concern us:

- Our children
- Our finances
- Our relationships
- Our jobs

If we cannot take care of our households, how can we use the authority God has given us to influence the world we live in?

Here's the deal: if the enemy can cause chaos in our families through his assaults, we will find ourselves consumed with those things, so stirred up that we will not be able to exercise our authority in our own households let alone beyond them to impact our world.

The enemy has sent out his assignments through things like alcohol and drugs, destruction of relationships and promiscuity, and if you allow it, Satan will keep you ineffective in Jerusalem (your home) and unable to push beyond the barriers there to impact the world around you.

Don't try to take on Judea, Samaria and the ends of the earth until you have sacrificed and committed to use your authority at home.

How Do We Take Care of Jerusalem?

So what do we do about it? How do we take care of Jerusalem and exercise the authority Jesus has given us and not allow the enemy to frustrate us and take our focus off our Lord? We must use the tools that God has given us through His Word, the disciplines of the faith. These very practical practices and disciplines will invite the Holy Spirit to lead and teach and empower us. They include but certainly are not limited to:

- Repentance
- Prayer (for God's will to be done)
- Claiming God's promises in His Word
- Fasting

Throughout the Word of God we have seen the men and women in the Bible practicing the disciplines of the faith. These disciplines are practical God-given ways to fight the enemy. And the fight begins at home.

Who is Our Enemy?

Any good general needs to know who the enemy is before he or she builds an effective battle plan. We know the battle belongs to the Lord, but we must also know how to cooperate with Him for victory. That requires discerning the reasons for our battles, the ploys of the enemy. The book of James illustrates the battle on all fronts: the world, the flesh and the devil. The battles begin in the flesh (our own stuff), progress into the influence the world has on us, and then move into the demonic. There are some questions to ask in order to determine the kind of battle you are fighting:

If The Battle Is Of the World

Does whatever I am struggling with line up with the principles of the world or with Scripture? Am I approaching this battle with a secular or a biblical worldview?

The world teaches us to be independent and self-assured, to look deeply within for the answers. Christian teaching is the opposite: Jesus teaches us to be centered on Him, dependent on Him. He very clearly wants us to be God-assured and to look to Him for the answers.

If The Battle Is Of the Flesh

Am I able to confront the battle with God confidence or does the way I live my life get in the way?

As Christians we are growing to be more like Christ. In the areas of our lives where sin reigns, where we are unforgiving, bitter, dishonest, gossiping, addicted – whatever runs contrary to living in the spirit – the battles cannot be fought effectively. Those things get in the way. It would be like going to battle with so much baggage that when it's time to move forward and engage in combat we are too weighed down.

If The Battle Is Of the Devil

Does the battle take on a life of its own? Am I able to confront the battle and press through to victory or do I find myself unable to press through?

The enemy will ride in on our hurts, places that need healing, our carnality, and he will find a foothold. He is very capable of causing even our best efforts to fail. He will whisper lies in our ears, and if we listen – if we allow him a foothold of any kind – he will delight in pushing us off course.

We battle from a place of being seated with Christ in heavenly places. The battle is won from a place of His victory, a place of rest in Him. The key to every battle is that we are seated; even this present battle was won on the cross.

Are you trying to stand in your own strength or wisdom or strategies against the battles of the world, the flesh and the devil when God has told you to sit? It is from the place of victory won on the cross that you have authority in the name of Christ to confront every battle of life.

So: confidently and joyfully take your seat in heavenly places with Christ and remember, remember, remember: the battle belongs to the Lord.

Notes

1. 1 John: 4:4
2. John 10:10
3. John Eldredge, Waking The Dead, 12-13
4. Matthew 28:20
5. John 17:18
6. Thomas White, The Believers Guide to Spiritual Warfare, 130
7. Ephesians 2:6-7
8. Ephesians 1:15-21
9. Ephesians 1:18-20
10. Ephesians 4:1-2
11. See Ephesians 5 for Paul's practical advice
12. Ephesians 6:10-11
13. 2 Chronicles 20:15
14. Psalm 9:9-10
15. Psalm 91
16. Acts 4:12
17. Luke 9:1
18. Matthew 7:28-29
19. Matthew 8:27
20. Matthew 28:18
21. Matthew 10
22. Acts 6:8-10
23. Acts 2:41
24. Acts 8:4-6
25. John 14:12-15
26. Matthew 25:21

22 HE CALLS ME FRIEND

We have come to the end of our journey together; a journey that places us at the feet of Jesus; a journey that challenges us to make space for God. Just like Mary made time and space to sit at her Master's feet, she also made space to hear Him call her friend. She worshipped and adored Him. She knew that in Him all her needs were met. But what she may not have known is that He wanted to be her friend. Before Jesus left He told His disciples that He would no longer call them servants, but He called them friends. How strange that must have sounded to them. The King of Kings, their Master, was calling them friend. And he called Mary friend and He calls you friend too. Yes you. He wants to go back to the Garden of Eden with you—the place where it all began and walk with you in the cool of the night and just be your friend. Things got messed up in the garden. A spirit of rebellion snuck in and for awhile (seemed like an eternity) mankind and God were separated. But the God of the universe who calls you friend found a way to reunite you and Him. He could not bear the thought of not having you as His friend. Yes you.

Does it make any sense to you that the very same One whose spoken command called into being the forests and the oceans and the galaxies, and everything in, on and under them, and every creature and every planet and every hair on your head wants to be your friend?

It does not really matter if it makes any sense to us, though I believe that the more we look into it, the more sense it will begin to make. Perhaps not logical, rational, human sense – but God-sense, Creator-sense. Perfect-Love-sense.

The truth is that the same unchangeable, un-begun and unending King of the Universe designed it that way: He created you and me to be in relationship with Him. Friendship. And the deeper the better as far as He is concerned.

God has written you a love letter – from Genesis to Revelation, God's letter – His Word – screams I LOVE YOU! Please take a moment right now, put your hand on your heart and say it: "God loves me. He loves me more than I even know how to love. " It's true – no doubt, no kidding. The King of the Universe is mad about you.

Perfect Design
Back in the Garden of Eden, when His creation was brand new and unbroken, God walked with His masterpiece, us. Adam and Eve were His friends and don't you agree that He must have taken great pleasure in the conversations they had together? Can you imagine? Can you imagine walking with Him as you would your best friend? No posing, no secrets, no fear of rejection. Pure, perfect, unselfconscious friendship.

He created them (us) to be in perfect unity with Him and with each other. It was His perfect design.

Problem was Adam and Eve overstepped the boundaries of that first-and-perfect friendship and disregarded their Father's one instruction to them. God had held one thing back from them and clearly told them to avoid it:

the Tree of the Knowledge of Good and Evil. But Eve
fell prey to the lies of the snake and caused a terrible
break in the relationship with her mate and with her
Father. Then Adam joined the scheme and together they
fell and fractured the bond of friendship.

The amazing thing is that God did not give up on them.
Most designers – at least the human variety
– would wipe the drawing board clean, destroy the
failed prototype, and start over fresh. Not our Creator.
Though Adam and Eve had to leave the garden and
abandon their intimate walk with God, restoration of
their friendship was already in the Designer's blueprints.
Jesus was sent to earth a long time after that scene in the
garden. He was sent to bring heaven back to earth and to
restore the relationship between the Creator and His
masterpiece.

What an incredible God we have. We fractured the
fellowship He had created and designed us for – we
committed spiritual suicide and began dying in that
moment of disobedience in the Garden – and He set in
motion His divine plan to bring us back alive. That kind
of eternal love is unimaginable. Or, more accurately: the
only one who can imagine that kind of love is Love
Himself, the Original Imaginer, the Creator who made us
to be in deep relationship with Him.

An Immutable Law
James 4:4 declares that anyone who loves the world is an
enemy of God – no friendship allowed. Wow. What a
radical declaration. Isn't this the world He died for?
Doesn't God's Word also say that *He so loved the world that
He gave His one and only Son*[1]...?

God loves the world more than we can comprehend, but not everyone in the world loves God. Those who love Him He calls friend. Those who love the world more He says are his enemies. Harsh? Revealing? True? Yes, all three. God is looking for friends who are fools for Him alone, those who are sold out to Him. Those who don't just sign up for the program of salvation but seek a relationship with the Savior. Those who walk and talk with Him, through thick and thin and everything in between. God is looking for some real friends.

It is impossible to love the world and have space available in your heart to love God completely. Luke-warm, half-hearted, maybe-today-but-I'm-not-so-sure-about-tomorrow love does not work for our Designer. The space in the living room of our lives gets crowded out by the world's time-bound me-centered messages, its *things*; things like love of money, desire for power and prestige, regret, shame, worry. Jesus said we cannot love money and Him. It is not possible. We can't strike an enduring balance between love of the world's stuff and love of our Lord. There just isn't space in the living room of our lives for both. Love for one or the other will rise to the top and squeeze the other out. That is an immutable law, like gravity. Like the speed of light. It is a guarantee. The King of the Universe says so.

Jesus said that if someone loves her father or mother more than Him, she is not worthy of Him and His friendship. Or if someone loves his son or daughter more than Him, he is not worthy. Does that pierce you like it does me? It hurts. I think of my husband, my children, grandchildren, parents, and I question who has first place in my heart. And that list is just the beginning of an almost endless list of things we might love more than we love God. You know what I mean: we can love money more, or friends, prestige, job, food, religion, the Yankees or Braves or Red Sox (name your favorite), or the environment, the Sunday church service, the time we volunteer at the homeless shelter or the soup kitchen, the delicious taste of chocolate.

What Kind of Friend Are You?
The question we all must answer is who or what do we love more than God? That is the question of the hour. God is looking for friends who have space at the center of their lives for Him; friends who want to walk with Him, talk to Him, listen to Him – today, tomorrow, always. Think of the best friend you have; God wants to be a better friend than that.

Recently I was in the check-out line at the grocery store. My groceries had already been bagged when I realized I'd left my wallet at home. The line behind me was long and as I shuffled through my purse I could hear the sighs and moans of impatience. Finally I found my checkbook and thought I was home free. Problem was that the clerk needed my drivers license, and of course that was in my wallet. She asked me if I knew my license number and I could hear more moans and chatter as I tried to recall a number I wasn't sure I ever really knew. 4400200? Uh … how about 4400100? As I continued to try different numbers I knew I was in trouble, and I thought it was time to give up, give in and go home without my groceries. Then I shot up a silent prayer: *God, you call me friend. I need a friend right now. Have mercy and* help me *remember my license number.* And voilà – my Friend spoke. The license number that I had not tried to remember for years came to my mind and the check went through. I started clapping, the clerk was impressed with my memory and the people behind me were relieved. With a smile, I thanked my Friend.

Do you have any other friends besides God who know what your license number is?

Anne Lamott says, *Here are the two best prayers I know: "Help me, help me, help me" and "thank you, thank you, thank you."* [2] I used both in the grocery store that day.

God calls us friend. He wants us to talk to Him, call on Him – share, confess, rage, beg, ask, thank. There is no request too small, no concern too trivial, no emotion He can't handle.

Jesus, John and Peter

In *No Wonder They Call Him Savior*, Max Lucado writes about the apostle John:

> But I like John most for the way he loved Jesus. His relationship with Jesus was again rather simple. To John, Jesus was a good friend with a good heart and a good idea. A once-upon-a-time storyteller with a some- where-over-the-rainbow promise. One gets the impression that to John, Jesus was above all a loyal companion. Messiah? Yes. Son of God? Indeed. Miracle worker? That too. But more than anything, Jesus was a pal. Someone you could go camping with or bowling with or count the stars with. [3]

John was one of the three disciples closest to Jesus. He was in the inner circle. So was Peter. The difference is

that when times got really tough – life-and-death tough –
John was the one who stayed and Peter ran.

Peter, the disciple who loved Jesus with such fervor that
when the Lord asked His disciples who the people
thought He was, Peter got it right. He probably shouted,
"You are the Christ, the Son of the living God." Peter,
who impetuously stepped out of the fishing boat and
onto the water to go to Jesus; Peter who got so excited
when Jesus took Him to the mountain and he saw the
Lord talking with Moses and Elijah he began to fantasize
about building altars for them.

It was Peter who said that if everyone fell away, if
everyone deserted Jesus, he never would. But when he
was cornered and scared, impetuous, passionate Peter ran.
Did John love Jesus more than Peter? Did Jesus love
John more than Peter? The answer to these questions is
revealed after the resurrection. Before that revelation,
though, Peter was scared to death and running. He
thought his friend Jesus was dead and gone forever. He
feared for his own life. He denied his hero and friend
three times. Interesting thing: Jesus had told Peter he
would do exactly that. Ever had a friend who knew you
like that – a friend who knew you inside-out … and loved
you in spite of you?

Jesus loved John, who was the only disciple we see at the
foot of the cross; and Jesus loved Peter, who ran like a
rabbit in high grass. He loves you and me, too – whether
we are close to Him or running, denying, hiding.

Our King doesn't back out on friendship. When He
offers and promises, He never goes back or di- lutes or

mitigates. He never renegotiates the deal. He never lets go of us. We let go of Him. We run. We run from fear, from disappointment, from worry, from sorrow ... from life.

But God never runs away from us. He moves toward us. He is always there. Always.

After the resurrection, when Jesus appeared for the third time to His followers, the disciples had been out all night trying to catch fish but had not caught any. Early in the morning, standing on the shore watching, the risen Christ asked them if they had caught any fish. They did not recognize who was calling to them. He told them to cast their nets on the right side of the boat, and when they did there were so many fish they could hardly haul them in. John recognized Jesus and cried out: "It is the Lord!"

Overwhelmed with joy, Peter jumped into the water. Impetuous, passionate Peter splashing around, waving his arms, desperate to get to his friend – his fears and regrets washing away with every splash, his brokenness dissolving and disappearing into the sea. The incredible sight and familiar voice of Jesus purified Peter's heart in an instant. The same Simon Peter who only a few days before had denied his best friend and run away. Well, the same but now changed forever.

Jesus had a fire going on the beach, waiting to cook the disciples' fish, and they had an extraordinarily fresh and revelatory breakfast together. Just imagine.

After they had eaten, Jesus spoke to his friend Peter. I suspect he looked at Peter with piercing eyes – not eyes filled with anger at Peter's denying Him, but eyes filled with the kind of deep unfailing love that the Father had for Adam and Eve in that perfect garden so long before.

It was the risen Lord's question that was piercing: *Simon, son of John, do you truly love me more than these?*[4] He could have been referring to the other disciples, or perhaps the fishing boat or gear. Maybe the supernatural catch of fish. Though it is interesting to speculate, we just don't know. But one thing we know for sure: Jesus was asking Peter what or who he loved the most?

There's that piercing question, from the lips of our Lord. In this scene, He is asking Peter, and the impetuous, passionate disciple stands for all of us. God is asking a question each one of us must answer, a question we have to wrestle honestly with again and again, day-in, day-out. What or who do we love more than we love Jesus? How we answer that question determines our friendship with Him and the amount of living room space we are willing to make available to Him.

Abiding in Him

Another time, Jesus took his disciples to a vineyard. He loved to use natural settings and props to describe and illustrate spiritual principles. He pointed out the vine and the branches, and as he described their relationship He painted a picture of what it means to love and abide and be obedient.

The disciples watched and listened, and they tried to absorb what He was saying. Seems like a fairly straight-forward lesson in vineyard tending, but there was so much more. Peter may have figured he could jump in and finish the lesson; John stayed next to Jesus, never leaving his side. Jesus held the vine in his hand and told them, *I am the vine; you are the branches. If a man remains in me and I in him, he will bear much fruit; apart from me you can do nothing.* [5] Apart from the vine the branch cannot survive. The branch is fed and nourished by the vine, its very existence is dependent on the vine.

Jesus looked at his followers and called them over. He told them clearly that His love was the bond between them, and that no greater love existed than the love that compels a person to lay down his life for his friends.

Did they get it? I doubt it. But at that moment, they must have known that something was different. This fellow they called friend was getting very serious. They were having fun up until then, but the climate was definitely changing. Maybe they felt a cloud settling in. Jesus tells them that now their relationship is changing – He would no longer call them servants, He would call them friends. Wait a second – weren't they already friends? In this moment Jesus takes their friendship to another level. He tells them, whether they heard it that day or not, *Greater love has no one than this, that he lay down his life for his friends.* [6]

Someday they would understand. Someday they would reflect on this scene in the vineyard and it would all become crystal clear. Maybe after the crucifixion, when they were huddled in the upper room waiting for the promised Spirit, they would recall the day when their Lord taught them about the vine and the branches, the day He called them friends. We don't know. One thing we do know is that God called those men (and us) His friends, and He redefined friendship in a way that would change the world forever.

The Lord called us His friends, and then died on the cross to prove it for all time.

Friends of God: Noah, Then and Now

The Bible is filled with friends of God. Noah was a friend. We are told that he lived in a wicked time when hearts were evil and God was grieved and filled with pain over the condition of the world. Sound familiar? Noah was a righteous, blameless man among corrupt people and God called him to build an ark. He found a way to preserve Noah and his family and He flooded the world. Scriptures say that Noah walked with God. *Walk* means to move along at a moderate pace by placing one foot on the ground before lifting the other. God walked beside Noah.

Last week I watched my two-year-old grandchildren, Noah and Ellison, walk down to our dock. They were holding hands and I sensed the Lord telling me to pay attention to Noah. God had been impressing on me as I worked on this chapter how the Old Testament Noah walked with God and how he was a friend of God. The Lord often speaks to me in the day- to-day activities of my life, so I watched.

Little Noah took Ellison by the hand and they proceeded down the long grassy path to the dock. Every time Ellison began to stray toward the water, Noah gently pulled her back toward him, not allowing her to get too close to the dangerous edge. Isn't that what our friend the Lord does for us – or will do if we allow Him?

He is a friend who sticks closer than a brother. He holds our hands and leads us at a moderate pace, one step at a time. He never lets go, though we sometimes do.

There were many other friends of God, including Abraham, Moses, Ruth, Esther, David, more than one Mary – all men and women who loved and trusted God as their faithful friend. How else could they have done the things God asked them to do?

Zacheus

Remember Zacheus? He was up in a tree when Jesus called him down and asked to have a meal with him. In those days when you went to someone's house to eat, it was a sign of friendship. Zacheus was a tax collector despised by his community, and no one wanted to be his friend. Except Jesus. He made a public point of inviting the hated tax collector into friendship. Zacheus came down and said Yes to the Lord's invitation.

What tree is God calling you down from? Are you in the tree of despair? The tree of loneliness? Fear? Worry? The King is calling you down to be His friend. Do you hear Him? Do you believe He means it?

Mary and Martha

How about Mary and Martha and their brother Lazarus? Jesus chose to stay in their home when He needed rest. He called them friends. How would you like to have been Lazarus? Pretty good deal, right? Jesus raised him from the dead. At first it didn't look like Jesus was treating Lazarus fairly because He waited three days to get to him when he was dying. Jesus allowed Lazarus to die. But Jesus' timing was actually perfect. He never made mistakes. He never forgot His friends. Everything worked out just as Jesus and His Father had planned, and Jesus proved his friendship by bringing Lazarus back from the dead.

Not long after that, the Lord proved His friendship to all of us by laying down His life.

Friendships Can Be Messy
The truth is that friendships can be messy here on earth, among imperfect humans like us. Sometimes we protect ourselves from close friendships because we fear intimacy; we are scared of being hurt because we have been hurt or have hurt others before. We think we cannot measure up as a friend or we have false expectations of friendship and are let down. We think we don't have time to develop and nurture friendship, or we are too selfish or fearful to lay our lives down for our friends; we are unwilling to consider others above ourselves. Our perceptions of our earthly friendships transfer to our friendship with God: fear, inadequacies, no time to develop the friendship, self centeredness – fill in the blank with what rings true for you in your life and experience.

Jesus boldly calls us friend. We know it is true because He spent precious time with us, nurtured intimacy, gave up the infinite rights and riches of divine Kingship, came to earth as a vulnerable child, became poor. He taught us and served us, and then He laid down His life for us.

The King did not demand that we serve Him, only that we love Him in return. Just as His life was dependent on His father, He wants us to depend on Him, a friend for life.

How To Be His Friend

How do we walk with God in friendship? We stay close, we remain in Him like the branch remains or *abides* in the life-giving vine. We say Yes and receive the unfailing love He offers. We stay as close as we can, and when we realize we are drifting away, toward the edge of the relationship, away from the one true Source of life, we confess and turn around and allow Him to gently pull us back. Like repentance, abiding requires a daily, even hourly, turning back and coming toward and saying Yes. God promises to tell His friends His secrets. If you draw near and listen closely, He has lots to tell you.

I know it seems unbelievable that the Creator of the universe calls us friend, but He does. He yearns for our friendship. We need do nothing but receive His love and pour it back out on a world that is starving for friendship.

Notes

1. John 3:16
2. Anne Lamott, Traveling Mercies
3. Max Lucado, No Wonder They Call Him Savior, 63-64
4. John 21:15
5. John 15:5
6. John 15:13

ABOUT THE AUTHOR

Founder of international nonprofit Drawing Near to God based in Mt. Pleasant, S.C., Joanne Ellison teaches women to make space for God so that God's presence keeps them from being overwhelmed with life.

Driven by a vision to motivate women to pursue a deeper relationship with God, Ellison founded Drawing Near to God in 2000 and has since reached tens of thousands of women through Christian radio and television, blogging, contributions to the Christian Broadcasting Network, social media, her weekly Bible teachings, livestreaming, speaking, books and other resources. She is the author of over 20 Bible study guides, the popular 365-day Bible devotional, *Drawing Near To God*, *Sitting at His Feet* devotional and *Tell Your Heart to Beat Again*.

She is a mother of three, grandmother, great-grandmother and is married to Dr. Blount Ellison. Making her home in the Charleston area for most of her life, Ellison is a graduate of the College of Charleston and an active member of Saint Andrew's Church, Mount Pleasant, SC. In her free time, she enjoys spending time with her grandchildren and traveling with her husband.

Ellison is an engaging speaker, writer and Bible teacher. Her speaking style includes both vulnerability and humor and is rooted in her passion for the Bible. She often incorporates stories about her children, grandchildren and travels into her teachings - cycling through Portugal and Copenhagen as well as hiking mountains all over the States have provided many challenges and adventures!

Made in the USA
Columbia, SC
31 October 2019